# A.W. TOZER

# *Renewed*

## DAY BY DAY

### *Volume 2*

A DAILY DEVOTIONAL
COMPILED BY GERALD B. SMITH

CHRISTIAN PUBLICATIONS
CAMP HILL, PENNSYLVANIA

Christian Publications
3825 Hartzdale Drive, Camp Hill, PA 17011
www.cpi-horizon.com


*Faithful, biblical publishing since 1883*


ISBN: 0-87509-461-9
LOC Catalog Card Number: 91-72566
© 1991 by Christian Publications
All rights reserved
Printed in the United States of America

98 99 00 01 02    7 6 5 4 3


Scripture is taken from the Holy Bible: King James Version.

# Preface

This second volume of brief, timely daily readings from the heart and mind of Dr. A.W. Tozer becomes a companion to the previous book, *Renewed Day By Day*, already in its 4th printing.

The compiler and publisher have followed a definite policy not to include any selections in this second volume which were used previously in the first.

Selections have been gleaned largely from Dr. Tozer's taped sermons, with additional quotations from his own published books and from his incisive editorials while he was the editor of *Alliance Life*. His helpful personal illustrations, testimonies, spiritual concerns and prayers have been scattered throughout these pages, all glorifying the Person of Jesus Christ, our Savior and Lord.

I remember telling you in the preface of the first *Renewed Day By Day* that Dr. Tozer would often rap your spiritual knuckles. Because much of the material in this second volume was spoken or written by Dr. Tozer nearer the time of his death in 1963, there are more warnings, more concerns for spiritual progress and more emphasis on the believer's readiness and preparation to meet his coming Lord and King.

Gerald B. Smith
Fort Myers, Florida

# YES, EVERYTHING IS WRONG . . .
# UNTIL JESUS MAKES IT RIGHT

*Having made peace through the blood of his cross, by him to reconcile all things unto himself . . . whether they be things in earth, or things in heaven. (Colossians 1:20)*

Men and women without God are helpless and hopeless human beings. We do well to remember that sin is to the human nature what cancer is to the human body!

Who can argue with the fact that sin has ruined us?

Our feverish activity is only one sign of what is wrong with us—sin has plunged us into the depths and so marked us with mortality that we have become brother to the clay—but God never meant it to be so.

I recall being invited to speak at a summer conference where much of the emphasis is upon fun and amusement and jokes, something like Hollywood, I suppose. After my sessions there, the pastor-director told me frankly of his wife's reaction: "Honey, after listening to Dr. Tozer, can it be true that there isn't anything good in this world?"

Well, I know she had a Bible in her house and I consider her query one of the foolish questions of our times. Of course the world makes its own argument that there are things that can be considered good on the human level—but they belong to us only for a brief day. Nothing is divinely good until it bears the imprint of our Lord Jesus Christ!

Men and women may argue and make excuses, but it does not change the fact that in our human society we are completely surrounded by three marks of the ancient curse: everything is recent, temporal and transient! That is why the Holy Spirit whispers faithfully, reminding us of the Christ of God, eternity walking in flesh, God Almighty come to live among us and to save—actually to give us eternity!

_____*January 1*

# IN THE BEGINNING

*In the beginning was the Word . . . and the Word was God.*
*(John 1:1)*

None of us can approach a consideration of the eternal nature and Person of Jesus Christ without sensing and confessing our human inadequacy in the face of the divine revelation.

John, in his gospel, provides a beautiful portrait of the eternal Christ, starting with those stark, incredible words: "In the beginning!" My brethren, that is where we start with the understanding and the revelation of Christianity!

Many others have made a variety of claims but only our Christ is the Christ of God. Certainly it was not Buddha and not Mohammed; not Joseph Smith, not Mrs. Eddy and not Father Divine! All of these and countless others like them had beginnings—but they all had their endings, too.

What an incredible difference! Our Christian life commences with the eternal Son of God. This is our Lord Jesus Christ: the Word who was with the Father in the beginning; the Word who was God; and the Word who is God! This is the only one who can assure us: "No man cometh unto the Father, but by Me!"

*January 2* _____

# MAN HAS LOST GOD

*Thou takest away their breath, they die, and return to dust.*
*(Psalm 104:29)*

The average person in the world today, without faith and without God and without hope, is engaged in a desperate personal search and struggle throughout his lifetime. He does not really know what he is doing here. He does not know where he is going.

The sad commentary is that everything he is doing is being done on borrowed time, borrowed money and borrowed strength—and he already knows that in the end he will surely die! It boils down to the bewildered confession of many humans that they have lost God somewhere along the way.

Man, made more like God than any other creature, has become less like God than any other creature. Created to reflect the glory of God, he has retreated sullenly into his cave—reflecting only his own sinfulness.

Certainly it is a tragedy above all tragedies in this world that love has gone from man's heart. Beyond that, light has gone from his mind. Having lost God, he blindly stumbled on through this dark world to find only a grave at the end!

# SAVIOR AND LORD

*For by grace are ye saved through faith . . . it is the gift of God. (Ephesians 2:8)*

God chose His only begotten Son as the channel for His grace and truth, for John witnesses that "grace and truth came by Jesus Christ!"

The Law was given by Moses—but that was all that Moses could do. He could only "command" righteousness. In contrast, only Jesus Christ produces righteousness.

All that Moses could do was to forbid us to sin. In contrast, Jesus Christ came to save us from sin.

Moses could not save anyone—but Jesus Christ is both Savior and Lord.

Grace came through Jesus Christ before Mary wept in the manger stall in Bethlehem. It was the grace of God in Christ that saved the human race from extinction when our first parents sinned in the Garden.

It is plain in history that God forgave Israel time and time again. It was the grace of God in Christ prior to the Incarnation that made God say: "I have risen early in the morning and stretched out my hands to you!"

*January 4* _____

# OUR CHARTER IS FROM GOD

*Upon this rock I will build my church; and the gates of hell shall not prevail against it. (Matthew 16:18)*

While we are right to thank God in appreciation for all of the great and good men in the history of the Christian church, we actually "follow" none of them. Our charter goes farther back and is from a higher source. They were rightly looked upon as leaders, but they were all servants of God, even as you and I are.

Luther sowed. Wesley watered. Finney reaped—but they were only servants of the living God.

In our local assemblies, we are part of the church founded by the Lord Jesus Christ and perpetuated by the mystery of the new birth. Therefore, our assembly is that of Christian believers gathered unto a Name to worship and adore the Presence. So, in that sense, the strain is gone. The strain and pressure to abide by traditional religious forms all begin to pale in importance as we function in faith as the people of God who glorify His Name and honor His Presence!

If all of this is true—and everything within me witnesses that it is—we may insist that God is able to do for us all that He did in the days of the apostles. There has been no revocation of our charter!

# YES, GOD LOVES US

*We love him, because he first loved us.* (1 John 4:19)

If we are to have any satisfying and lasting understanding of life, it must be divinely given. It begins with the confession that it is indeed the God who has revealed Himself to us who is the central pillar bearing up the universe. Believing that, we then go on to acknowledge that we have discovered His great eternal purpose for men and women made in His own image.

I heard a brilliant Canadian author being interviewed on the radio concerning world conditions, and he said: "I confess that our biggest mistake is the fond belief that we humans are special pets of Almighty God and that God has a special fondness for us as people."

We have a good answer: man as he was originally created is God's beloved. Man in that sense is the beloved of the universe. God said, "I have made man in My image and man is to be above all other creatures. Redeemed man is to be even above the angels in the heavens. He is to enter into My presence pardoned and unashamed, to worship me and to look on My face while the ages roll on!" No wonder we believe that God is the only certain foundation!

*January 6* _____

# RICHES OF GRACE

*God hath in these last days spoken by his Son . . . by whom also he made the worlds. (Hebrews 1:2)*

Would it startle you if I dared to say that the living God has never done anything in His universe apart from Jesus Christ?

Christians seem to be woefully unaware of the full meaning and measure of the grace of God. Why should we question God's provision when the Holy Spirit tells us through the Apostle John that the Word who became flesh is "full of grace and truth"? Brethren, the stars in their courses, the frogs that croak beside the lake, the angels in heaven above and men and women on earth below—all came out of the channel we call the eternal Word!

In the book of Revelation, John bears record of the whole universe joining to give praise to the Lamb that was slain. Under the earth and on the earth, and above the earth John heard creatures praising Jesus Christ, all joining in a great chorus: "Worthy is the Lamb that was slain to receive power, and riches, and wisdom, and strength, and honor, and glory and blessing!"

Yes, surely the entire universe is beneficiary of God's rich grace in Jesus Christ!

# BENEFITS OF GRACE

*But now in Christ Jesus . . . ye are made nigh by the blood of Christ.* (Ephesians 2:12)

Only a believing Christian can testify, "I am a sinner—saved by the grace of God!" But that is not the whole story. All that we have is cut of His grace. Jesus Christ, the eternal Word who became flesh and dwelt among us, is the open channel through whom God moves to provide all the benefits He gives, both to saints and to sinners—yes, even to sinners!

Even though you may still be unconverted and going your own way, you have received much out of the ocean of His fullness. You have received the pulsing life that beats in your bosom.

You have received the brilliant mind and the brain without which you could not function. You have received a memory that strings the events you cherish as a jeweler strings pearls into a necklace.

When we say to an unbelieving man, "Believe on the Lord Jesus Christ," we are actually saying to him: "Believe on the One who sustains you and upholds you and who has given you life. Believe in the One who pities you and spares you and keeps you. Believe on the One out of whom you came!"

*January 8* _____

# GOD'S GRACIOUS ACT

*The Word was made flesh . . . and dwelt among us.*
*(John 1:14)*

We do well to remember that mankind is only one order of God's beings or creatures. So we wonder: *How could the Infinite ever become finite?* And: *How could the Limitless One deliberately impose limitations upon Himself?*

In the book of Hebrews we learn to our amazement that God took not upon Him the nature of angels, but He took upon Him the seed of Abraham.

We would suppose that God in stepping down would step down just as little as possible. But instead He came down to the lowest order and took upon Himself the nature of Abraham—the seed of Abraham.

I like what John Wesley said concerning this mysterious act of God in stooping down to tabernacle with us: we should be sure to distinguish the act from the method by which the act is performed. Do not reject a fact because we do not know how it was done, Wesley advised.

With the saints of all ages, we do well just to throw up our hands and confess: "Oh Lord, Thou knowest!"

# GRACE CAN BE COSTLY

*For it is a good thing that the heart be established with grace . . . grace be with you all. Amen. (Hebrews 13:9, 25)*

Christians all around us are trying every shortcut they can think of, to get "something for nothing" in the kingdom of God. Talk to them and they will predictably flare up: "Isn't grace something for nothing?"

That depends upon what kind of grace we are talking about.

Pastor Dietrich Bonhoeffer gave his life as a martyr in Hitler's Germany, but he left a book now known around the world: *The Cost of Discipleship.* He pointed out a sharp distinction between "cheap grace" and "costly grace." Although God's grace has been given freely to humans who do not deserve it, Bonhoeffer believed it rightly could be called "costly grace" because it cost our Lord Jesus Christ even the suffering of death.

Some men and women have actually turned God's grace into lasciviousness. They do not know what the word grace means—that God gives us out of His rich and full goodness although we are unworthy of it. When I preach about the grace of God and point out that Jesus commanded us to take up our cross and follow Him, those who do not know the meaning of grace respond: "Oh, Tozer is now preaching legalism."

*January 10* _____

# UNITED WITH CHRIST

*We are in him that is true, even in his Son Jesus Christ.*
*(1 John 5:20)*

The Spirit of God has impelled me to preach and write much about the believer's conscious union with Christ—a union that must be felt and experienced. I will never be through talking about the union of the soul with the Savior, the conscious union of the believer's heart with Jesus.

Remember, I am not talking about a "theological union" only. I am speaking also of a conscious union, a union that is felt and experienced.

I have never been ashamed to tell my congregations that I believe in feelings. I surely believe in what Jonathan Edwards termed "religious affections." That is man's perspective.

I am aware also that from God's perspective there are qualities in the Divine Being that can only be known by the heart; never by the intellect!

Long ago John wrote: "Hereby perceive we the love of God, because he laid down his life for us" (1 John 3:16). So it is best for us to confess that as humans we have difficulty in understanding what God has said when He says that He loves us!

# DEALING WITH SIN

*For the wages of sin is death; but the gift of God is eternal life. (Romans 6:23)*

Many evangelical teachers insist so strongly upon free, unconditional grace as to create the impression that sin is not a serious matter and that God cares very little about it!

They make it seem that God is only concerned with our escaping the consequences.

The gospel, then, in practical application, means little more than a way to escape the fruits of our past!

But the heart that has felt the weight of its own sin and has seen the dread whiteness of the Most High God will never believe that a message of forgiveness without transformation is a message of good news. To remit a man's past without transforming his present is to violate the moral sincerity of his own heart.

To that kind of thing God will be no party! For to offer a sinner the gift of salvation based upon the work of Christ, while at the same time allowing him to retain the idea that the gift carries with it no moral implications, is to do him untold injury where it hurts him most!

*January 12* _____

# LOVE WITHOUT MEASURE

*Yea, I have loved thee with an everlasting love.*
*(Jeremiah 31:3)*

I once wrote something about how God loves us and how dear we are to Him. I was not sure I should put it down on paper—but God knows what I meant.

I wrote: "The only eccentricity that I can discover in the heart of God is the fact that a God such as He is should love sinners such as we are!"

On this earth a mother will love the son who has betrayed her and shamed her and is now on his way to a life in prison. That seems to be a natural thing for a mother. But there is nothing natural about this love of God. It is a divine thing. It is forced out by the inward pressure within the heart of the God of all grace. That is why He waits for us, puts up with us, desires to lead us on—He loves us!

My brethren, this should be our greatest encouragement in view of all that we know about ourselves: God loves us without measure, and He is so keenly interested in our spiritual growth and progress that He stands by in faithfulness to teach and instruct and discipline us as His own dear children!

# THE WONDER OF REDEMPTION

*For in him dwelleth all the fullness of the Godhead bodily.*
*(Colossians 2:9)*

My brethren in the Christian faith, stand with me in defense of this basic doctrine: The living God did not degrade Himself in the Incarnation. When the Word was made flesh, there was no compromise on God's part!

It is plain in the ancient Athanasian Creed that the early church fathers were cautious at this point of doctrine. They would not allow us to believe that God, in the Incarnation, became flesh by a coming down of the Deity into flesh, but rather by the taking of mankind into God. That is the wonder of redemption!

In the past, the mythical gods of the nations were not strangers to compromise. But the holy God who is God, our heavenly Father, could never compromise Himself!

He remained ever God and everything else remained not God. That gulf still existed even after Jesus Christ had become man and dwelt among us. This much, then, we can know about the acts of God—He will never back out of His bargain. This amazing union of man with God is effected unto perpetuity!

*January 14* _____

# OUR LIFE IS IN CHRIST

*Thanks be unto God, which always causeth us to triumph in Christ. (2 Corinthians 2:14)*

Certainly not all of the mystery of the Godhead can be known by man—but just as certainly, all that men can know of God in this life is revealed in Jesus Christ!

When the Apostle Paul said with yearning, "That I may know Him," he was not speaking of intellectual knowledge. Paul was speaking of the reality of an experience of knowing God personally and consciously, spirit touching spirit and heart touching heart.

We know that people spend a lot of time talking about a deeper Christian life—but few seem to want to know and love God for Himself.

The precious fact is that God is the deeper life! Jesus Christ Himself is the deeper life, and as I plunge on into the knowledge of the triune God, my heart moves on into the blessedness of His fellowship. This means that there is less of me and more of God—thus my spiritual life deepens and I am strengthened in the knowledge of His will!

# GOD SETS NO LIMIT

*Let no man deceive you with vain words. (Ephesians 5:6)*

Do you know that there are Bible "interpreters" now who believe they can set up rules as to how much we can have of God? However, the Lord Himself has promised that as far as He is concerned, He is willing to keep the candles of my soul brightly burning!

So, my heart tells me to ignore the modern scribes whose interpretations, I fear, are forcing the Spirit, the blessed Dove, to fold His wings and be silent. I turn rather to one of Dr. A.B. Simpson's hymns rarely sung now, probably because very few believers have this experience of which he wrote:

> I take the hand of love divine,
> I count each precious promise mine
> With this eternal countersign—
> I take—He undertakes!
>
> I take Thee, blessed Lord,
> I give myself to Thee;
> And Thou, according to Thy Word
> Dost undertake for me!

*January 16* _____

# EXPLORE GOD'S WORD

*Thy word have I hid in mine heart. (Psalm 119:11)*

What a strange paradox! The atheistic free-thinker rants and raves about the Bible being a "dangerous" book at the very same time that the Word of God is speaking life to my soul!

Strange indeed that some humans have the idea that the Word of God can only be approached with shivering fears. But that is true only of those who *love their sin* and *hate their Savior*.

The blessed truth is that if I hate my sin and love my Savior, the Word of God is a wonderful revelation, indeed, and a trustworthy guide.

We need to be aware always that if we do not keep the Word of God on our side, we will be miserable in our souls continually. It is up to us. What do we sincerely will to do with God and His revealed Word?

Years ago, the saintly George Mueller said he had read the Bible hundreds of times, and then he added: "with meditation!"

Let us see to it that we read the Word. More than that, we should actually explore it!

# FAITH AND OBEDIENCE

*For whosoever shall call upon the name of the Lord shall be saved. (Romans 10:13)*

What is our answer to the many confused persons who keep asking: "How can we know that we have come into a saving relationship with Jesus Christ?"

First, we stand together on the basic truth that Christ Jesus came into the world to save sinners. A second fact is that men and women are saved by faith in Christ, alone; without works and without our merit.

However, the fact that Christ came to save sinners is not enough—that fact in itself cannot save us. Now, in our day, the issues of believing faith and the gift of eternal life are clouded and confused by an "easy acceptance" that has been fatal to millions who may have stopped short in matters of faith and obedience.

Faith is believing and receiving, as in Acts 16:31: "Believe on the Lord Jesus Christ and thou shalt be saved;" and as in John 1:12: "But as many as received him, to them gave he power to become the sons of God, even to them that believe in his name."

*January 18* _____

# SALVATION'S PRICE

*But without faith it is impossible to please him.*
*(Hebrews 11:6)*

Too many Christian leaders, acting like enthusiastic promoters, are teaching that the essence of faith is this: "Come to Jesus—it will cost you nothing!"

The price has all been paid—"it will cost you nothing!" Brethren, that is a dangerous half-truth. There is always a price connected with salvation and with discipleship.

God's grace is free, no doubt about that. No one in the wide world can make any human payment towards the plan of salvation or the forgiveness of sins.

I take issue on Bible grounds with the statement that "everyone in the world has faith—all you have to do is turn your faith loose."

That is truly a misconception of what the Bible teaches about men and God and faith. Actually, faith is a rare and wonderful plant that lives and grows only in the penitent soul.

The teaching that every one has faith is simply a form of humanism in the guise of Christianity. I warn you that any faith that belongs to everybody is not the faith that saves. It is not that faith which is a gift of God to the broken and contrite heart!

# GOD'S FAITHFUL VOICE

*And take heed to yourselves . . . and cares of this life.*
*(Luke 21:34)*

In a day when judgments are soon to come upon the earth, we are often warned by doctors that we eat too much—and that we worry too much. More of us suffer from mental illness than suffer from major physical illnesses.

In our self-centered lives, even those who are professing believers are prone to think they will hear the trumpets of woe in time to do something about all this. But at that time, it will be too late!

The voice of God is a quiet voice. The voice of God's love and grace is constant—never strident, never compulsive. God has sent His messengers to every generation. He has spoken urgently and faithfully through His prophets; through the concerns of preachers and evangelists; even through the sweet voices of the gospel singers. Further, God has spoken through witnessing men and women: plain, sincere, loving men and women transformed by a spiritual birth which is from above.

This is the voice of God we hear in this day of grace—the voice of the Savior calling wandering sinners home.

*January 20* _____

# THE TRUE SON OF MAN

*One like unto the Son of man . . . out of his mouth went a*
*sharp two-edged sword. (Revelation 1:13, 16)*

The Christian message has ceased to be a
pronouncement and has become instead a proposition.
Scarcely anyone catches the imperious note in the words
spoken by Jesus Christ.

The invitational element of the Christian message has
been pressed far out of proportion in the total scriptural
scene. Christ with His lantern, His apologetic stance and
His weak pleading face has taken the place of the true Son
of Man whom John saw—His eyes as a flame of fire, His
feet like burnished brass and His voice as the sound of
many waters.

Only the Holy Spirit can reveal our Lord as He really is,
and He does not paint in oils. He manifests Christ to the
human spirit, not to our physical eyes.

These are strenuous times and men and women are
being recruited to devote themselves to one or another
master. But anything short of complete devotion to Christ
is inadequate and must end in futility and loss.

# GUIDANCE IS BY THE SPIRIT

*Bringing into captivity every thought to the obedience of Christ. (2 Corinthians 10:5)*

We can always trust the moving and the leading of the Holy Spirit in our lives and experiences, but we cannot always trust our human leanings and our fleshly and carnal desires. That calls for another word of balance. We know that the emotional life is a proper and noble part of our total personality. But by its very nature, it is of secondary importance, for religion lies in the will, and so does righteousness.

God never intended that such a being as mankind should become the mere plaything of his or her feelings. The only good that God recognizes is the willed good. The only valid holiness is a willed holiness. That is why I am always a little suspicious of the overly bubbly Christian who talks too much about himself or herself—and not enough about Jesus. That is also why I am more than a little concerned about the professing Christian whose experience does not seem to have resulted in a true inner longing to be more like Jesus every day in thought, word and deed!

*January 22* _____

# MAJESTY—AND MEEKNESS

*I will speak of the glorious honour of thy majesty, and of thy wondrous works. (Psalm 145:5)*

When the prophets try to describe for me the attributes, the graces, the worthiness of the God who appeared to them and dealt with them, I feel that I can kneel down and follow their admonition: "He is thy Lord—worship thou Him!"

They described Him as radiantly beautiful and fair. They said that He was royal and that He was gracious. They described Him as a mysterious being, and yet they noted His meekness.

The meekness was His humanity. The majesty was His deity. You find them everlastingly united in Him. So meek that He nursed at His mother's breast, cried like any baby and needed all the human care that every child needs.

But He was also God, and in His majesty He stood before Herod and before Pilate. When He returns, coming down from the sky, it will be in His majesty, the majesty of God; yet it will be in the majesty of the Man who is God!

This is our Lord Jesus Christ. Before His foes He stands in majesty. Before His friends, He stands in meekness!

# BRINGING US TO GLORY

*For it became him . . . bringing many sons unto glory.*
*(Hebrews 2:10)*

As Christian believers (I am assuming you are a believer), you and I know how we have been changed and regenerated and assured of eternal life by faith in Jesus Christ and His atoning death. On the other hand, where this good news of salvation by faith is not known, religion becomes an actual bondage. If Christianity is known only as a religious institution, it may well become merely a legalistic system of religion, and the hope of eternal life becomes a delusion.

I have said this much about reality and assurance to counter the shock you may feel when I add that God wants to fully prepare you in your daily Christian life so that you will be ready indeed for heaven! Many of us have been in God's household for a long time. Remember that God has been trying to do something special within our beings day after day, year after year.

Why? Because His purpose is to bring many sons—and daughters, too—unto glory!

*January 24* _____

# SPIRITUAL READINESS

*The end of all things is at hand: be ye therefore sober, and watch unto prayer. (1 Peter 4:7)*

When the Bible says that God is calling a special people out of the nations to bear the name of His eternal Son, I believe it—and His name is Jesus!

Our pious forefathers believed in spiritual preparation, and they said so. They saw themselves as a bride being prepared to meet the Bridegroom. They regarded this earth as the dressing room to outfit themselves for heaven.

The evangelical church has come through a period when nearly everyone has believed that there is just one prerequisite to readiness: being born again. We have made being born again almost like receiving a pass to a special event—when Jesus returns we whip out the pass to prove our readiness.

Frankly, I do not think it will be like that. I do not believe that all professed believers are automatically ready to meet the Lord. Our Savior Himself was joined by Peter and John and Paul in warning and pleading that we should live and watch and pray, so to be ready for Jesus' coming.

# JOURNEY OF THE HEART

*And they said, Believe on the Lord Jesus Christ and thou shalt be saved. (Acts 16:31)*

I object to the charge that "Tozer preaches experience." I preach Christ, the Savior—that is my calling! But I am positive about the validity, the reality and the value of genuine Christian experience. We can talk to Jesus just as we talk to our other friends.

As a boy, I was not a Christian. I did not have the privilege of growing up in a home where Christ was known and loved. God spoke to me through a street preacher who quoted the words of Jesus, "Come unto me, all ye that labour and are heavy laden, and I will give you rest."

That invitation let me know that Jesus is still calling "Come now!" I went home and up into the attic. There in earnest prayer I gave my heart and life to Jesus Christ. My feet had taken me home and into the attic. But it was my heart that went to Jesus! Within my heart I consented to go to Jesus. I have been a Christian ever since that moment.

# WE GET AROUND IT

*If I then, your Lord and Master, have washed your feet; ye also ought to wash one another's feet. (John 13:14)*

The Lordship of Jesus is not quite forgotten among Christians, but it has been relegated to our hymn book, where all responsibility toward it may be comfortably discharged in a glow of pleasant religious emotion.

The idea that the Man Christ Jesus has absolute and final authority over all its members in every detail of their lives is simply not accepted as true by the rank and file of evangelical Christians.

To avoid the necessity of either obeying or rejecting the plain instruction of our Lord in the New Testament, we take refuge in a liberal interpretation of them. We find ways to avoid the sharp point of obedience, comfort carnality and make the words of Christ of none effect. And the essence of it all is that "Christ simply could not have meant what He said." Dare we admit that His teachings are accepted even theoretically only after they have been weakened by "interpretation"? Dare we confess that even in our public worship, the influence of the Lord is very small? We sing of Him and preach about Him, but He must not interfere!

# MINISTRY OF THE CHURCH

*The house of God, which is the church of the living God, the pillar and ground of the truth. (1 Timothy 3:15)*

Not all of the pooled efforts of any church can make a Christian out of a lost man!

The Christian life begins with the individual; a soul has a saving encounter with God and the new life is born.

All else being equal, every individual. Christian will find in the communion of a local church the most perfect atmosphere for the fullest development of his spiritual life. There he will also find the best arena for the largest exercise of those gifts and powers with which God may have endowed him.

Unfortunately, the word "church" has taken on meanings which it did not originally have. The meaning of the word for the true Christian was fixed by our Lord and His apostles, and no man and no angel has authority to change it!

The universal Church is the Body of Christ, the Bride of the Lamb, the habitation of God through the Spirit, the pillar and the ground of the Truth.

Without doubt, the most important body on earth is the Church of God which He purchased with His own blood!

*January 28* _____

# A BELIEVING REMNANT

*Even so then at this present time also there is a remnant according to the election of grace. (Romans 11:5)*

What is God trying to do with His believing people?—the Bible calls us a remnant according to grace, believers taken out of the great, teeming swarm of so-called religious people in today's world.

I am inclined to join others in wondering if the Lord is postponing His coming because He is trying to get His Bride ready?

For years it has been the popular idea in evangelical Christianity that the whole body of believers in Christ would rise like a flock of frightened birds when the Lord comes. But A.B. Simpson and William MacArthur and others in the past generation said, "Oh no! The Lord will take with Him those who are prepared and ready for His coming!"

I do not presume to give an answer satisfying to everyone in our churches. But I know that many Christians are too smug about this, saying in effect: "I am converted to Christ through grace, so I can live as I please!"

Of some things we cannot be dogmatic; but we know this for sure—God has no halfway house between heaven and hell where He takes us to fumigate us!

# CHRIST WILL RULE

*I pray God your whole spirit and soul and body be preserved blameless unto the coming of our Lord Jesus Christ.* (1 Thessalonians 5:23)

I am not surprised that I still meet people who do not believe that Jesus Christ is going to return to earth. In fact, some of them, armed with their own Bibles and interpretations, are insistent on setting me "straight."

One gentleman has written saying that I have it all wrong, and that Paul did not mean what I had said he meant, as I applied Paul's statement to everyday life.

I took time to write a reply: "When it comes to saying what he meant, Paul's batting average has been pretty good up to now. So, I will string along with what Paul plainly, clearly said."

I did not figure I needed someone to straighten me out—particularly someone who had decided the Bible does not mean what it says.

No one is going to argue me out of my faith in what God has revealed and what God has said. As far as I am concerned, it is a fact that Jesus is coming again! The question I do raise is this: Are we prepared spiritually for His coming? Are we tolerating conditions in our midst that will cause us embarrassment when He does come?

*January 30* _____

# A PRAYER OF CONCERN

Gracious Father in heaven, I am a pastor in the flock of God and I confess that I am a troubled man. It is too late in my ministry for me to be engaged week after week with men and women who do not hear Thy pleading voice.

0 Lord, we often wonder if Thou wilt be forced to turn from those who have heard all of the Bible truths over and over again, in order to find willing and responsive listeners elsewhere? We recognize that Thou hast given us plain warnings in Thy Word. We remember all too well that the Jews of Jesus' day held stubbornly to their attitudes of presumption: "We are Abraham's descendents. We know who we are. If God is going to bless anyone, He is going to bless us." Yet at that very time those same self-serving men were planning to kill their promised Messiah, the eternal Son whom Thou hadst sent in the fullness of time.

We pray earnestly, 0 God, that we may not be found among those with hardened hearts, no longer able to hear Thy voice.

# OUR GOD: ALL SUFFICIENT

*In the beginning, God created the heaven and the earth.*
*(Genesis 1:10)*

Have we modern men and women never given thought or meditation concerning the eternal nature of God? Who are we to imagine that we are "bailing out" the living God when we drop a $10 bill in the Sunday offering plate?

Let us thank God for the reality of His causeless existence. Our God only is all sufficient, uncreated, unborn, the living and eternal and self-existent God!

I refer often to the great worshiping heart of Frederick William Faber, who in these words celebrated his vision of God's eternal self-existence:

> Father! the sweetest, dearest Name,
>   That men or angels know!
> Fountain of life, that had no fount
>   From which itself could flow.
>
> Thy vastness is not young or old,
>   Thy life hath never grown;
> No time can measure out Thy days,
>   No space can make Thy throne!

*February 1* _____

# SHARING GOD'S NATURE

*Precious promises, that by these ye might be partakers of the divine nature. (2 Peter 1:4)*

Our heavenly Father disciplines us for our own good, "that we may share in His holiness." God's motives are always loving!

I have known people who seemed to be terrified by God's loving desire that we should reflect His own holiness and goodness. As God's faithful children, we should be attracted to holiness, for holiness is God-likeness—likeness to God!

God encourages every Christian believer to follow after holiness. We know who we are and we know who God is. He does not ask us to be God and He does not ask us to produce the holiness that only He Himself knows. Only God is holy absolutely: all other beings can be holy only in relative degrees.

Actually, it is amazing and wonderful that God should promise us the privilege of sharing in His nature. He remembers we were made of dust. So He tells us what is in His being as He thinks of us: "It is My desire that you grow in grace and in the knowledge of Me. I want you to be more like Jesus, My eternal Son, every day you live!"

# GOD REVEALS HIMSELF

*I saw also the Lord . . . then said I, woe is me! for I am undone. (Isaiah 6:1, 5)*

I often wonder how so many people can live with a continuing hope that they will in some way be able to commune with God through their intellectual capacities. When will they realize that if they could possibly "discover" God they realize that with the intellect, they would be equal to God?

Isaiah is a dramatic example of God's revelation of Himself to mankind. Isaiah could have tried for a million years to reach God by means of his intellect. But brainpower is not the means by which we find God!

Brethren, it is true that all of us would still be far from God if He had not graciously and in love revealed Himself to us. In the space of a short second of time, the Lord who loves us can reveal Himself to the willing spirit of a man or woman. It is only then that an Isaiah, or any one of us, can say with humble assurance, "I know Him!"

A committed Christian, then, should have upon him an element that is beyond psychology—beyond all natural laws and into spiritual laws!

*February 3* _____

# JESUS SAID HE WAS GOD

*But unto the Son he saith, Thy throne, 0 God, is for ever and ever. (Hebrews 1:8)*

The more we study the words of our Lord Jesus Christ when He lived on earth among us, the more certain we are about who He is.

Some critics have scoffed: "Jesus did not claim to be God. He only said He was the Son of Man."

It is true that Jesus used the term, "Son of Man" frequently. But He testified boldly, even among those who were His sworn enemies, that He was God. He said with great forcefulness that He had come from the Father in heaven and that He was equal with the Father.

Bible-believing Christians stand together on this. They may differ about the mode of baptism, church polity or the return of the Lord. But they agree on the deity of the eternal Son. Jesus Christ is of one substance with the Father—begotten, not created (Nicene Creed). In our defense of this truth we must be very careful and old—belligerent, if need be!

Christ is the brightness of God's glory, and the express image of God's Person!

_____ *February 4*

# BOTH LORD AND CHRIST

*God hath made this same Jesus . . . both Lord and Christ.*
*(Acts 2:36)*

No Christian believer should ever forget what the Bible says about the Person and the offices of the eternal Son, the Christ of God.

"God hath made this same Jesus whom ye have crucified both Lord and Christ" (Acts 2:36). Jesus means Savior; Lord means Sovereign; Christ means Anointed One.

The Apostle Peter did not proclaim Jesus only as Savior—he preached to them Jesus as Lord and Christ and Savior, never dividing His Person or His offices.

Remember, also, the declaration of Paul: "If thou shalt confess with thy mouth the Lord Jesus, thou shalt be saved."

Three times in the passage to the Roman Christians telling how to be saved, Paul calls Jesus "Lord." He says that faith in the Lord Jesus plus confession of that faith to the world brings salvation to us!

*February 5* _____

# TRUTH IS A PERSON

*Then said Jesus . . . And ye shall know the truth, and the truth shall make you free. (John 8:31–32)*

Let me say boldly that it is not the difficulty of discovering truth, but the unwillingness to obey it, that makes it so rare among men.

Our Lord said, "I am the Truth." And again He said, "The Son of Man is come to seek and to save that which was lost." Truth, therefore, is not hard to find for the very reason that it is seeking us!

So we learn that Truth is not a thing for which we must search, but a Person to whom we must hearken! In the New Testament, multitudes came to Jesus for physical help, but only rarely did one seek Him out to learn the Truth. The whole picture in the gospels is one of a seeking Savior, not one of seeking men.

The Truth was hunting for those who would receive it, and relatively few did, for "many are called, but few are chosen."

# CHRIST IS NOT DIVIDED

*Jesus answered, If a man love me, he will keep my words.*
*(John 14:23)*

Much of our full gospel literature and much of our preaching tend to perpetuate a misunderstanding of what the Bible says about obedience and Christian discipleship.

I think the following is a fair statement of what I was taught in my early Christian experience and before I began to pray and study and anguish over the whole matter:

> "We are saved by accepting Christ as our Savior."
> "We are sanctified by accepting Christ as our
> Lord."
> "We may do the first without doing the second."

What a tragedy that in our day we often hear the gospel appeal made in this way:

"Come to Jesus! You do not have to obey anyone. You do not have to give up anything. Just come to Him and believe in Him as Savior!"

The fact that we hear this everywhere does not make it right! To urge men and women to believe in a divided Christ is bad teaching—for no one can receive a half or a third or a quarter of the divine Person of Christ!

*February 7* _____

# WHO HEARS THE CALL OF GOD?

*Lord, to whom shall we go? thou hast the words of eternal life. (John 6:68)*

Who can deny that there are certain persons who, though still unconverted, nevertheless differ from the crowd, marked out of God, stricken with an interior wound and susceptible to the call of God?

In the prayer of Jesus in John 17:11b, He said: "Father, keep through thine own name those whom thou hast given me." Surely no man is ever the same after God has laid His hand upon him. He will have certain marks, perhaps some not easy to detect.

First might be a deep reverence for divine things. A sense of the sacred must be present or there can be no receptivity to God and truth.

Another mark is great moral sensitivity. When God begins to work in a man to bring him to salvation He makes him acutely sensitive to evil.

Another mark of the Spirit's working is a mighty moral discontent. It does take a work of God in a man to sour him on the world and to turn him against himself; yet until this has happened he is psychologically unable to repent and believe!

# WHO WILL COME TO JESUS?

*Whosoever will, let him take the water of life freely.*
*(Revelation 22:17)*

God's invitation to men is broad but not unqualified. The words "whosoever will may come" throw the door open, indeed, but the church is carrying the gospel invitation far beyond its proper bounds, turning it into something more human and less divine than that found in the sacred Scriptures.

What we tend to overlook is that the word "whosoever" never stands by itself. Always its meaning is modified by the word "believe" or "will" or "come."

According to the teachings of Christ no one will or can come and believe unless there has been done within him a prevenient work of God enabling him to do so.

In the sixth chapter of John, Jesus teaches as that no one can come of himself; he must first be drawn by the Father. "It is the spirit that quickeneth; the flesh profiteth nothing," Jesus said.

Before any man or woman can be saved, he or she must feel a consuming spiritual hunger. Where a hungry heart is found, we may be sure that God was there first—"Ye have not chosen me, but I have chosen you" (John 15:16).

*February 9* _____

# CHRIST CAME TO SAVE

*For God sent not his Son into the world to condemn the world. (John 3:17)*

Millions who have rejected the Christian gospel have generally been too busy and too involved to ask themselves a simple question: "What really is God's intention toward me?"

They could have found the plain and simple answer given by the Apostle John: "For God sent not his Son into the world to condemn the world: but that the world through him might be saved."

This is a gravely significant message from the heart of God Himself! Yet, even in the full light it provides, people are indifferent. Upon our eyes there seems to have fallen a strange dimness; within our ears, a strange dullness. It is a wonder, and a terrible responsibility, that we should have this message in our possession and be so little stirred about it!

I confess that it is very hard for me to accept the fact that it is now very rare for anyone to come into the house of God, silently confessing: "Dear Lord, I am ready and willing to hear what you will speak to me today!"

# WE ARE NOT ORPHANS

*The steps of a good man are ordered by the Lord.*
*(Psalm 37:23)*

I once wrote in an editorial that Christian believers are not orphans in this world, making the point that the divine Shepherd goes before us and that we travel an appointed way.

A reader wrote to question my allusion to our traveling an "appointed" way, asking: "I was brought up a Methodist. In your comments, do you mean this to be foreordination? That is what the Presbyterians believe. Just what did you mean?"

I replied that I had not meant to go down that deep into doctrine—that I had not been thinking of foreordination, predestination or the eternal decrees.

"I was just satisfied that if a consecrated Christian will put himself in the hands of God, even the accidents may be turned into blessings," I told him.

Anyway, I am sure the Methodist brother can go to sleep at night knowing that he does not have to become a Presbyterian to be certain that God is looking after him!

*February 11* _____

# THINK LIKE GOD THINKS

*Search me, 0 God . . . and try me, and know my thoughts.*
*(Psalm 139:23)*

If God knows that your intention is to worship Him with every part of your being, He has promised to cooperate with you. On His side is the love and grace, the promises and the atonement, the constant help and the presence of the Holy Spirit.

On your side there is determination, seeking, yielding, believing. Your heart becomes a chamber, a sanctuary, a shrine in which there may be continuous, unbroken fellowship and communion with God. Your worship rises to God moment by moment!

We have all found that God will not dwell in spiteful and proud and selfish thoughts. He treasures our pure and loving thoughts, our meek and charitable and kindly thoughts. They are the thoughts like His own!

As God dwells in your thoughts, you will be worshiping—and God will be accepting. He will be smelling the incense of your high intentions even when the cares of life are intense and there is activity all around you.

This leaves us no argument. We know what God wants us to be. He wants us to be worshipers!

*February 12*

# OUR HIGHEST HAPPINESS

*If ye know these things, happy are ye if ye do them.*
*(John 13:17)*

Let me call it to your attention that the happiness of all moral creatures lies in the giving of obedience to God, the Creator.

The psalmist cries out in Psalm 103:20: "Bless the Lord, ye his angels; that excel in strength, that do his commandments, hearkening unto the voice of his word."

The angels in heaven find their complete freedom and highest happiness in obeying the commandments of God. They do not find it a tyranny—they find it a delight!

Here is something that we should know and realize: heaven is a place of surrender to the whole will of God and it is heaven because it is such a place.

I thank God that heaven is the world of God's obedient children. Whatever else we may say of its pearly gates, golden streets and jasper walls, heaven is heaven because children of the Most High God find they are in their normal sphere as obedient moral beings.

*February 13* _____

# ACTIVITY IS NOT ENOUGH

*And he said unto them, Come ye yourselves apart . . . and rest awhile. (Mark 6:31)*

Those who try to give warnings to the Christian church are never very popular. Still, I must voice the caution that our craze for "activity" brings very few enriching benefits into our Christian circles. Look into the churches, and you will find groups of half-saved, half-sanctified, carnal people who know more about social niceties than they do about the New Testament.

It is a fact that many of our church folks are activists—engaged in many religious journeys—but they do not seem to move up any closer to Jesus in heart and in spirit.

This modern religious emphasis on activity reminds me of the Japanese mice I have seen in the pet store windows. They are called waltzing mice—but they do not waltz. They just run continually!

Many in our churches hope to have a part in "something big and exciting." But God calls us back—back to the simplicity of the faith; back to the simplicity of Jesus Christ and His unchanging Person!

_____ *February 14*

# PLAYING AT RELIGION

*Whatsoever is born of God overcometh the world.*
*(1 John 5:4)*

When our faith becomes obedience to our Savior, then it is true faith, indeed! The difficulty we modern Christians face is not misunderstanding the Bible, but persuading our untamed hearts to accept its plain instruction. Our problem is to get the consent of our world-loving minds to make Jesus Lord in fact, as well as in word. For it is one thing to say, "Lord, Lord," and quite another thing to obey the Lord's commandments.

We may sing "Crown Him Lord of all," and rejoice in the tones of the loud organ and the deep melody in harmonious voices, but still we have done nothing until we have left the world and set our faces toward the City of God in hard practical reality.

The world's spirit is strong and it can play at religion with every appearance of sincerity. It can have fits of conscience (particularly during Lent)! It will contribute to charitable causes and campaigns on behalf of the poor, but all with its own condition: "Let Christ keep His distance and never assert His Lordship." This it positively will not endure!

*February 15* _____

# WE SEE GOD'S PURPOSE

*That he might gather together in one, all things in Christ
. . . in heaven and on earth. (Ephesians 1:10)*

We trust the Word of God—and the inspired revelation
makes it plain to the believing Christian that all things in
the universe have derived their form from Christ, the
eternal Son!

We are assured that even as an architect-builder gathers
the necessary materials needed to fashion the structure he
has designed, so God will ultimately gather all things
together under one head, even Christ (Ephesians 1:9–10).

Everything in the universe has received its meaning by
the power of His word; each has maintained its place and
order through Him.

Jesus Christ is God creating!

Jesus Christ is God redeeming!

Jesus Christ is God completing and harmonizing!

Jesus Christ is God bringing together all things after the
counsel of His own will!

I can only hope that as we grow and mature and delight
in our faith we are beginning to gain a new appreciation
of God's great eternal purpose!

_____ *February 16*

# MAN'S WASTED POTENTIAL

*Depart from me, ye cursed, into everlasting fire, prepared for the devil and his angels. (Matthew 25:41)*

God has made it plain that hell is a real place—a final abode for people who do not want to love God and serve Him!

The sadness and the tragedy of this fact is that these are human beings, all dear to God because He created them in His own image. Of nothing else in the Creation is it said that it was created in the likeness of God!

Because fallen and perishing man is still nearer to God's likeness than any other creature on earth, God offers him conversion, regeneration and forgiveness. It was surely because of this great potential in the human personality that the eternal Word could become flesh and dwell among us.

We are assured in many ways in the Scriptures that God the Creator does not waste human personality but it is surely one of the stark tragedies of life that human personality can waste itself!

A man by his own sin may waste himself, which is to waste and lose that which on earth is most like God. The man who dies out of Christ is said to be lost, and hardly a word in our language expresses his condition with greater accuracy!

*February 17* _____

# WE WERE OUTCASTS, TOO

*As the Father hath loved me, so have I loved you.*
*(John 15:9)*

We confess, do we not, that we have a Christian responsibility to believe God's Word and to obey God's Truth?

Then we should accept the fact that it is our task to practice the Christian virtues in the power of the Holy Spirit as we await the coming of Him who will come.

The great spiritual needs around us should drive us back to the gospel records of the life and ministry of our Lord Jesus. When evil men crucified Jesus, killed Him, they had no power to change Him. They could not alter the Person or the personality of the Son of God. Putting Him on the cross did not drain away any of His divine affection for a lost race.

The best thing we know about our Lord and Savior is that He loves the sinner. He has always loved the outcast—and for that we should be glad, for we, too, were once outcasts! We are descended from that first man and woman who failed God and disobeyed. They were cast out of the garden, and God set in place a flaming sword to keep them from returning!

*February 18*

# GOD'S HIGHEST WILL

*Then said he, Lo, I come to do thy will, O God.*
*(Hebrews 10:9)*

Let us consider three simple things reinforced in the Word of God for those who would discern God's highest will.

First, be willing to put away known sin!

Second, separate yourself from all of the attractions of the world, the flesh and the devil!

Finally, offer yourself to your God and Savior in believing faith!

God has never yet turned away an honest, sincere person who has come to know the eternal value of the atonement and the peace that is promised through the death and resurrection of our Lord Jesus Christ.

The only person who will never be cleansed and made whole is the one who insists he or she needs no remedy. The person who comes in faith to God and confesses, "I am unclean; I am sin-sick; I am blind," will find mercy and righteousness and life.

Our Lord Jesus Christ is the Savior, the Cleanser. He is the Purifier, the Healer. He is the Sight-giver and the Life-giver. He alone is the Way, the Truth and the Life!

*February 19* _____

# EVERY HINDRANCE REMOVED

*Being justified by faith, we have peace with God through our Lord Jesus Christ. (Romans 5:1)*

There are many legal and governmental reasons why lost men and women should not go to heaven!

It should not be difficult for us to acknowledge that a holy and righteous God must run His universe according to holy laws—and we do not belong there because we have broken every one of those holy laws in some way!

Therefore, there must be an effective redemption, a justification of some kind if we are to have God and He is to have us!

Thank God, it has been done!

The New Testament language is as plain as can be—in Christ through His death and resurrection, every legal hindrance has been met and satisfied: taken away! There is nothing that can keep us from assurance except our own selves.

Let us quit trying to think our way in, to reason our way in. The only way to get in is to believe Him with our hearts forevermore!

*February 20*

# WE HAVE IT ALL

*Seek ye first the kingdom . . . all these things shall be added unto you. (Matthew 6:33)*

How much time have you spent in your Christian life meditating on the plain instruction from our Savior?—"Seek ye first the kingdom of God and his righteousness; and all these things shall be added unto you."

The God who has revealed Himself to needy men and women wants us to know that when we have Him, we have everything—we have all the rest!

Any of us who have experienced a life and ministry of faith can tell how the Lord has met our needs—even for food and the essentials of life.

Brethren, we ought to learn, and learn it soon, that it is much better to have God first and have God Himself, even if we have only a thin dime, than to have all the riches and all the influence in this world and not have God with it!

Let us go on to know Him and to love Him more dearly; not for His gifts and benefits but for the pure joy of His presence. Thus we will fulfill the purpose for which He created us and redeemed us!

*February 21* _____

# OUR INDIVIDUAL WORTH

*For Christ is the end of the law for righteousness to every one that believeth. (Romans 10:4)*

Our lost race has always been prone to discount and reject the wonderful fact of the individual factor in the love of God. Far, far too many men and women in this world are convinced that God's love for the world is just one big lump—and the individual is not involved.

We have only to look around us with serious observation to confirm the fact that the devil has been successful in planting his lie that no one cares for the individual person.

Even in nature around us, there appears to be very little individual concern. The burden of concern is always for the species.

But Jesus did not preach to the multitudes as though they were a faceless crowd. He preached to them as individuals, and with a knowledge of the burdens and the needs of each one. Our Savior did not come into the world to deal with statistics!

Each of us must come with full confidence that it is a personal word God has spoken to us in Christ, that "whosoever believeth in Him shall not perish."

# THE SPIRIT ILLUMINATES

*Your faith should not stand in the wisdom of men, but in the power of God. (1 Corinthians 2:5)*

When we study the New Testament record, we see plainly that Christ's conflict was with the theological rationalists of His day.

John's gospel record is actually a long, inspired, passionately-outpoured account trying to save us from evangelical rationalism—the doctrine that says the text is enough.

Divine revelation is the ground upon which we stand. The Bible is the book of God and I stand for it with all my heart; but before I can be saved, there must be illumination, penitence, renewal, inward deliverance.

In our Christendom, we have tried to ease many people into the kingdom but they have never been renewed within their own beings. The Apostle Paul told the Corinthians that their faith should not stand in the wisdom of men, but in the power of God! There is a difference.

We must insist that conversion to Christ is a miraculous act of God by the Holy Spirit—it must be wrought in the Spirit. There must be an inward illumination!

*February 23* _____

# GIVE TIME TO GOD

*In his law doth he meditate day and night. (Psalm 1:2)*

I have often wished that there were some way to bring modern Christians into a deeper spiritual life painlessly by short easy lessons; but such wishes are vain. No shortcut exists!

God has not bowed to our nervous haste nor embraced the methods of our machine age. It is well that we accept the hard truth now: the man who would know God must give time to Him!

He must count no time wasted which is spent in the cultivation of His acquaintance.

He must give himself to meditation and prayer hours on end. So did the saints of old, the glorious company of the apostles, the goodly fellowship of the prophets and the believing members of the holy Church in all generations.

And so must we if we would follow in their train!

May not the inadequacy of much of our spiritual experience be traced back to our habit of skipping through the corridors of the kingdom like little children through the marketplace, chattering about everything but pausing to learn the true value of nothing?

# "NOW IT IS THE LORD"

*In Christ Jesus, who of God is made unto us . . .*
*sanctification. (1 Corinthians 1:30)*

Is it possible to become so enamored of God's good gifts that we fail to worship Him, the Giver?

Dr. Albert B. Simpson, the founder of The Christian and Missionary Alliance, invited to preach in a Bible conference in England discovered on his arrival that he was to follow two other Bible teachers. All three had been given the same topic, "Sanctification."

From the pulpit, the first speaker made clear his position that sanctification means eradication—the old carnal nature is removed. The second, a suppressionist, advised: "Sit on the lid and keep the old nature down!"

Dr. Simpson in his turn quietly told his audience that he could only present Jesus Christ Himself as God's answer.

"Jesus Christ is your Sanctifier, your all and in all! God wants you to get your eyes away from the gifts. He wants your gaze to be on the Giver—Christ Himself," he said.

This is a wonderful word for those who would worship rightly:

> Once it was the blessing;
> Now it is the Lord!

*February 25* _____

# "BE STILL AND KNOW"

*Be still, and know that I am God. (Psalm 46:10)*

Prayer among evangelical Christians is always in danger of degenerating into a glorified "gold rush." Almost every book on prayer deals with the "get" element mainly. How to get things we want from God occupies most of our space.

Christians should never forget that the highest kind of prayer is never the making of requests.

Prayer at its holiest moment is the entering into God to a place of such blessed union as makes miracles seem tame and remarkable answers to prayer appear something very far short of wonderful, by comparison.

We should be aware that there is a kind of school where the soul must go to learn its best eternal lessons. It is the school of silence. "Be still and know," said the psalmist.

It might well be a revelation to some Christians if they were to get completely quiet for a time—a time to listen in the silence for the deep voice of the Eternal God!

# THE END OF THE AGE

*All of these things shall be dissolved . . . what manner of persons ought ye to be? (2 Peter 3:11)*

Everywhere around us we are experiencing a great new wave of humanity's interest in spiritism and devil worship. I must take this as one of the signs that God's age of grace and mercy is approaching the end point. It tells us that the time may be near when God proclaims: "I have seen enough of mankind's sin and rebellion. It is time for the trumpets of judgment to sound!"

If we are willing to add the appeals from the book of Revelation to the weight of the other Scriptures, we discover God saying to us that the earth on which we live is not self-explanatory and certainly not self-sufficient.

Although the earth on which we spin is largely populated by a rebel race, it had a divine origin. Now God is about to enforce His claim upon it and judge those who are usurpers. He is saying that there is another and better world, another kingdom, that is always keeping an eye on the world we inhabit!

*February 27* _____

# PRAYER FOR ANOINTING

It is time, 0 God, for Thee to work, for the enemy has entered into Thy pasture, and the sheep are torn and scattered. False shepherds abound who deny the danger and laugh at the perils which surround Thy flock.

Lord Jesus, I come to Thee for spiritual preparation. Lay Thy hand upon me, anoint me with the oil of the New Testament prophet. Save me from the error of judging a church by its size, its popularity or the amount of its yearly offering.

Help me to remember that I am a prophet—not a promoter, not a religious manager. Let me never become a slave to crowds. Heal my soul of carnal ambitions and deliver me from the itch for publicity.

Lay Thy terror upon me, 0 God, and drive me to the place of prayer, where I may wrestle with principalities and powers and the rulers of the darkness of this world.

Teach me self-discipline, that I may be a good soldier of Jesus Christ.

# BEGIN WITH GOD

*Not as pleasing men, but God, which trieth our hearts.*
*(1 Thessalonians 2:4)*

I am really sad for the great throngs of men and women who have never known the satisfaction of believing what God says about all of the good things He has created—and everything having its purpose!

This is an area in which you must begin with God. Then you begin to understand everything in its proper context. All things fit into shape and form when you begin with God!

In Christian circles, there is now an undue deference to intellectual knowledge and accomplishment. I insist that it ought to be balanced out. We appreciate the efforts and hours that go into academic progress, but we must always keep God's wisdom and God's admonitions in mind.

Search and study as we will and we discover that we have only learned fragments of truth. On the other hand, the newest Christian believer has already learned many marvelous things at the center of truth. He has met and knows God!

That is the primary issue, my brother and sister. That is why we earnestly invite men and women to become converted, taking Jesus Christ as their Savior and Lord!

*March 1* _____

# THE GODHEAD—FOREVER ONE

*Father, into thy hands I commend my spirit. (Luke 23:46)*

When Christ Jesus died on that unholy, fly-infested cross for mankind, He never divided the Godhead! We are assured from the earliest church fathers that the Father in heaven, His eternal Son, and the Holy Ghost are forever One—inseparable, indivisible—and can never be anything else.

Not all of Nero's swords could ever cut down through the substance of the Godhead to cut off the Father from the Son.

It was Mary's son who cried out, "Why hast Thou forsaken me?" It was the human body which God had given Him. It was the sacrifice that cried—the lamb about to die! The Son of Man knew himself forsaken. God dumped that vast, filthy, slimy mass of human sin on the soul of the Savior—and then backed away.

Believe it that the ancient and timeless Deity was never separated. He was still in the bosom of the Father when He cried, "Into Thy hands I commend my spirit!"

Little wonder that we are amazed and marvel every day at the wonder of the ancient theology of the Christian church!

# GLORY OF THE TRINITY

*Three that bear record in heaven, the Father, the Word, and the Holy Ghost: and these three are one. (1 John 5:7)*

The more I read my Bible, the more I believe in the triune God!

With the prophet Isaiah, I am stirred by the vision of the heavenly creatures, the seraphim around the throne of God, engrossed in their worship and praise.

I have often wondered why the rabbis and saints and hymnists of the olden times did not come to the knowledge of the Trinity just from the seraphims' chorus: "Holy! Holy! Holy!"

I am a trinitarian—I believe in one God, the Father Almighty, maker of heaven and earth. I believe in one Lord Jesus Christ, Son of the Father, begotten of Him before all ages. I believe in the Holy Spirit, the Lord and Giver of life, who with the Father and the Son together is worshiped and glorified.

Isaiah was an astonished man. He could only manage this witness: "Mine eyes have seen the King!" Only the King of glory can reveal Himself to the willing spirit of a man, so that an Isaiah or any other man or woman, can say with humility but with assurance, "I know Him!"

*March 3* _____

# PREACH A WHOLE CHRIST

*God is faithful, by whom ye were called unto the fellowship of his Son Jesus Christ our Lord. (1 Corinthians 1:9)*

I reject the human insistence among us that Christ may sustain a divided relationship toward us in this life.

I am aware that this is now so commonly preached that to oppose it or object to it means that you are sticking your neck out and you had best be prepared for what comes.

But, I am forced to ask: how can we insist and teach that our Lord Jesus Christ can be our Savior without being our Lord?

How can so many continue to teach that we can be saved without any thought of obedience to our Sovereign Lord?

I am satisfied in my own heart that when a man or a woman believes on the Lord Jesus Christ he or she must believe on the whole Lord Jesus Christ—not making any reservation! How can a teaching be justified when it encourages sinners to use Jesus as a Savior in their time of need, without owing Him obedience and allegiance?

I believe we need to return to preaching a whole Christ to our needy world!

# LORD OF RIGHTEOUSNESS

*But of him are ye in Christ Jesus, who of God is made unto us wisdom, and righteousness. (1 Corinthians 1:30)*

In the midst of all the confusions of our day, it is important that we find out that Jesus Christ is the Lord of all righteousness and the Lord of all wisdom.

Righteousness is not a word easily acceptable to lost men and women in a lost world. Outside of the Word of God, there is no book or treatise that can give us a satisfying answer about righteousness, because the only One who is Lord of all righteousness is our Lord Jesus Christ, Himself. A scepter of righteousness is the scepter of His kingdom. He is the only One in all the universe who perfectly loved righteousness and hated iniquity.

Our great High Priest and Mediator is the righteous and holy One—Jesus Christ, our risen Lord. He is not only righteous, He is the Lord of all righteousness!

Then, there is His wisdom. The sum total of the deep and eternal wisdom of the ages lies in Jesus Christ as a treasure hidden away. All the deep purposes of God reside in Him because His perfect wisdom enables Him to plan far ahead! Thus history itself becomes the slow development of His purposes.

*March 5* _____

# THE GOSPEL WARNING

*As he reasoned of righteousness, temperance, and judgment to come, Felix trembled. (Acts 24:25)*

We who rejoice in the blessings that have come to us through the Savior, need to bear in mind that the gospel is not good news only!

The message of the Cross is good news indeed for the penitent, but to those who obey not the gospel it carries an overtone of warning.

The Spirit's ministry to the impenitent world is to tell of sin and righteousness and judgment. For sinners who want to cease being willful sinners and become obedient children of God, the gospel message is one of unqualified peace, but it is by its very nature also an arbiter of the future destinies of man.

Actually, the message of the gospel may be received in either of two ways: in word only without power, or in word with power.

The truth received in power shifts the bases of life from Adam to Christ—a new and different Spirit enters the personality and makes the believing man new in every department of his being!

# THE ETERNAL VERITY

*Jesus Christ the same yesterday, today and forever.*
*(Hebrews 13:8)*

There is a great deal of discussion now taking place about the lack of spiritual power in our Christian churches. What about the New Testament patterns?

Brethren, the apostolic method was to provide a foundation of good, sound biblical reasons for following the Savior, for our willingness to let the Spirit of God display the great Christian virtues in our lives.

That is why we come in faith and rejoicing to the eternal verity of Hebrews 13:8, "Jesus Christ, the same yesterday, today and forever!" This proclamation gives significance to every other section of teaching and exhortation in the letter to the Hebrews. In this verse is truth that is morally and spiritually dynamic if we will exercise the faith and the will to demonstrate it in our needy world.

I think this fact, this truth that Jesus Christ wants to be known in His church as the ever-living, never-changing Lord of all, could bring back again the power and testimony of the early church!

*March 7* _____

# WE KNOW WHAT WE BELIEVE

*If ye continue in the faith grounded and settled . . . not moved away from the hope of the gospel. (Colossians 1:23)*

The hope of the Christian church still lies in the purity of her theology, that is, her beliefs about God and man and their relation to each other.

It is a fact that positive beliefs are not popular these days. I sense that the modern efforts to popularize the Christian faith have been extremely damaging to that faith. The purpose has been to simplify truth for the masses by using the language of the masses instead of the language of the church. It has not succeeded, but has added to rather than diminished religious confusion.

A mistaken desire to maintain a spirit of tolerance among all races and religions has produced a breed of Janus-like Christians with built-in swivels, remarkable only for their ability to turn in any direction gracefully!

Our Christian beliefs have been revealed by the inspiration of the Holy Spirit in the sacred Scriptures. Everything there is clear-cut and accurate. We dare not be less than accurate in our treatment of anything so precious!

# "AUTOMATIC" SAINTS?

*Always bearing about in the body the dying of the Lord
Jesus, that the life also of Jesus might be made manifest.*
*(2 Corinthians 4:10)*

Not everyone agrees with me that full qualification for
eternity is not instant or automatic or painless.

I can only hope that you are wise enough, desirous
enough and spiritual enough to face up to the truth that
every day is another day of spiritual preparation, another
day of testing and discipline with our heavenly
destination in mind.

I hope, too, that you may begin to understand why
many evangelical churches are in such a mess. It has
become popular to preach a painless Christianity and
automatic saintliness. It has become a part of our
"instant" culture—"just pour a little water on it, stir
mildly, pick up a gospel tract, and you are on your
Christian way!"

"Lo," we are told, "this is Bible Christianity!"

"It is nothing of the sort!"

To depend upon that kind of a formula is to experience
only the outer fringe, the edge of what Christianity really
is. For when the new birth is real and the wonder of
regeneration has taken place, then comes the lifetime of
preparation  with the guidance of the Holy Spirit!

*March 9* _____

# NORMAL—OR NOMINAL?

*Where your treasure is, there will your heart be also.*
*(Luke 12:34)*

Is the Lord Jesus Christ your most precious treasure in the whole world? If so, count yourself among "normal" Christians, rather than among "nominal" Christians!

My old dictionary gives this definition as the meaning of nominal:

> Existing in name only, not real or actual;
> hence so small, slight, as to be hardly
> worth the name.

With that as a definition, those who know they are Christians "in name only" should never make the pretense of being normal Christians. Thankfully those who are "normal" are constantly being drawn to praise and worship, charmed by the moral beauty which is found only in Jesus.

I cannot understand how anyone can profess to be a follower and a disciple of our Lord Jesus Christ and not be overwhelmed by His attributes. Those divine attributes faithfully attest that He is indeed Lord of all, completely worthy of our worship and praise!

*March 10*

# THE GREAT PHYSICIAN

*When Jesus saw him . . . he saith unto him, Wilt thou be made whole? (John 5:6)*

If you are a discouraged and defeated Christian believer, you may have accepted the rationalization that your condition is "normal for all Christians."

You may now be content with the position that the progressive, victorious Christian life may be suitable for a few Christians—but not for you! You have been to Bible conferences; you have been to the altar—but the blessings are for someone else.

Now, that attitude on the part of Christian believers is neither modesty nor meekness. It is a chronic discouragement resulting from unbelief. It is rather like those who have been sick for so long that they no longer believe they can get well.

Jesus is still saying, as He said to the man lying by the gate at the Jerusalem pool, "Do you want to be made whole?" Jesus made him whole—because of his desire! His need was great, but he had never lapsed into that state of chronic discouragement.

*March 11* _____

# WISDOM FROM GOD

*Things which are seen are temporal . . . things which are*
*not seen are eternal. (2 Corinthians 4:18)*

The thinking of our generation often reflects a
willingness to exchange a high view of God's eternity for
a short-term concept called "here and now." Technology
is presumed to be paramount but the answers science
gives us are short-term answers.

The scientists may be able to keep us alive for a few
extra years but believing Christians know some things
that Einstein did not know!

For instance, we know why we are here. We can say
why we were born. We also know what we believe about
the value of things eternal.

We are thankful that we have found the promise from
the God of all grace that deals with the long-term and the
eternal. We belong to a company of the plain people who
believe the truth revealed in the Bible.

Actually, the wisest person in the world is the person
who knows the most about God; the person who realizes
that the answer to creation and life and eternity is a
theological answer—not a scientific answer!

# THE IMAGE WE PROJECT

*O come, let us worship and bow down; for he is our God.*
*(Psalm 95:6–7)*

Are we presently missing important elements of worship in our churches? I speak of the genuine and sacred offering of ourselves as we worship the God and Father of our Lord Jesus Christ.

We must ask the question, even though we are building great churches and large congregations. We are boasting about high standards and talking about revival. But as evangelical Christian believers, are we as concerned as we should be about the image we really project to the community around us? It cannot be denied that many who profess the name of Christ still fail to show forth His love and compassion!

It should say something to us that the often-quoted Jean-Paul Sartre described his turning to philosophy and hopelessness as a turning away from a secularistic church.

His indictment: "I did not recognize in the fashionable God who was taught me, Him who was waiting for my soul. I needed a creator: I was given a big businessman!"

*March 13* _____

# WORSHIP—AND WORK

*And the Lord make you to increase and abound in love one toward another, and toward all men. (1 Thessalonians 4:12)*

I must take issue with those in the churches who insist that the worshiping saints do not get anything done but worship! Such an attitude reveals that they have not done their homework. The beautiful part of worship is that it prepares you and enables you to zero in on the important things that must be done for God.

Listen to me! Practically every great deed done in the church of Christ all the way back to the apostles was done by people blazing with the radiant worship of their God!

The great hospitals and the mental institutions have grown out of the hearts of worshiping and compassionate disciples. It is true, also, that wherever the church has come out of her lethargy and into the tides of revival and spiritual renewal, always the worshipers were back of it.

A survey of church history will prove that it was those who were the yearning worshipers who also became the great workers and the selfless servants. If we give ourselves to God's call for worship, everyone will do more for the Savior than they are doing now!

# "TEARS OF JOY—AMEN!"

*He shall baptize you with the Holy Ghost and with fire.*
*(Luke 3:16)*

We need not be afraid of a genuine visitation of the Spirit of God!

Blaise Pascal, the famed 17th-century French scientist and philosopher, experienced in his lifetime a personal, overwhelming encounter with God that changed his life. Those who attended him at his death found a worn, creased paper in his clothing, close to his heart; apparently a reminder of what he had felt and sensed in God's very presence.

In Pascal's own hand it read:

> From about half-past ten at night, to about half after midnight—fire! 0 God of Abraham, God of Isaac, God of Jacob—not the God of philosophers or the wise. The God of Jesus Christ who can be known only in the ways of the Gospel. Security. Feeling. Peace. Joy. Tears of joy—Amen!

Were these the expressions of a fanatic, an extremist? No; it was the ecstatic utterance of a yielded man during two awesome hours in the presence of God. The astonished Pascal could only describe the visitation in one word—"Fire!"

*March 15* _____

# EXCEPT YE REPENT

*The rest of mankind . . . still did not repent.*
*(Revelation 9:20)*

There are many compelling lessons to be drawn from the Scriptures and one of the clearest is that sinful and rebellious people can never be forced into repentance.

The same act that may cause one person to repent and believe will cause others to hate and despise God!

The same Bible sermon that brings the person to tearful submission at an altar of prayer will send others out with pride and a resolve to have their own human way.

Students of the Scriptures are aware that the Old Testament prophets and the writing apostles of New Testament times foresaw and proclaimed God's coming day of judgment—the consummate settling of accounts between the Sovereign God and his rebellious and sinful creation.

How desperately we would like to believe that in the face of coming judgment, all lost men and women will cry out to God, but such will not be the case: "The rest of mankind that were not killed by these plagues still did not repent" (Revelation 9:20).

# RESPONSE TO THE WORD

*The word of God . . . is sharper than any two-edged sword.*
*(Hebrews 4:12)*

Men and women who read and study the Scriptures for their literary beauty alone have missed the whole purpose for which they were given.

God's Word is not to be enjoyed as one might "enjoy" a Beethoven symphony or a poem by Wordsworth.

The reason: the Bible demands immediate action, faith, surrender, committal. Until it has secured these, it has done nothing positive for the reader, but it has increased his responsibility and deepened the judgment that must follow.

The Bible was called forth by the fall of man. It is the voice of God calling men home from the wilds of sin; it is a road map for returning prodigals. It is instruction in righteousness, light in darkness, information about God and man and life and death and heaven and hell.

Further, the destiny of each individual depends upon the response to that Voice in the Word!

*March 17* _____

# THE CROWD TURNS BACK

*From that time many of his disciples went back, and walked no more with him. (John 6:66)*

Our Lord Jesus Christ called men to follow Him, but He plainly taught that "no man can come unto me, except it were given him of my Father" (John 6:65).

It is not surprising that many of His early followers, upon hearing these words, went back and walked no more with Him. Such teaching cannot but be deeply disturbing to the natural mind. It takes from sinful men much of the power of self-determination. It cuts the ground out from under their self-help and throws them back upon the sovereign good pleasure of God—and that is precisely where they do not want to be!

These statements by our Lord run contrary to the current assumptions of popular Christianity. Men are willing to be saved by grace, but to preserve their self-esteem, they must hold that the desire to be saved originated with them.

Most Christians today seem afraid to talk about these plain words of Jesus concerning the sovereign operation of God—so they use the simple trick of ignoring them!

# MONEY IS NOT TRUTH

*The blessing of the Lord, it maketh rich, and he addeth no sorrow with it. (Proverbs 10:22)*

It is a fact in human history that men and women have never in any great numbers sought after truth.

The young people who stream from our halls of learning each year confess to having no more than a passing and academic interest in truth. The majority admit that they go to college only to improve their social standing and increase their earning power.

So, the average American will confess that he most wants success in his chosen field; and he wants success both for prestige and for financial security.

The ominous thing about all this is that everything men and women want can be bought with money, and it would be difficult to think of an indictment more terrible than that!

Real seekers after truth are almost as rare as albino deer! Why? Because truth is a glorious but hard master. Jesus said, "I am the Truth," and followed Truth straight to the Cross. The Truth seeker must follow Him there and that is the reason few men seek the Truth!

*March 19* _____

# TELL THE WHOLE TRUTH

*In hope of eternal life, which God, that cannot lie, promised before the world began.* (Titus 1:2)

It is sad indeed to know that there are Christian leaders among us who are too timid to tell the people all the truth. They are now asking men and women to give to God only that which costs them nothing!

The contemporary moral climate does not favor a faith as tough and fibrous as that taught by our Lord and His apostles.

Christ calls men to carry His cross; we call them to have fun in His name!

He calls them to suffer; we call them to enjoy all the bourgeois comforts modern civilization affords!

He calls them to holiness; we call them to a cheap and tawdry happiness that would have been rejected with scorn by the least of the Stoic philosophers!

When will believers learn that to love righteousness it is necessary to hate sin? That to accept Christ it is necessary to reject self? That a friend of the world is an enemy of God? Let us not be shocked by the suggestion that there are disadvantages to the life in Christ!

# POUR YOURSELF OUT

*How be it when he, the Spirit of truth, is come, he will guide you into all truth.* (John 16:13)

Science declares that nature abhors a vacuum. It should be happy knowledge to us, then, that the same principle is true in the kingdom of God—when you empty yourself, God Almighty rushes in!

The Creator God who fills the universe and overflows into immensity can never be surrounded by that little thing we call our brain, our mind, our intellect. Never can we rise to face God by what we are and by what we know! Only by love and faith are we lifted thus to know Him and adore Him!

What a happy hour it becomes when we are drawn out of ourselves, and into that vacuum rushes the blessed Presence.

How wonderful in our humanity to sense the reality of the Holy Spirit's invitation: "Pour yourself out! Give yourself to Me! Empty yourself! Bring your empty earthen vessels! Come in meekness like a child!"

Drawn out of ourselves by the Holy Spirit of God—for who knows the things of God but the Holy Spirit?

We are delivered from ourselves when we finally seek God for Himself alone!

*March 21* _____

# GOD'S OVERCOMERS

*These have washed their robes, and made them white in the blood of the Lamb. (Revelation 7:14)*

I insist that if we are burdened with genuine concern, we have the responsibility of examining the true spiritual condition of men and women within the church's ranks.

We do live in a time of soft, easy Christianity. It is an era marked by a polite "nibbling" around the edges of the Word of God. There is a mindset within present day Christianity that supposes one should get into trouble or suffer embarrassment for Christ's sake!

My brethren, what does it mean to be loyal to Jesus Christ? To confess that Jesus Himself is more important to us than anything else in the world?

Many find it hard to understand how large numbers of Christian believers could have died for their faith in our own generation! With a sense of distant admiration, we call them simple-hearted nationals. God calls them overcomers!

Professing Christians in our North American churches can hardly comprehend so costly a price for the faith we take for granted. Material prosperity and popular acceptance have sapped the vitality of our Christian witness!

# HERE FOR OUR TIME

*Who knowest whether thou art come to the kingdom for such a time as this? (Esther 4:14)*

Just as those who lived in the past had the privilege of being God's people of faith then, so do we in our own day! It is good to come to the understanding that while God wants us to be holy and Spirit-filled, He does not expect us to look like Abraham or to play the harp like David or to have the same spiritual insights given to Paul.

All of the former heroes of the faith are dead. You are alive in your generation. A Bible proverb says that it is better to be a living dog than a dead lion. You may wish to be Abraham or Isaac or Jacob, but remember they have been asleep for centuries, and you are still around!

You can witness for our Lord today! You can still pray! You can still give of your substance to help those who are in need!

In this, your own generation, give God all your love, all your devotion. You do not know what holy, happy secret God may want to whisper to your responsive heart!

*March 23* _____

# "BORN OF GOD!"

*By his own blood he entered in once into the holy place.
(Hebrews 9:12)*

I think most of us remember with assurance the words
of the Charles Wesley hymn which was his own personal
testimony:

> His Spirit answers to the blood,
> And tells me I am born of God!

Wesley testified here and in many other hymns to an
inner illumination!

When I became a Christian, no one had to come to me
and tell me what Wesley meant. That is why Jesus taught
that whosoever is willing to do His will shall have a
revelation in his own heart. He shall have an inward
revelation that tells him he is a child of God.

Too many persons try to make Jesus Christ a
convenience. They reduce Him simply to a Big Friend
who will help us when we are in trouble.

That is not biblical Christianity! Jesus Christ is Lord,
and when an individual comes in repentance and faith,
the truth flashes in. For the first time he finds himself
saying, "I will do the will of the Lord, even if I die for it!"

# CONVICTION AND PAIN

*Nicodemus answered and said unto him, How can these things be? (John 3:9)*

I consider it a good sign that some people are still asking questions like these in our churches: "What should happen in a genuine conversion to Christ?" and "What should a man or woman feel in the transaction of the new birth?"

If I am asked, my answer is this: "There ought to be a real and genuine cry of pain!"

That is why I am not impressed with the kind of evangelism that tries to invite people into the fellowship of God by signing a card. There should be a birth within, a birth from above. There should be the terror of seeing ourselves in violent contrast to the holy, holy God!

Unless we come into this place of conviction and pain concerning our sin, I am not sure how deep and real our repentance will ever be.

The man whom God will use must be undone, humble and pliable. He must be, like the astonished Isaiah, a man who has seen the King in His beauty!

*March 25* _____

# BREAK WITH THIS WORLD

*Come out from among them, and be ye separate, saith the Lord. (2 Corinthians 6:17)*

I dare to say that Christians who have genuinely come to love and trust Jesus Christ have also renounced this world and have chosen a new model after which to pattern their lives.

Further, we should say that this is the aspect of the Christian life that most people do not like. They want comfort. They want blessing. They want peace. But they recoil from this radical, revolutionary break with the world.

To follow Christ in this rough and thorough-going way is too much for them!

Actually, the true Christian dissents from the world because he knows that it cannot make good on its promises. As Christ's believing disciple, he is not left without a "norm" to which he seeks to be adjusted. The Lord Jesus Christ is Himself the norm, the ideally perfect model, and the worshiping soul yearns to be like Him. Indeed, the whole drive behind the Christian life is the longing to be conformed to the image of Christ!

# THE WORLDLY "VIRUS"

*Let all bitterness, and wrath, and anger, and clamour . . . be put away from you. (Ephesians 4:31)*

As Christian believers, we must stand together against some things. So, if you hear anyone saying that A.W. Tozer preaches a good deal that is negative, just smile and agree: "That is because he preaches the Bible!"

Here are some of the things we oppose: we are against the many modern idols that have been allowed to creep into the churches; we are against the "unauthorized fire" that is being offered on the altars of the Lord; we are against the modern gods that are being adopted in our sanctuaries.

We are against the world's ways and its false values. We are against the world's follies and its vain pleasures. We are against this world's greed and sinful ambitions. We are against this world's vices and its carnal habits.

We believe this spells out clearly the Bible truth of separation. God asks us to stand boldly against anything or anyone who hurts or hinders this New Testament body of Christians. Where the church is not healed it will wither. The Word of God is the antibiotic that alone can destroy the virus that would plague the life of the church!

*March 27* _____

# LET FEAR BECOME TRUST

*Ye have not received the spirit of bondage again to fear.*
*(Romans 8:15)*

What can we do but pray for the throngs of defiant men and women who believe that their humanistic view of life is all-sufficent? They believe that they are responsible "captains" of their own souls.

The sad fact is that even while they are joining in the age-old rejection of Jesus Christ—"We will not have this Man to rule over us"—they still are beset with fears within.

The present competitive world and its selfish society have brought many new fears to the human race. I can sympathize with those troubled beings who lie awake at night worrying about the possible destruction of the race through some evil, misguided use of the world's store of nuclear weapons. The tragedy is that they have lost all sense of the sovereignty and omnipotence and faithfulness of the living God.

Although the material world has never understood it, our faith is well-placed in the Scriptures! Those who take God's Word seriously are convinced of an actual heavenly realm as real as this world we inhabit!

# OUR FUTURE REWARDS

*Every man shall receive his own reward.* (1 Corinthians 3:8)

Our motives in the Christian life should be both right and genuine. God is the Faithful One. We are to love Him and serve Him because He is God—not because of the gracious things He does for us or for the rewards He promises us!

However, it should be said that God does not expect us to forget or ignore the gracious future promises He has made to us. It is a glorious truth that if we believe God and honor His Word, if we walk by faith in love and obedience, there will be eternal rewards for each of us in that great coming day. The rewards will differ. Wisdom and knowledge and love reside in Him who is our God. He will make the right judgments for His people.

I for one will not be surprised if some of God's faithful people serving Him today should rise as high and shine as brightly as the heroes of faith listed in the book of Hebrews.

I say that in all truthfulness because I do not think that all of the heroes of faith are dead and gone!

*March 29*

# WHICH CROSS DO WE CARRY?

*Having made peace through the blood of his cross.*
*(Colossians 1:20)*

One of the strange things under the sun is a "crossless" Christianity. The cross of Christendom is a "no-cross," an ecclesiastical symbol. The cross of our Lord Jesus Christ is a place of death!

Let each one be careful which cross he carries!

Thousands turn away from Jesus Christ because they will not meet His conditions. He watches them as they go, for He loves them, but He will make no concessions.

Admit one soul into the kingdom by compromise and that kingdom is no longer secure. Christ will be Lord, or He will be Judge. Every man must decide whether he will take Him as Lord now, or face Him as Judge then!

"If any man will . . . let him follow me." Some will rise and go after Him, but others give no heed to His voice. So the gulf opens between man and man, between those who will and those who will not.

The Man, the kindly Stranger who walked this earth, is His own proof. He will not put Himself again on trial; He will not argue. But the morning of the judgment will confirm what men in the twilight have decided!

# POWER OF THE CROSS

*The cross . . . by whom the world is crucified unto me, and I unto the world. (Galatians 6:14)*

Only a person with a perfect knowledge of mankind could have dared to set forth the terms of discipleship that our Lord Jesus Christ expects of His followers.

Only the Lord of men could have risked the effect of such rigorous demands: "Let him deny himself!"

Can the Lord lay down such severe rules at the door of His kingdom? He can—and He does!

If He is to save the man, He must save him from himself. It is the "himself" which has enslaved and corrupted the man. Deliverance comes only by denial of that self.

No man in his own strength can shed the chains with which self has bound him, but in the next breath the Lord reveals the source of the power which is to set the soul free: "Let him take up his cross."

The cross was an instrument of death—slaying a man was its only function. "Let him take his cross," said Jesus, and thus he will know deliverance from himself!

*March 31* _____

# THE PRESENCE OF GOD

*The righteous shall give thanks . . . the upright shall dwell in thy presence. (Psalm 140:13)*

The spiritual giants of old were those who at some time became acutely conscious of the presence of God. They maintained that consciousness for the rest of their lives.

How otherwise can the saints and prophets be explained? How otherwise can we account for the amazing power for good they have exercised over countless generations?

Is it not that indeed they had become friends of God? Is it not that they walked in conscious communion with the real Presence and addressed their prayers to God with the artless conviction that they were truly addressing Someone actually there?

Let me say it again, for certainly it is no secret: we do God honor in believing what He has said about Himself and coming boldly to His throne of grace than by hiding in a self-conscious humility!

Those unlikely men chosen by our Lord as His closest disciples might well have hesitated to claim friendship with Christ. But Jesus said to them, "You are my friends!"

_____ *April 1*

# GOD HAS A REMEDY

*If we confess our sins, he is faithful and just to forgive us our sins. (1 John 1:9)*

Seekers and inquirers have often voiced this deep question of concern: "Why does God forgive? and how does God forgive sin?"

There is plain teaching throughout the Old and New Testaments concerning God's willingness to forgive and forget. Yet there are segments of the Christian church which appear to be poorly taught concerning God's clear remedy, through the atonement of Christ, for the believer who has yielded to temptation and failed his Lord.

God knows that sin is the dark shadow standing between Him and His highest creation, man. God is more willing to remove that shadow than we are to have it removed!

He wants to forgive us—and that desire is a part of God's character. In the sacrificial death of a lamb in the Old Testament, God was telling us that one day a perfect Lamb would come to actually take away sin.

That is how and why God forgives sin now. In John's words: "We have an advocate with the Father, Jesus Christ the righteous: And he is the propitiation for our sins" (1 John 2:1–2a).

*April 2* _____

# SPIRITUAL UNANIMITY

*Finally, be ye all of one mind, having compassion one of another, love as brethren. (1 Peter 3:8)*

The Holy Spirit knew what He was doing when He moved the Apostle Peter to write to the early Christian church about the reality of being "of one mind" in their fellowship.

Peter was not asking all the brothers and sisters to settle for some kind of regulated uniformity. He was recommending a spiritual unanimity—which means that the Spirit of God making Christ real within our beings will also give us a unity in certain qualities and disposition.

Peter leaves little doubt about the fruits of genuine Christian unanimity within: "Be alike in compassion. Be alike in loving. Be alike in pity. Be alike in courtesy. Be alike in forgiving!" Then he sums it all up: "Finally, be ye all of one mind!"

God's love shed abroad in our hearts—compassion and love which can only be found in Jesus Christ—these are the only elements of true unity among men and women today!

# HOPE—OR DESPAIR?

*A man can receive nothing, except it be given him from heaven. (John 3:27)*

John the Baptist gave his questioners a brief sentence that I have called the "hope and the despair" of mankind. He told them that "a man can receive nothing, except it be given him from heaven."

John was not referring to men's gifts. He was speaking of spiritual truth. Divine truth is of the nature of the Holy Spirit, and for that reason it can be received only by spiritual revelation.

In his New Testament letters, the Apostle Paul declares again and again the inability of human reason to discover or comprehend divine truth. In that inability we see human despair.

John the Baptist said, ". . . except it be given him from heaven"—and this is our hope! These words do certainly mean that there is such a thing as a gift of knowing, a gift that comes from heaven. Jesus promised His disciples that the Holy Spirit of truth would come and teach them all things.

Jesus also prayed: "I thank thee, O Father, because thou hast hid these things from the wise, and hast revealed them unto babes" (Luke 10:21).

*April 4* _____

# THE EASTER TRIUMPH

*Why seek ye the living among the dead? He is not here, but is risen.* (Luke 24:5–6)

I do not mind telling you that within me I find the Easter message and the reality of the Resurrection more beautiful and glorious than the Christmas scene.

Christmas tells us that Jesus was born; that He was born for the humiliation of suffering and death and atonement.

But Easter is the radiant and glory-filled celebration of Christ's mighty triumph over the grave and death and hell!

When Easter comes, our voices are raised in the triumphant chorus:

> The three sad days had quickly sped;
> He rises glorious from the dead!

There is the real beauty! This is more than the beauty of color; more than the beauty of outline or form; more than the beauty of physical proportion.

In the living Christ is the perfection of all beauty; and because He lives, we too shall live in the presence of His beauty and the beauties of heaven, forever!

# RESURRECTION POWER

*Jesus came and spake unto them, saying, All power is given unto me in heaven and in earth. (Matthew 28:18)*

Let us be confident, Christian brethren, that our power does not lie in the manger at Bethlehem nor in the relics of the Cross. True spiritual power resides in the victory of the mighty, resurrected Lord of glory, who could pronounce after spoiling death: "All power is given me in heaven and in earth."

The power of the Christian believer lies in the Savior's triumph of eternal glory!

Christ's resurrection brought about a startling change of direction for the believers. Sadness and fear and mourning marked the direction of their religion before they knew that Jesus was raised from the dead—their direction was towards the grave. When they heard the angelic witness, "He is risen, as He said," the direction immediately shifted away from the tomb—"He is risen, indeed!" If this is not the meaning of Easter, the Christian church is involved only in a shallow one-day festival each year.

Thankfully, the resurrection morning was only the beginning of a great, vast outreach that has never ended—and will not end until our Lord Jesus Christ comes back again!

*April 6* _____

# RESURRECTION: A FACT

*Be established in the present truth . . . for we have not*
*cunningly devised fables. (2 Peter 1:12, 16)*

The resurrection of Christ and the fact of the empty
tomb are not a part of this world's complex and
continuing mythologies. This is not a Santa Claus tale—it
is history and it is a reality!

The true church of Jesus Christ is necessarily founded
upon the belief and the truth that there was a real death, a
real tomb and a real stone!

But, thank God, there was a sovereign Father in heaven,
an angel sent to roll the stone away and a living Savior in
a resurrected and glorified body, able to proclaim to His
disciples, "All power is given unto me in heaven and in
earth!"

Brethren, He died for us, but ever since the hour of the
resurrection, He has been the mighty Jesus, the mighty
Christ, the mighty Lord!

Our business is to thank God with tearful reverence for
the Cross, but to go on to a right understanding of what
the resurrection meant both to God and to men. We
understand and acknowledge that the Resurrection has
placed a glorious crown upon all of Christ's sufferings!

# EASTER—AND MISSIONS

*That I may know him, and the power of his resurrection.*
*(Philippians 3:10)*

Do we really believe that the resurrection of Jesus Christ is something more than making us the "happiest fellows in the Easter parade"?

Are we just to listen to the bright cantata and join in singing, "Up from the Grave He Arose," smell the flowers and go home and forget it?

No, certainly not!

It is truth and a promise with a specific moral application. The resurrection certainly commands us with all the authority of sovereign obligation—the missionary obligation!

I cannot give in to the devil's principal, deceitful tactic which makes so many Christians satisfied with an "Easter celebration" instead of experiencing the power of Christ's resurrection. It is the devil's business to keep Christians mourning and weeping with pity beside the cross instead of demonstrating that Jesus Christ is risen, indeed.

When will the Christian church rise up, depending on His promise and power, and get on the offensive for the risen and ascended Savior?

*April 8* _____

# "I WILL NOT FORSAKE YOU!"

*And, lo, I am with you alway, even unto the end of the
world. Amen. (Matthew 28:20)*

Men without God suffer alone and die alone in times of
war and in other circumstances of life. All alone!

But it can never be said that any true soldier of the
Cross of Jesus Christ, no man or woman as missionary or
messenger of the Truth has ever gone out to a ministry
alone!

There have been many Christian martyrs—but not one
of them was on that mission field all alone. Jesus Christ
keeps His promise of taking them by the hand and
leading them triumphantly through to the world beyond.

We can sum it up by noting that Jesus Christ asks us
only to surrender to His lordship and obey His
commands. When the Spirit of God deals with our young
people about their own missionary responsibility, Christ
assures them of His presence and power as they prepare
to go: "All power is given unto Me! I am no longer in the
grave. I will protect you. I will support you. I will go
ahead of you. I will give you effectiveness for your
witness and ministry. Go, therefore, and make disciples of
all nations—I will never leave you nor forsake you!"

# LEANING TOWARD HERESY

*The mighty God, even the Lord, hath spoken . . . thou*
*thoughtest that I was altogether such an one as thyself.*
*(Psalm 50:1, 21)*

When large numbers of adherents in the Christian
churches come to believe that God is different from what
He actually is, that concept becomes heresy of the most
insidious and deadly kind!

When the Christian church surrenders her once lofty
concept of God and substitutes for it ideas so low, so
ignoble as to be utterly unworthy, her situation is tragic
indeed. Into the life and the practices of the church
comes a whole new philosophy; and the sense of the
divine Presence and the majesty of God is no longer
known.

Although "morality" is no longer a popular word in our
world, it is apparent that such low and unworthy
concepts of God's Person actually constitute a moral
calamity for professed believers in great segments of
Christianity. The records of both sacred and secular
history show that low views of God will surely destroy
the appeal of the Christian for all who hold them!

To all sinners, Jesus said, "You must be born
again—from above!" He knew that the gods begotten in
the shadowy thoughts of the fallen sons and daughters of
Adam will quite naturally be no true likeness of the true
and living God!

*April 10* _____

# TO SIN IS TO REBEL

*Sin, when it is finished, bringeth forth death.* (James 1:15)

Some of you will object to my saying this—but it is my opinion that in Christianity we have over-emphasized the psychology of the lost sinner's condition.

We spend time describing the sinner's woes and the great burden he carries until we almost forget the principal fact that the sinner is actually a rebel against properly constituted authority!

That is what makes sin SIN! We are rebels, we are sons of disobedience. Sin is the breaking of the Law and we are fugitives from the just laws of God while we are sinners. We are fugitives from divine judgment.

But thankfully, the plan of salvation reverses that, and restores the original relationship, so that the first thing the returning sinner does is confess: "Father, I have sinned against heaven and in Thy sight and I am no more worthy to be called Thy son. Make me as one of Thy hired servants!"

Thus, in repentance, we reverse that relationship and we fully submit to the Word of God and the will of God, as obedient children!

# THE TRANSFORMED LIFE

*He that taketh not his cross . . . is not worthy of me.*
*(Matthew 10:38)*

Many of the great evangelists who have touched the world for God, including such men as Jonathan Edwards and Charles Finney, have declared that the church is being betrayed by those who insist on Christianity being made "too easy."

Jesus laid down the terms of Christian discipleship and there are some among us who criticize: "Those words of Jesus sound harsh and cruel."

This is where we stand: receiving Jesus Christ into your life means that you have made an attachment to the Person of Christ that is revolutionary, in that it reverses the life and transforms it completely! It is complete in that it leaves no part of the life unaffected. It exempts no area of the life of the total man.

By faith and through grace, you have now formed an exclusive relationship with your Savior, Jesus Christ. All of your other relationships are now conditioned and determined by your one relationship to your Savior.

To receive Jesus Christ, then, is to attach ourselves in faith to His holy person, to live or die, forever! He must be first and last and all!

*April 12* _____

# RUNNING LIFE'S RACE

*Let us run with patience the race that is set before us.*
*(Hebrews 12:1)*

The writer to the Hebrews gives us good New Testament counsel: "Let us run the race with patience."

The Holy Spirit here describes Christian believers as runners on the track, participants in the race which is the Christian life. He provides both strong warning and loving encouragement, for there is always the danger of losing the race, but there is also the victor's reward awaiting those who run with patience and endurance. So, there are important things each of us should know and understand about our struggles as the faithful people of God.

For instance, it is a fact that the Christian race is a contest. But in no sense is it a competition between believers or between churches! As we live the life of faith, we Christians are never to be in competition with other Christians. The Bible makes this very plain!

Christian churches are never told to carry on their proclamation of the Savior in a spirit of competition with other Jesus-churches. The Holy Spirit tells us to keep our eyes on Jesus not on others who are also running the race!

# ARE WE MIRED DOWN?

*I know thy works, that thou art neither cold nor hot.*
*(Revelation 3:1)*

God will speak to us if we read and study and obey the Word of God! But when He does speak, we should speak back to Him in prayer and devotion. Otherwise, we are among the Christians who are mired down right where we are.

Many in our congregations have grown older and yet are not one inch farther up the mountain than on that day when the sun first arose on them in conversion. In fact, some are not even as far advanced along the way with God as they were a few years ago.

If these things are true, I can only conclude that there are "common" Christians, men and women who no longer hear the Lord speaking to them as they should.

Can they really think that this half-way Christian life is the best that we can know?

In the face of what Christ offers us, how can we settle for so little?

It is a tragedy of our time that so many are settling for less than the Lord is willing to give!

*April 14* _____

# MEDIOCRE CHRISTIANITY

*I, brethren, could not speak unto you as unto spiritual, but as unto carnal. (1 Corinthians 3:1)*

Read your New Testament again and you will agree that mediocrity in the Christian life is not the highest that Jesus offers. Certainly God is not honored by our arrested spiritual development—our permanent half-way spiritual condition.

We all know that the Bible tells us that we honor God by going on to full maturity in Christ!

Why, then, do we settle for those little pleasures that tickle the saintlets and charm the fancy of the carnal?

It is because we once heard a call to take up the cross and instead of following toward the heights, we bargained with the Lord like a street huckster! We felt an urge to be spent for Christ, but instead of going on, we started asking questions. We began to bicker and bargain with God about His standards for spiritual attainment.

This is plain truth—not about unbelieving "liberals"— but about those who have been born again and who dare to ask, "Lord, what will it cost me?"

_April 15

# INSTRUCT—THEN EXHORT

*Let the word of Christ dwell in you richly . . . teaching and admonishing one another. (Colossians 3:16)*

The godly men of old through whom the Scriptures came to us were faithful in their exhortations to personal faith and godliness, characteristic of the early church.

The apostolic method of teaching, instructing and encouraging was based on solid and fundamental Christian doctrine. This was Paul's method in his New Testament letters. First he gives his readers the scriptural reasons for certain Christian actions and attributes. He provides the basis and reason—then he exhorts the readers to respond appropriately.

We do not know if Paul was the human writer to the Hebrews, but the method of exhortation is like Paul's. We are assured that Christ is greater than Moses and greater than the angels and that He purchased mankind's salvation.

Then the exhortation: if all of these things are true, then we should keep on loving one another, keep on praying for one another. It is a good and gracious argument: because we have reasons for doing something, we ought to do it without delay and without reservation!

*April 16* _____

# NOT READY FOR HEAVEN?

*My meditation of him shall be sweet; I will be glad in the Lord. (Psalm 104:34)*

I can safely say on the authority of all that is revealed in the Word of God, that any man or woman on this earth who is bored and turned off by worship is not ready for heaven!

Now, I can almost hear someone saying, "Is Tozer getting away from justification by faith?"

I assure you that Martin Luther never believed in justification by faith more strongly than I do. But nowadays there is a deadly, automatic quality about getting saved.

This bothers me greatly: "Sinner, just put a nickel's worth of faith in the slot, pull down the lever and take out the little card of salvation." Tuck it in your wallet and off you go—a justified believer!

But really, my brother or sister, we are brought to God and to faith and to salvation that we might worship. We do not come to God that we might be automatic Christians stamped out with a die!

God has provided His salvation that we might be, individually and personally, vibrant children of God, loving God with all our heart and worshiping Him in the beauty of holiness!

# KNOWING HIS PRESENCE

*Lo, I am with you alway, even unto the end of the world.*
*(Matthew 28:20)*

Do not try to short-circuit God's plans for your discipleship and spiritual maturity here. If you and I were already prepared for heaven in the moment of our conversion, God would have taken us home instantly!

We must remember that God exists in Himself. His holy nature is such that we cannot comprehend Him with our minds. He is of a substance not shared by any other being. Hence, God can be known only as He reveals Himself!

I have found this to be a fact: every redeemed human being needs the humility of spirit that can only be brought about by the manifest Presence of God.

This mysterious yet gracious Presence is the air of life eternal. It is the music of existence, the poetry of the Christian life. It is the beauty and wonder of being one of Christ's own—a sinner born again, regenerated, created anew to bring glory to God!

To live surrounded by this sense of God is not only beautiful and desirable, but it is imperative!

*April 18* _____

# COME AS YOU ARE

*Being justified by his grace . . . heirs according to the hope of eternal life. (Titus 3:7)*

Let me say this to any of you who are still trying to add up your human merits—look away in faith to the Lord of abundant mercy!

Fixing yourself over and trying to straighten yourself out will never be sufficient—you must come to Jesus as you are!

Our Lord told about two men who went up into the temple to pray. One said, "God, here I am—all fixed up. Every hair is in place!"

The other said, "Oh God, I just crawled in off Skid Row. Have mercy on me!"

God forgave the Skid Row bum, but sent the other man away, hardened and unrepentant and unforgiven.

We come to Him just as we are but in humble repentance. When the human spirit comes to God knowing that anything it receives will be out of God's mercy, then repentance has done its proper work!

God promises to forgive and forget and to take that man into His heart and teach him that all of God's kindnesses are due to His mercy. What more can a sinner ask?

*April 19*

# SEEKING AFTER TRUTH

*We have received . . . that spirit which is of God; that we might know the things that are freely given us of God.*
*(1 Corinthians 2:12)*

We live in a mixed-up kind of world in which many people are not at all sure of what they believe or what they ought to believe.

Some churches advertise that way—you do not have to believe anything: "just be a seeker after truth." Some actually settle for poetry, siding with Edwin Markham who "saw his bright hand sending signals from the sun."

I, for one, never had any such signals from God. We have Bibles everywhere and the gospel is preached faithfully. Yet men and women seek God in old altars and tombs—in dark and dusty places, and finally wind up believing that God is sending signals from the sun.

Some folks get mad at me when I say that this kind of "seeking after truth" needs to be exposed. We need to double our efforts in telling the world that God is spirit and those who worship Him must worship in spirit and in truth.

It must be the Truth of God and the Spirit of God! Far from being an optional luxury in our Christian lives, the presence and the power of the Holy Spirit is a necessity!

*April 20* _____

# SPIRITUAL TESTING

*Do therefore as the Lord your God hath commanded you: ye
shall not turn aside to the right hand or to the left.*
*(Deuteronomy 5:32)*

In the scriptural accounts, there are many examples of
men and women being tested, and I think it is plain that
the Holy Spirit rarely tells a believer that he is about to be
tested.

Abraham was being tested when the Lord asked him to
take his only son up into the mountain. He thought he
was being ordered. He did not know he was being tested.

Peter was unconsciously tested. Paul was tested and
tried. There does come a time when we have heard
enough truth and the Holy Spirit says, "Today this
disciple is going to be tested."

The people of Israel in their time of testing came to
Kadesh-Barnea and instead of crossing into the promised
land, they said, "We will not go over!" God simply let
them make their own test and they flunked it!

Are there any among us who have an honest desire to
be Christlike? We should all be aware that every day is a
day of testing. Some come to their own Kadesh-Barnea
and turn back.

What a solemn thought: that many of the persons
whom God is testing will flunk the test!

# GLORIOUS CONTRADICTIONS

*The life which I now live in the flesh I live by the faith of the Son of God, who loved me. (Galatians 2:20)*

God has revealed so many glorious contradictions in the lives and conduct of genuine Christian believers that it is small wonder that we are such an amazement to this world.

The Christian is dead and yet he lives forever. He died to himself and yet he lives in Christ.

The Christian saves his own life by losing it and he is in danger of losing it by trying to save it.

It is strange but true that the Christian is strongest when he is weakest and weakest when he is strongest. When he gets down on his knees thinking he is weak, he is always strong.

The Christian is in least danger when he is fearful and trusting God and in the most danger when he feels the most self-confident.

He is most sinless when he feels the most sinful and he is the most sinful when he feels the most sinless.

The Christian actually has the most when he is giving away the most; and in all of these ways, the Christian is simply putting into daily practice the teachings and example of Jesus Christ, his Savior and Lord!

*April 22* _____

# REJOICING IN TRIALS

*But rejoice, inasmuch as ye are partakers of Christ's suffering.* (1 Peter 4:13)

The Apostle Peter stated a great Christian truth in the form of an amazing paradox: the obedient Christian believer will continue to rejoice and praise God even in the midst of continuing trials and suffering in this earthly life!

God's people know that things here on this earth are not all they ought to be, but they refuse to join the worry brigade. They are too busy rejoicing in the gracious prospect of all that will take place when God fulfills His promises to His redeemed children.

This ability to rejoice is demonstrated throughout the Bible and in the New Testament it rings forth like a silver bell!

The life of the normal believing child of God can never become a life of gloom and pessimism, for it is the Holy Spirit of God who keeps us above the kind of gloomy resignation that marks the secularism of the day.

We are still able to love the unlovely and to weep with those who weep, for in Peter's words, "when Christ's glory shall be revealed you may be glad with exceeding joy!"

# CONFESSING OUR LOVE

*He brought me to the banqueting house, and his banner over me was love. (Song of Solomon 2:4)*

Consider with me the appealing Old Testament story of the beautiful young woman in the Song of Solomon. Deeply in love with the young shepherd, she is also actively sought out by the king, who demands her favor. She remains loyal to the simple shepherd, who gathers lilies and comes to seek her and calls to her through the lattice.

In many ways, this is a beautiful picture of the Lord Jesus, of His love and care for His Bride, the Church. In the scriptural account, she does turn her loved one away with simple excuses. But condemned in heart, she rises to go out and search for him. As she seeks, she is asked: "What is he above others that you should seek him?"

"Oh, he is altogether lovely," she replies. "He came and called for me, and I had not the heart to go!"

But at last she is able to confess, "I have found him whom my soul loveth!"

He had been grieved but He was not far away. So it is with our Beloved—He is very near to us and He awaits our seeking!

*April 24* _____

# "AS I WAS, SO I WILL BE!"

*As I was with Moses, so I will be with thee. (Joshua 1:5)*

For all things, God is the great Antecedent!
Because He is, we are and everything else is.

We cannot think rightly of God until we begin to think of Him as always being there—and being there first!

Joshua had this to learn. He had been so long the servant of God's servant Moses, and had with such assurance received God's word at his mouth, that Moses and the God of Moses had become blended in his thinking; so blended that he could hardly separate the two thoughts. By association they always appeared together in his mind.

Now Moses is dead and lest the young Joshua be struck down with despair God spoke to assure him: "As I was with Moses, so I will be with thee!"

Moses was dead, but the God of Moses still lived! Nothing had changed and nothing had been lost, for nothing of God dies when a man of God dies.

"As I was—so I will be." Only the Eternal God could say this!

_____ *April 25*

# THE WALK OF FAITH

*Enoch walked with God . . . and God took him.*
*(Genesis 5:24)*

There are spiritual lessons for every Christian believer in the life of godly Enoch, seventh generation from Adam through Adam's third son, Seth.

We are impressed that he could resist the devil and find fellowship with his Creator-God, for he lived in a worldly society headed for destruction.

Enoch's daily walk was a walk of faith, a walk of fellowship with God. The Scriptures are trying to assure us that if Enoch could live and walk with God by faith in the midst of his sinful generation, we likewise should be able to follow his example because the human race is the same and God is the same!

Beyond that, Enoch reminds us that the quality and boldness of our faith will be the measure of our preparation for the return of Jesus Christ to this earth. We walk by faith as Enoch did, and although it is now 20 centuries after Christ's sojourn on earth, we hold firmly to the New Testament promise that our risen Lord will return to earth again!

*April 26* _____

# ENOCH ESCAPED DEATH

*By faith Enoch was translated that he should not see death
. . . he had this testimony, that he pleased God.*
*(Hebrews 11:5)*

The Genesis record concerning Enoch should speak to
us of our own troubled times—for that is the purpose of
the Word of God. It should be our concern that we hear
and that we obey!

The faith and deportment of the man Enoch compose a
vivid picture—a powerful object lesson—to encourage
every believer in his or her faith. There is only one
conclusion to be drawn—Enoch was translated into the
presence of God because of his faith, and thus he escaped
death!

It is my strong conviction that Enoch's experience of
translation is a type, or preview, of the coming rapture of
the Church, the Bride of Christ, described in the
Scriptures.

It is evident that there was no funeral for Enoch.
Perhaps members of his family did not fully understand
his walk with God, but they could answer with the facts!
"He is gone! We thought he was extreme in his beliefs
but now he is gone, and we are still here in a troubled
world!"

# A MAN SENT FROM GOD

*Among them that are born of women there hath not risen a greater than John the Baptist. (Matthew 11:11)*

The Bible record is very plain when it assures us that John the Baptist was a man sent from God.

Our generation would probably decide that such a man ought to be downright proud of the fact that God had sent him. We would urge him to write a book. Seminary leaders would line up to schedule him as guest lecturer.

Actually, John the Baptist would never have fit into the contemporary religious scene in our day—never! He did not keep his suit pressed. He was not careful about choosing words that would not offend. He did not quote beautiful passages from the poets. The doctors of psychiatry would have quick advice for him: "John, you really need to get adjusted to the times and to society!"

"Adjust"—that is a modern word I have come to hate. It was never an expression used to speak about human beings until we forgot that man has a soul. Now we have weird guys with mental "screwdrivers" adjusting one person a little tighter and another a little looser. John needed no adjustment. He gladly stepped down, so that all eyes could turn to Jesus, the Lamb of God!

*April 28* _____

# DEMONSTRATE YOUR FAITH

*It is the spirit that quickeneth . . . the words that I speak
unto you, they are spirit, and they are life. (John 6:63)*

We know of many who have been deceived into
believing that the learning and the memorizing of
Christian doctrine is all-sufficient. They actually think
that somehow they are better off for having learned the
doctrines of religion.

God actually asks of us what He asked of Noah long
ago! "Demonstrate your faith in God in your everyday
life!"

It is evident that God did not say to Noah, "I am
depending on you to hold the proper orthodox doctrines.
Everything will be just fine if you stand up for the right
doctrines."

I have read a statement by Martin Lloyd-Jones, the
English preacher and writer, in which he said: "It is
perilously close to being sinful for any person to learn
doctrine for doctrine's sake."

I agree with his conclusion that doctrine is always best
when it is incarnated—when it is seen fleshed out in the
lives of godly men and women. Our God Himself
appeared at His very best when He came into our world
and lived in our flesh!

# PRAYER OF A SERVANT

O Lord, I have heard Thy voice and was afraid. Thou hast called me to an awesome task in a grave and perilous hour. Thou art about to shake all nations and the earth and also heaven, that the things that cannot be shaken may remain.

O Lord my Lord, Thou hast stooped to honor me to be Thy servant. No man taketh this honor upon himself save he that is called of God as was Aaron. Thou hast ordained me Thy messenger to them that are stubborn of heart and hard of hearing.

They have rejected Thee, the Master and it is not to be expected that they will receive me, the servant.

My God, I shall not waste time deploring my weaknesses nor my unfittedness for the work. The responsibility is not mine but Thine. Thou hast said, "I know thee; I ordained thee; I sanctified thee."

Who am I to argue with Thee or to call into question Thy sovereign choice? The decision is not mine but Thine. So be it, Lord; Thy will, not mine be done.

*April 30* _____

# YOUR DEVOTIONAL LIFE

*Be strong in the Lord, and in the power of his might.*
*(Ephesians 6:10)*

Too many of us object, perhaps unconsciously, to the rather evident fact that the maintenance of the devotional mood is indispensable to success in the Christian life.

And what is the devotional mood?

It is nothing else than constant awareness of God's enfolding presence, the holding of inward conversations with Christ and private worship of God in spirit and in truth!

To establish our hearts in the devotional mood we must abide in Christ, walk in the Spirit, pray without ceasing and meditate in the Word of God day and night. Of course this implies separation from the world and obedience to the will of God, as we are able to understand it.

No matter how we may argue, true holiness and spiritual power are not qualities that can be once received and thereafter forgotten, as one might wind a clock or take a vitamin pill. Every advance in the spiritual life must be made against the determined resistance of the world, the flesh and the devil!

# PRACTICING THE TRUTH

*Cleanse your hands . . . and purify your hearts, ye double minded.* (James 4:8)

Christians habitually weep and pray over beautiful truth, only to draw back from that same truth when it comes to the difficult job of putting it into practice!

Actually, the average church simply does not dare to check its practices against biblical precepts. It tolerates things that are diametrically opposed to the will of God, and if the matter is pointed out to its leaders, they will defend its unscriptural practices with a casuistry equal to the verbal dodgings of the Roman moralists.

Can it be that there is no vital connection between the emotional and the volitional departments of life? Since Christ makes His appeal directly to the will, are we justified in wondering whether or not these divided souls have ever made a true commitment to the Lord? Or whether they have been inwardly renewed?

It does appear that too many Christians want to enjoy the thrill of feeling right but not willing to endure the inconvenience of being right! Jesus Himself left a warning: "Thou hast a name that thou livest, and art dead" (Revelation 3:1b).

*May 2* _____

# AN EXCLUSIVE ATTACHMENT

*But now, after ye are known of God, how turn ye again to the weak and beggarly elements? (Galatians 4:9)*

I am not in the business of trying to downgrade any other believer's efforts to win souls. I am just of the opinion that we are often too casual and there are too many tricks that can be used to make soul winning encounters completely "painless" and at "no cost" and without any "inconvenience."

Some of the unsaved with whom we deal on the "quick and easy" basis have such little preparation and are so ignorant of the plan of salvation that they would be willing to bow their heads and "accept" Buddha or Zoroaster if they thought they could get rid of us in that way.

To "accept Christ" in anything like a saving relationship is to have an attachment to the Person of Christ that is revolutionary, complete and exclusive!

It is more than joining some group that you like. It is more than having enjoyable social fellowship with other nice people. You give your heart and life and soul to Jesus Christ—and He becomes the center of your transformed life!

# A BIRTH FROM ABOVE

*Marvel not that I said unto thee, Ye must be born again.*
*(John 3:7)*

This may sound like heresy in some quarters, but I have come to this conclusion—that there are far too many among us who have thought that they accepted Christ, but nothing has come of it within their own lives and desires and habits!

This kind of philosophy in soul-winning—the idea that it is "the easiest thing in the world to accept Jesus"—permits the man or woman to accept Christ by an impulse of the mind or of the emotions.

It allows us to gulp twice and sense an emotional feeling that has come over us, and then say, "I have accepted Christ."

These are spiritual matters about which we must be legitimately honest and in which we must seek the discernment of the Holy Spirit. These are things about which we cannot afford to be wrong; to be wrong is still to be lost and far from God.

Let us never forget that the Word of God stresses the importance of conviction and concern and repentance when it comes to conversion, spiritual regeneration, being born from above by the Spirit of God!

*May 4* _____

# SPIRITUAL CONFIRMATION

*Let us draw near with a true heart in full assurance of faith.*
*(Hebrews 10:22)*

The human personality has a right to be consciously aware of a meeting with God. There will be a spiritual confirmation, an inward knowledge or witness!

This kind of confirmation and witness was taught and treasured by the great souls throughout the ages.

Conscious awareness of the presence of God! I defy any theologian or teacher to take that away from the believing church of Jesus Christ!

But be assured they will try. And I refer not just to the liberal teachers. God has given us the Bible for a reason—so it can lead us to meet God in Jesus Christ, in a clear, sharp encounter that will burn on in our hearts forever and ever.

When the Bible has led us to God and we have experienced God in the crisis of encounter, then the Bible has done its first work. That it will continue to do God's work in our Christian lives should be evident!

# THE ETHICS OF JESUS

*And ye shall be witnesses unto me. (Acts 1:8)*

The teachings of Jesus belong to the Church, not to society, for in society is sin, and sin is hostility to God!

Christ did not teach that He would impose His teachings upon the fallen world. He called His disciples to Him and taught them, and everywhere throughout His teachings there is the overt or implied idea that His followers will constitute an unpopular minority group in an actively hostile world.

The divine procedure is to go into the world of fallen men, preach to them the necessity to repent and become disciples of Christ and, after making disciples, to teach them "the ethics of Jesus," which Christ called "all things which I have commanded you."

The ethics of Jesus cannot be obeyed or even understood until the life of God has come to the heart of a man or woman in the miracle of the new birth.

The righteousness of the law is fulfilled in those who walk in the Spirit. Christ lives again in His redeemed followers the life He lived in Judea, for righteousness can never be divorced from its source, which is Jesus Christ Himself!

*May 6* _____

# FAITH AND EXPERIENCE

*O taste and see that the Lord is good. (Psalm 34:8)*

I insist that the effective preaching of Jesus Christ, rightly understood, will produce Christian experience in Christian believers. Moreover, if preaching does not produce spiritual experience and maturing in the believer, that preaching is not being faithful to the Christ revealed in the Scriptures.

Let me say it again another way: the Christ of the Bible is not rightly known until there is an experience of Him within the believer, for our Savior and Lord offers Himself to human experience.

When Jesus says, "Come unto me, all ye that labour and are heavy laden," it is an invitation to a spiritual experience. He is saying, "Will you consent to come? Have you added determination to your consent? Then come; come now!"

Yes, our Lord gives Himself to us in experience. David says in Psalm 34: "O taste and see that the Lord is good." I think David said exactly what he meant.

Surely the Holy Spirit was saying through David: "You have taste buds in your soul for tasting, for experiencing spiritual things. Taste and experience that God is good!"

# WE ARE NOT ALL ALIKE

*For we are his workmanship, created in Christ Jesus unto good works. (Ephesians 2:10)*

We ought to be fully aware that in the body of Christ we are not interested in the production of "cookie-cutter" Christians.

This is a word of caution in the matter of Christian experience—there is no pattern or formula for identical Christian experiences. It is actually a tragic thing for believers to try to be exactly like each other in their Christian faith and life.

I have probably been overly cautious about testifying to my own experiences because I do not want anyone to be tempted to try to copy anything the Lord has done for me.

God has given each of us an individual temperament and distinct characteristics. Therefore it is the office of the Holy Spirit to work out as He will the details of Christian experience. They will vary with personality.

Of this we may be sure: whenever a person truly meets God in faith and commitment to the gospel, he will have a consciousness and a sharp awareness of the details of that spiritual transaction!

*May 8* _____

# QUESTIONS WE ASK

*A living sacrifice, holy, acceptable unto God, which is your reasonable service. (Romans 12:1)*

I am convinced that anyone who brings up the question of consequences in the Christian life is only a mediocre and common Christian!

I have known some who were interested in the deeper life, but began asking questions: "What will it cost me—in terms of time, in money, in effort, in the matter of my friendships?" Others ask of the Lord when He calls them to move forward: "Will it be safe?" This question comes out of our constant bleating about security and our everlasting desire for safety above all else.

A third question that we want Him to answer is: "Will it be convenient?"

What must our Lord think of us if His work and His witness depend upon the security and the safety and the convenience of His people? No element of sacrifice, no bother, no disturbance—so we are not getting anywhere with God!

We have stopped and pitched our tent halfway between the swamp and the peak. We are mediocre Christians!

# BEYOND EMPTY PROFESSION

*Examine yourself, whether ye be in the faith; prove your own selves. (2 Corinthians 13:5)*

Preaching from the pulpit about the Christian "deeper life" does not automatically produce a deeper life church and congregation. The profession of men and women that they believe in "the deeper Christian life" is no assurance that their fellowship is actually a deeper life church.

The deeper spiritual life many people say they want is not a message; it is not a sermon; it is not a profession.

I am a pastor and I think I major in telling the truth. It is true that it is about time we stop coddling and apologizing for congregations that have reputations for being deeper life churches.

The deeper spiritual life is not something just to be talked about—it is a quiet enjoyment of daily blessing and peace and victory that is lived day by day; beyond empty profession and without any two-faced circumstances!

*May 10* _____

# CONFESS CHRIST'S LORDSHIP

*As ye have therefore received Christ Jesus the Lord, so walk ye in him. (Colossians 2:6)*

I think it is a completely wrong concept in Christian circles to look upon Jesus as a kind of divine nurse to whom we can go when sin has made us sick, and after He has helped us, to say, "Goodbye, Jesus"—and go on our own way.

Suppose I go into a hospital in need of a blood transfusion. After the staff has ministered to me and given their services, do I just slip out with a cheery "goodbye"—as though I owe them nothing and it was kind of them to help me in my time of need?

That may sound far out to you, but it draws a picture of attitudes among us today.

But the Bible never in any way gives us such a concept of salvation. Nowhere are we ever led to believe that we can use Jesus as a Savior and not own Him as our Lord. He is the Lord and as the Lord He saves us, because He has all of the offices of Savior, Christ, High Priest, and Wisdom and Righteousness and Sanctification and Redemption!

He is all of these—and all of these are embodied in Him as Christ, the Lord!

# HOW DO WE LISTEN?

*I will hear what God the Lord will speak . . . peace unto his people (Psalm 85:8)*

The living God has spoken to lost mankind in a variety of ways. The general response among us has been, "We did not hear His voice. We did not hear anything."

John recorded in his gospel the reactions of an audience of people who heard God speak audibly. When Jesus talked of His coming death, asking God to glorify His name through it, "a voice came from heaven, 'I have glorified it, and will glorify it again':" (John 12:28).

And what were the reactions of the bystanders? "The crowd that was there heard it and said it had thundered; others said an angel had spoken to him" (John 12:29).

People prefer their own logic, their own powers of reason. even when God speaks, they refuse to recognize His voice. They will not confess that God has spoken through Jesus Christ, the eternal Son. When He confronts them with their sin, they consult a psychiatrist and hope they can get their personalities "properly adjusted."

But in a coming day every knee will bow and every tongue will confess that Jesus Christ is Lord of all!

*May 12* _____

# UNCLEAN BY COMPARISON

*And when I saw him, I fell at his feet as dead.*
*(Revelation 1:17)*

In the Old Testament, whenever the living God revealed Himself in some way to humankind, terror and amazement were the reactions. People saw themselves as guilty and unclean by comparison!

In the book of Revelation, the Apostle John describes the overwhelming nature of his encounter with the Lord of glory. Although a believer and an apostle, John sank down in abject humility and fear when the risen, glorified Lord Jesus appeared before him on Patmos.

Our glorified Lord did not condemn John. He knew that John's weakness was the reaction to revealed divine strength. He knew that John's sense of unworthiness was the instant reaction to absolute holiness. Along with John, every redeemed human being needs the humility of spirit that can only be brought about by the manifest Presence of God.

Jesus at once reassured John, stooping to place a nail-pierced hand on the prostrate apostle, and saying: "Do not be afraid. I am the Living One. I was dead, and behold I am alive for ever and ever, and I hold the keys of death and hades."

# GOD KNOWS THE HYPOCRITES

*Let us therefore not judge one another anymore.*
*(Romans 14:13)*

I do not consider that it is my place as a Christian to stand around making judgments and calling other people "hypocrites."

Our Lord Jesus Christ is the only man I know who was holy and perfect enough to call the religious leaders of the day hypocrites.

I am just a man with faults and shortcomings of my own, and I must always consider myself lest I be tempted!

I preach to my own congregation about our faults and our failings, with the warning that some of our professions of blessing and victory may get into the area of "unintentional hypocrisy." Through the grace of God and the kindness of our spiritual ancestors we may have spiritual light that some others do not have—but in all honesty, we are wretchedly far below what we should be in living up to it, day by day.

It helps us to be honest and frank and humble to know that the great God Almighty knows the secrets of every person's heart!

*May 14* _____

# MORE THAN RELIGION

*Walk worthy of God, who hath called you unto his kingdom and glory. (1 Thessalonians 2:12)*

Contrary to much that is being said and practiced in churches, true worship is not something that we "do" in the hope of appearing to be religious!

True worship must be a constant and consistent attitude or state of mind within the believer, a sustained and blessed acknowledgement of love and admiration. If we have this awareness in our own lives and experience, then it is evident that we are not just waiting for Sunday to come to church and worship.

Having been made in His image, we have within us the capacity to know God and the instinct that we should worship Him. The very moment that the Spirit of God has quickened us to His life in regeneration, our whole being senses its kinship to God and leaps up in joyous recognition!

That response within our beings, a response to the forgiveness and pardon and regeneration, signals the miracle of the heavenly birth—without which we cannot see the kingdom of God. Thus the primary work of the Holy Spirit is to restore the lost soul to intimate fellowship with God through the washing of regeneration.

# HOLY SPIRIT, ALL DIVINE

*It is the Spirit that beareth witness, because the Spirit is truth. (1 John 5:6)*

I wonder if any Christian can ever show forth the transforming radiance of the love of God without a complete surrender to the indwelling Person of the Holy Spirit?

Surely that was in the mind of the songwriter, as he prayed and sang:

> Holy Ghost, with light divine,
> Shine upon this heart of mine;
> Chase the shades of night away,
> Turn my darkness into day.
>
> Holy Spirit, all divine,
> Dwell within this heart of mine;
> Cast down every idol throne,
> Reign supreme—and reign alone.

Our world is filled with hatred and conflict, violence and bloodshed. Through the plan of redemption God has dealt graciously with this global problem of hatred in the hearts of men and women. He has sent the source of love and light and radiance to the human bosom; Paul himself testifying: "The love of God is shed abroad in our hearts by the Holy Ghost which is given to us" (Romans 5:5).

*May 16* _____

# HONOR GOD'S SPIRIT

*Grieve not the Holy Spirit of God, whereby ye are sealed unto the day of redemption. (Ephesians 4:30)*

I think there are great numbers of Christian believers who ought to go home and go into their places of prayer and apologize to God for their demeaning attitudes toward the Holy Spirit of God.

Included in their numbers are Bible teachers who are guilty of leading us astray. They have dared to teach Christians that the Holy Spirit will never speak of His own person or position, as though the third Person of the Godhead may be ignored and His ministry downgraded!

Jesus said, "[When He comes] He shall not speak of himself, but whatever He shall hear, that shall He speak" (John 16:13b).

Jesus was actually telling His disciples: The Comforter will not come to stand on His own, to speak on His own authority. He will guide you into all truth—He will speak and act on the authority of the divine Godhead: Father, Son and Holy Spirit.

If you do not yield and honor the Holy Spirit, your lives will not show forth the blessed fruits of the Spirit!

*May 17*

# RESPONDING TO THE SPIRIT

*Quench not the Spirit. Hold fast to that which is good.*
*(1 Thessalonians 5:19–20)*

Are we raising a whole generation of young men and women without any sensitivity to the voice of God's Holy Spirit?

I am on record, and I will be as long as I live, that I would rather lose a leg and hobble along throughout the rest of my life than to lose my sensitivity to God and to His voice and to spiritual things!

Oh, how I want to keep that sensitivity within me—within my soul!

I am thinking about a great throng of men and women raised in Christian homes. They have been brought up in Sunday school. They probably cut their first baby tooth on the edge of a hymn book when the mother was not watching.

Still, to this day, they are not right with God. Some have made a kind of profession but have never been able to delight themselves in the Lord.

The reason? They have lost sensitivity to the message and the voice of God. If the Holy Spirit cannot move something within their beings every day they are not going to be effective Christians—if they are Christians at all!

*May 18* _____

# WHEN PENTECOST CAME

*But ye shall receive power, after that the Holy Ghost is*
*come upon you: and ye shall be witnesses. (Acts 1:8)*

As we read the New Testament, we find a very simple
and very plain and very forceful truth—the Holy Spirit
makes a difference!

Consider the early disciples—Jesus Himself had taught
them for more than three years—the greatest Bible
school! But still He had to caution them and encourage
them not to depend on their own wisdom and strength:
"Tarry ye . . . until ye be endued with power from on
high" (Luke 24:49b). He promised that they would
receive the Person of the Holy Spirit to carry out His plan
of world evangelization.

After Pentecost, the Spirit brought them a new and
vivid consciousness of the actual Presence of God. He
gave them the gifts of divine joy and peace. He gave them
great and continuing delight in prayer and communion
with God!

Finally, we recall that before Pentecost the disciples
could only ask questions. After Pentecost, throughout the
record in the book of Acts, they stood in the authority of
the Spirit and answered all of the questions of the people
concerning God's plan of salvation through the crucified
and risen Christ!

# THE PROMISE OF THE SPIRIT

*This Jesus . . . being by the right hand of God exalted, and
having received of the Father the promise of the Holy Ghost.
(Acts 2:32–33)*

The miraculous events wrought in Jerusalem by the
Holy Spirit on the day of Pentecost indicated to the
disciples that Jesus Christ, the Messiah-Savior, had indeed
taken His place at the right hand of the Majesty on high.

With Jewish critics all around, Peter lifted his voice and
said that all who were in Jerusalem on that day were
seeing the fulfillment of prophecy—the words of Jesus
that He would send the Holy Spirit after His death and
resurrection and exaltation.

"Therefore," Peter cried, "let all the house of Israel
know assuredly, that God hath made that same Jesus
whom ye have crucified, both Lord and Christ" (Acts
2:36).

Many, many have failed to note Peter's Pentecostal
emphasis: the important thing in God's plan was the fact
that Jesus had been exalted in heaven, and that His
glorification there had been the signal for the coming of
the promised Holy Spirit. What a lesson! The Spirit does
not have to be begged—He comes when the Savior is
honored and exalted!

*May 20* _____

# GEARED INTO THINGS ETERNAL

*Christ, who through the eternal Spirit offered himself without spot to God. (Hebrews 9:14)*

The coming of the Holy Spirit on the day of Pentecost was a gracious experience of fulfillment and blessing and direction for the Christian church.

It was the continuing emphasis for believers that we must live to gear ourselves into things eternal and to live the life of heaven here upon earth. We must yield our first obedience and loyalty to Jesus Christ, at any cost!

Anything we try to offer God that is less than that really is a degradation of the Christian church.

Frankly, I would rather be a member of a group that meets in a little room on a side street than to be part of a great activity that is not New Testament in its doctrine, in its spirit, in its living, in its holiness, in all of its texture and tenor. The Spirit-filled and Spirit-led congregation will be a joyful people. Beyond that, it will be useful and caring and compassionate! I do believe that the Christian church ought to be a helpful influence to the whole community!

# GOD IS SOVEREIGN

*We are in him that is true, even in his Son Jesus Christ.*
*(1 John 5:20)*

Oh, how I wish that I could adequately set forth the glory of the One who is worthy to be the object of our worship!

I do believe that if our new converts—the babes in Christ—could be made to see His thousand attributes and even partially comprehend His being, they would become faint with a yearning desire to worship and honor and acknowledge Him, now and forever!

I know that many discouraged Christians do not truly believe in God's sovereignty. In that case, we are not filling our role as the humble and trusting followers of God and His Christ.

And yet, that is why Christ came into our world. The old theologians called it "theanthropism"—the union of the divine and human natures in Christ. This is a great mystery and I stand in awe before it!

The theanthropy is the mystery of God and man united in one Person—not two persons but two natures. So, the nature of God and the nature of man are united in this One who is our Lord Jesus Christ!

*May 22* _____

# BLAME SOMEONE ELSE

*And the man said, The woman . . . gave me of the tree, and I did eat. (Genesis 3:12)*

In the earliest day of failure and tragedy in the garden of Eden, Adam came out of hiding, knowing full well his own guilt and shame.

Adam confessed: "We ate from the fruit of the tree that was forbidden—but it was the woman who enticed me!"

When God said to Eve, "What did you do?" she said: "It was the serpent that beguiled me!"

In that brief time our first parents had learned the art of laying the blame on someone else. That is one of the great, betraying evidences of sin—and we have learned it straight from our first parents. We do not accept the guilt of our sin and iniquity. We blame someone else.

If you are not the man you ought to be, you are likely to blame your wife or your ancestors. If you are not the young person you ought to be, you can always blame your parents. If you are not the wife you ought to be, you may blame your husband or perhaps the children.

Sin being what it is, we would rather lay the blame on others. We blame, blame, blame! That is why we are where we are.

# UNHOLY, UNRIGHTEOUS, UNHAPPY

*And so death passed upon all men, for that all have sinned.*
*(Romans 5:12)*

All of history and the daily newspaper testify that the human race lies in ruin—spiritually, morally and physically.

The long parade of gods, both virtuous and obscene, and a thousand varieties of vain and meaningless religious practices declare our spiritual degeneration, while disease, old age and death testify sadly to the completeness of our physical decay.

By nature, men and women are unholy; and by practice we are unrighteous. That we are also unhappy is of small consequence.

But it is of overwhelming importance to us that we should seek the favor of God while it is possible to find it, and that we should bring ourselves under the plenary authority of Jesus Christ in complete and voluntary obedience.

To do this is to invite trouble from a hostile world and to incur such unhappiness as may naturally follow. Add the temptation of the devil and a life-long struggle with the flesh and it will be obvious that we will need to defer most of our enjoyments to more appropriate time!

*May 24* _____

# BRAGGING ABOUT GOD

*That God in all things may be glorified through Jesus
Christ, to whom be praise and dominion. (1 Peter 4:11)*

Basic beliefs about the Person and the nature of God
have changed so much that there are among us now men
and women who find it easy to brag about the benefits
they receive from God—without ever a thought or a
desire to know the true meaning of worship!

I have immediate reactions to such an extreme
misunderstanding of the true nature of a holy and
sovereign God, for I believe that the very last thing God
desires is to have shallow-minded and worldly Christians
bragging about Him.

Beyond that, it does not seem to be very well recognized
that God's highest desire is that every one of His believing
children should so love and so adore Him that we are
continually in His presence, in spirit and in truth.

Something wonderful and miraculous and life-changing
takes place within the human soul when Jesus Christ is
invited in to take His rightful place. That is what God
anticipated when He wrought the plan of salvation. He
intended to make worshipers out of rebels; to restore the
place of worship which our first parents knew when they
were created!

*May 25*

# MAN'S VIEW OF THIS WORLD

*Choose you this day whom ye will serve . . . but as for me and my house, we will serve the Lord. (Joshua 24:15)*

If you have ever given much thought to this present world in which we live, you have some idea of the power of interpretation. The world is a stable fact, quite unchanged by the passing of years, but how different is modern man's view of the world from the view our fathers held.

The world is for all of us not only what it is; it is what we believe it to be, and a tremendous load of weal or woe rides on the soundness of our interpretation!

In the earlier days, when Christianity exercised a dominant influence over American thinking, men conceded this world to be a battleground. Man, so our fathers held, had to choose sides. He could not be neutral—for him it must be life or death, heaven or hell!

In our day, the interpretation has changed completely. We are not here to fight, but to frolic! We are not in a hostile foreign land; we are at home! It now becomes the bounden duty of every Christian to reexamine his spiritual philosophy in the light of the Bible. So much depends on this that we cannot afford to be careless about it!

# THE HUMBLE PLACE

*All of you be subject one to another, and be clothed with humility. (1 Peter 5:5)*

I have met two classes of Christians; the proud who imagine they are humble, and the humble who are afraid they are proud!

There should be another class: the self-forgetful men and women who leave the whole thing in the hands of Christ and refuse to waste any time trying to make themselves good. They will reach the goal far ahead of the rest.

The truly humble person does not expect to find virtue in himself, and when he finds none he is not disappointed. He knows that any good deed he may do is the result of God's working within him.

When this belief becomes so much a part of any man or woman that it operates as a kind of unconscious reflex, he or she is released from the burden of trying to live up to the opinion they hold of themselves. They can relax and count upon the Holy Spirit to fulfill the moral law within them.

Let us never forget that the promises of God are made to the humble: the proud man by his pride forfeits every blessing promised to the lowly heart, and from the hand of God he need expect only justice!

# ASHAMED OF SIN

*Verily every man at his best state is altogether vanity . . .*
*Surely every man walketh in a vain shew. (Psalm 39:5–6)*

Brethren, I am not ashamed of this world God created—I am only ashamed of man's sin!

If you could take all of man's sin out of this world, there would be nothing to be ashamed of and nothing to be afraid of.

Our apologies must be for humanity—and for our sins. I keep repeating that we have no business making excuses for God.

It is popular now to talk about Christ being a guest here. I dare to tell people that they should stop patronizing Jesus Christ!

He is not the guest here—He is the Host!

We have apologists who write books and give lectures—apologizing for the person of Christ, trying to "explain" to our generation that the Bible does not really mean "exactly" what it says. But God has revealed Himself in Jesus Christ and thus we know where we stand, believing that all things were made by Him and "without Him was not anything made that was made."

*May 28* _____

# A GREAT MORAL BLUNDER

*By the name of Jesus Christ of Nazareth, whom ye crucified*
*. . . This is the stone which was set at nought of you*
*builders. (Acts 4:10–11)*

Of all the people on the earth, the nation of Israel surely was the best prepared to receive the Christ of God. The children of Abraham, they were called to be a chosen people in an everlasting covenant with God, the Father.

Yet they failed to recognize Jesus as Messiah and Lord. There is no doubt that theirs was the greatest moral blunder in the history of mankind. He came to His own people and they rejected Him!

Jesus taught frankly that He was asking His followers to throw themselves out on the resources of God. For the multitude, He was asking too much. He had come from God but they received Him not!

It seems to be a comfort to some Christians to sit back and blame and belabor the Jews, refusing to acknowledge that they have information and benefits and spiritual light that the Jews never had.

It is surely wrong for us to try to comfort our own carnal hearts by any emphasis that Israel rejected Him. If we do that, we only rebuild the sepulchers of our fathers as Jesus said!

# ASTONISHED REVERENCE

*Come and hear, all ye that fear God, and I will declare what he hath done for my soul. (Psalm 66:16)*

In my own being, I could not exist very long as a Christian without the inner consciousness of the Presence and nearness of God! I can only keep right by keeping the fear of God on my soul and delighting in the fascinating rapture of worship.

I am sorry that the powerful sense of godly fear is a missing quality in churches today.

The fear of God is that "astonished reverence" of which the saintly Faber wrote. I would say that it may grade anywhere from its basic element—the terror of the guilty soul before a holy God—to the fascinated rapture of the worshiping saint.

There are few unqualified things in our lives but I believe that the reverential fear of God, mixed with love and fascination and astonishment and adoration, is the most enjoyable state and the most purifying emotion the human soul can know. A true fear of God is a beautiful thing, for it is worship, it is love, it is veneration. It is a high moral happiness because God is!

*May 30* _____

# GOD KNOWS MY PRAYER

*Blessed are the dead which die in the Lord . . . that they may rest from their labors. (Revelation 14:13)*

We modern Christians seem to be a strange breed in many of our ways. We are so completely satisfied with earthly things and we enjoy our creature comforts so much that we would just rather stay on here for a long, long time!

Probably most of us do not tell God about that kind of desire when we pray. But for years I have made a practice of writing many of my earnest prayers to God in a little book—a book now well worn. I remind God often of what my prayers have been.

One prayer in the book—and God knows it well by this time—is an honest supplication:

> Oh, God,
> Let me die rather than to go on day by day living wrong. I do not want to become a careless, fleshly old man.
>
> I want to be right so that I can die right! Lord, I do not want my life to be extended if it would mean that I should cease to live right and fail in my mission to glorify You all of my days!

I would rather go home right now than to live on—if living on was to be a waste of God's time and my own!

# GOD'S GRACE IS ETERNAL

*Much more the grace of God, and the gift by grace, which is by one man, Jesus Christ, hath abounded unto many.*
*(Romans 5:15)*

It is a typical and accepted teaching in Christian churches today that Moses and the Old Testament knew only God's law, and that Christ and the New Testament know only God's grace.

I repeat: that is the "accepted" teaching of the hour—but I also hasten to add that it is a mistaken concept, and that it was never the concept held and taught by the early Christian church fathers.

God has always been the God of all grace, and He does not change. Immutability is an attribute of God; therefore God at all times and in all of history must act like Himself!

He is the God of all grace; therefore the grace of God does not ebb and flow like the ocean tides. There has always been the fullness of grace in the heart of God. There is no more grace now than there was previously and there will never be any more grace than there is now!

The flow of God's grace did not begin when Christ came to die for us. It was part of God's ancient plan of redemption and was manifested in the blood and tears and pain and death at Calvary's cross!

*June 1*  _____

# HIS CROSS IS MY CROSS

*The disciple is not above his master, nor the servant above his lord. (Matthew 10:24)*

To take Jesus Christ into your life without reservation is to accept His friends as your friends and to know that His enemies will be your enemies! It means that we accept His rejection as our rejection. We knowingly accept His cross as our cross.

If you then find yourself in an area where Christ has no friends, you will be friendless—except for the one Friend who will stick closer than a brother. I made up my mind a long time ago. Those who declare themselves enemies of Jesus Christ must look upon me as their enemy, and I ask no quarter from them! And if they are friends of Christ they are my friends—and I do not care what color they are or what denomination they belong to.

If the preachers would faithfully tell the people what it actually means to receive Christ and obey Him and live for Him, we would have fewer converts backsliding and foundering.

Preachers who are not faithful one day will stand before the judgment seat of Christ and answer to a faithful Savior why they betrayed His people in this way!

# NEW TESTAMENT ROOTS

*For by one Spirit are we all baptized into one body . . . and have been all made to drink into one Spirit.*
*(1 Corinthians 12:13)*

It is really a blessed thing in our Christian fellowship and in our congregations that God never asks whether it is a big church or a little church!

A young pastor, when introduced to a well-known church leader, said, "You do not know me. I am the pastor of a little rural church."

I think it was a wise reply that came from the churchman: "Young man, there are no little churches; all churches are the same size in God's sight!"

But, whether large or small, it must be an assembly of believers brought together through the Name of Jesus, to worship in God's Presence; and with the right to receive all that God bestows.

With these roots, we should ask ourselves if we are truly interested in spiritual attainment as were the New Testament believers. We must confess that the spiritual temperature among us may often be lower than in the early church. But we hold to the message that those who truly honor the Presence of the Savior are included in this relationship that goes back to the New Testament and to the apostles!

*June 3* _____

# SPECTATOR CHRISTIANS

*By love serve one another. (Galatians 5:13)*

This we have heard: "I am a born again Christian and I am happy that my sins are forgiven and I go to church on Sunday because I like the fellowship!"

We ask: "Do you not go to put yourself in the way of spiritual blessing?"

The answer: "No, I am saved and I do not need anything!"

We ask: "Have you offered to witness, to pray, to encourage, to assist, to participate in your church's life and outreach?"

The answer: "No. My church seems to get along very well without my help!"

Brethren, this "non participation" kind of faith is a strange parody on Bible Christianity. Men and women who say they are believers just cancel themselves out. Is it something we have learned from the sporting events?—the great majority are spectators. They come and sit!

If there is any true spiritual life within us, God will give us a gift of some kind and the humble soul will find something to do for God!

# DO THINGS POSSESS US?

*Nor trust in uncertain riches, but in the living God, who giveth us richly all things to enjoy. (1 Timothy 6:17)*

I think a lot of people in our congregations get confused when some learned brother advises us that we must all join in a fervent fight against "materialism."

If men and women do not know what materialism is, how can they be expected to join the battle?

Materialism in its crisis form occurs when men and women created in the image of God accept and look upon matter as "the ultimate"—the only reality.

The advice, "We must fight materialism," does not mean that everyone should get a sword, and run after a fellow named Material, and cut him down.

What it does mean is that we should start believing in the fact of God's Creation and that matter is only a creature of the all-wise and ever-loving God! The believer is not deceived into believing that the physical things we know and enjoy are the ultimate end, in themselves.

*June 5* _____

# WITHOUT FEELING?

*Singing and making melody in your heart to the Lord.*
*(Ephesians 5:19)*

I do know something of the emotional life that goes along with conversion to Jesus Christ. I came into the kingdom of God with joy, knowing that I had been forgiven.

I have had people tell me very dogmatically that they will never allow "feeling" to have any part in their spiritual life and experience.

"Too bad for you!" is my reply.

I say that because I have voiced a very real definition of what I believe true worship to be: "Worship is to feel in the heart!"

In the Christian faith, we should be able to use the word "feel" boldly and without apology. What worse thing could be said of us as the Christian church if it can be said of us that we are a feelingless people?

I think we must agree that those of us who have been blest within our own beings would not join in any crusade to "follow your feelings." But if there is no feeling at all in our hearts, then we are dead!

# WHO IS YOUR EXAMPLE?

*Be thou an example . . . in word, in conversation, in charity, in spirit, in faith, in purity.* (1 Timothy 4:12)

The Christian churches of our day have suffered a great loss in rejecting the example of good men, choosing instead the "celebrity of the hour" for their pattern.

We must agree that it is altogether unlikely that we know who our "greatest" men are.

One thing is sure, however—the greatest man alive today is the best man alive today. That is not open to debate.

Spiritual virtues run deep and silent. The holy and humble man will not advertise himself nor allow others to do it for him.

The Christian who is zealous to promote the cause of Christ can begin by living in the power of God's Spirit, and so reproducing the life of Christ in the sight of men. In deep humility and without ostentation he can let his light shine.

To sum it all up: the most effective argument for Christianity is still the good lives of those who profess it!

*June 7* _____

# MAKE GOD'S WILL OUR WILL

*And he trembling and astonished said, Lord, what wilt thou have me to do? (Acts 9:6)*

The mystery of man's free will is far too great for us!

God said to Adam and Eve: "Thou shalt not eat from this tree." Here was a divine requirement calling for obedience on the part of those who had the power of choice and will. When they disobeyed they usurped the right that was not theirs!

The poet Tennyson must have thought about this for he wrote in his *In Memoriam:* "our wills are ours, we know not how; our wills are ours to make them Thine!"

"We know not how;" then Tennyson girds himself and continues, "Yes, our wills are ours to make them Thine."

As created beings, that is our only right—to make our wills the will of God, to make the will of God our will!

God is sovereign, and we are the creatures. He is the Creator and therefore His is the right to command us with the obligation that we should obey.

It is a happy obligation, I might say, for "His yoke is easy and His burden is light!" It is important to agree that true salvation restores the right of a Creator-creature relationship, acknowledging God's right to our fellowship and communion!

# WHY SETTLE DOWN?

*That ye might be filled with all the fullness of God.*
*(Ephesians 3:19)*

Why should a Christian "settle down" as soon as he has come to know the Lord?

I blame faulty exposition of the New Testament for stopping many Christians dead in their tracks, causing them to shrug off any suggestion that there is still spiritual advance and progress beckoning them on.

It is the position of some would-be teachers that everyone who comes into the kingdom of God by faith immediately obtains all there is of God's spiritual provision.

I believe that such a teaching is as deadly as cyanide to the individual Christian life. It kills all hope of spiritual advance and causes many believers to adopt what I call "the creed of contentment."

I am sure you agree with me that there is always real joy in the heart of the person who has become a child of God. Sound teaching of the Word will then hold out the goal of moving forward, emulating the Apostle Paul's desire to become a special kind of Christian!

*June 9* _____

# FALSE PRETENDERS

*When the young man heard that saying, he went away*
*sorrowful; for he had great possessions.* (Matthew 19:22)

All persons who are alienated from God and outside of
Christ are part and parcel of a mighty deception!

They are called upon to pretend that they can have
peace of mind within and that they can be relatively
happy and make a big success of their human lives if they
have youth and wealth and morality and high position.

In that sense of what is going on all around us, David
never had to apologize for writing that "every man is a
liar!" The whole human concept of success and happiness
and inner peace, based upon who we are and what we
have, is completely false.

The rich young ruler who came to question Jesus had
wealth, morality, position and youth. But his very first
question gave the clue to his own inner emptiness of life:
"What good thing should I do, that I may have eternal
life?"

He knew very well that there is not a person alive who
has eternal youth or eternal position or eternal
righteousness. So, like every other man, he had to make a
choice!

# COMPROMISE IS COSTLY

*I pray . . . that thou shouldest keep them from the evil.*
*(John 17:15)*

Christianity today is so entangled with this present world that millions never guess how radically they have missed the New Testament pattern.

Compromise is everywhere—but actually no real union between the world and the Church is possible. When the Church joins up with the world it is the true Church no longer but only a pitiful hybrid thing, an object of smiling contempt to the world, and an abomination to the Lord!

Nothing could be clearer than the pronouncements of the Scriptures on the Christian's relation to the world. The confusion which gathers around this matter results from the unwillingness of professing Christians to take the Word of the Lord seriously.

This whole thing is spiritual in its essence. A Christian is what he is not by ecclesiastical manipulation but by the new birth. He is a Christian because of a Spirit which dwells in him. Only that which is born by the Spirit is spirit, no matter how many church dignitaries work on it!

*June 11* _____

# CHRIST MADE THE WORLD

*God hath spoken unto us by his Son . . . by whom he made the worlds. (Hebrews 1:12)*

Think about the world into which our Lord Jesus Christ came—it is actually Christ's world!

Every section of this earth that we buy and sell and kick around and take by force of arms is a part of Christ's world. He made it all and He owns it all.

Jesus Christ, the eternal Word, made the world. He made the very atoms of which Mary was made; the atoms of which His own body was made. He made the straw in the manger upon which He was laid as a new-born baby.

Let me digress here. I hear an occasional devotional exercise on the radio, in which the participants ask: "Mary, mother of God, pray for us!" It is only right that we should express our position based on the Word of God, and the truth is that Mary is dead and she is not the "mother of God."

Mary was the mother of that tiny babe, for God in His loving and wise plan of redemption used the body of the virgin Mary as the matrix to give the eternal Son a human body. We join in giving her proper honor when we refer to her as Mary, mother of Christ.

# LOVING GOD ONLY

*And because iniquity shall abound, the love of many shall
wax cold. (Matthew 24:12)*

The first and greatest commandment is to love God
with every power of our entire being. Where love like that
exists, there can be no place for a second object.

Yet popular Christianity has as one of its most effective
talking points the idea that God exists to help people to
get ahead in this world! The God of the poor has become
the God of an affluent society. We hear that Christ no
longer refuses to be a judge or a divider between
money-hungry brothers. He can now be persuaded to
assist the brother that has accepted Him to get the better
of the brother who has not!

Whoever seeks God as a means toward desired ends will
not find God. God will not be one of many treasures. His
mercy and grace are infinite and His patient
understanding is beyond measure, but He will not aid
men in selfish striving after personal gain. If we love God
as much as we should, surely we cannot dream of a loved
object beyond Him which He might help us to obtain!

*June 13* _____

# NO ONE CHANGES GOD'S LAW

*I delight to do thy will, O my God: yea, thy law is within my heart. (Psalm 40:8)*

Because we live in a period known as the age of God's grace, it has become a popular thing to declare that the Ten Commandments are no longer valid, no longer relevant in our society.

With that context, it has become apparent that Christian churches are not paying attention to the Ten Commandments.

But Dwight L. Moody preached often in the commandments. John Wesley said he preached the commands of the Law to prepare the way for the gospel. R. A. Torrey told ministers if they did not preach the Law they would have no response to the preaching of the gospel. It is the Law that shows us our need for the gospel of salvation and forgiveness!

It is accurate to say that our binding obligation is not to the Old Testament Law. As sincere Christians we are under Christ's higher law—that which is represented in His love and grace. But everything that is morally commanded in the Ten Commandments still comprises the moral principles that are the will of God for His people. God's basic moral will for His people has not changed!

# ASCRIPTION OF GLORY

*Yet believing, ye rejoice with joy unspeakable and full of glory.* (1 Peter 1:18)

I am discovering that many Christians are not really comfortable with the holy attributes of God. In such cases, I am forced to wonder about the quality of their worship.

The word "holy" is much more than an adjective saying that God is a holy God. It is an ecstatic ascription of glory to the triune God. Everything that appears to be good among men and women must be discounted, for we are humans. Abraham, David and Elijah, Moses, Peter and Paul—all were good men, but each had his human flaws and weaknesses as members of Adam's race. Each had to find his own place of humble repentance. Because God knows our hearts and our intentions, He is able to restore His believing children in the faith!

So, we should be honest and confess that much of our problem in continuing fellowship with a holy God is that many Christians only repent for what they do, rather than for what they are!

*June 15* _____

# THE MYSTERY IN WORSHIP

*Behold, the bush burned with fire, and the bush was not consumed. (Exodus 3:2)*

Consider the experience of Moses in the desert as he beheld the fire that burned in the bush without consuming it. Moses had no hesitation in kneeling before the bush and worshiping God. Moses was not worshiping a bush; it was God and His glory dwelling in the bush whom Moses worshiped!

This is an imperfect illustration, for when the fire departed from that bush, it was a bush again.

But this Man, Christ Jesus, is eternally the Son. In the fullness of this mystery, there has never been any departure, except for that awful moment when Jesus cried, "My God, my God, why hast thou forsaken me?" (Matthew 27:46). The Father turned His back for a moment when the Son took on Himself that putrifying mass of sin and guilt, dying on the cross not for His own sin, but for ours.

The deity and the humanity never parted, and to this day, they remain united in that one Man.

When we kneel before Him and say, "My Lord and my God, Thy throne, O God, is forever and ever," we are talking to God!

# "YET SHALL HE LIVE"

*He that believeth in me, though he were dead, yet shall he live. (John 11:25)*

This may sound strange—but it is a fact that death is not the worst thing that can happen to a believing Christian!

I can recall the first time I heard that statement, in a quiet conversation with Harry M. Shuman, for many years the president of the international Christian and Missionary Alliance.

He was a soft-spoken yet forceful man of God, rich in the wisdom of God's Word. We were talking of the serious issues of life and death. When he had something especially important to say, Dr. Shuman had an unusual way of lowering his voice and tilting his head just a bit. I can see him yet as he looked out from under his shaggy brows straight into my eyes.

"Remember, Tozer," he said, "death is not the worst thing that can happen to a person!"

For the Christian, death is a journey to the eternal world. It is a victory, a rest, a delight. I am sure my small amount of physical suffering has been mild compared to Paul's, but I feel as Paul did: "I desire to depart and be with Christ, which is better by far!" (Philippians 2:23).

*June 17*

# TRUTH HAS A SOUL

*Neither knoweth any man the father, save the Son, and he*
*to whomsoever the Son shall reveal him. (Matthew 11:27)*

I believe there is a positive warning in the gospels that a
person's faith may stand in the revealed Bible text—and
still be as dead as the proverbial doornail!

Consider the prayer of our Lord in Matthew 11: "All
things are delivered unto me of my Father; and no man
knoweth the Son, but the Father; neither knoweth any
man the Father, save the Son, and he to whomsoever the
Son will reveal him."

There is more than a body of truth—and if we do not
get through to the soul of truth, we have only a dead
body on our hands.

When the power of God moves in on the text and sets
the sacrifice on fire, then you have genuine Christianity!
We try to call that revival, but it is not revival at all. It is
simply New Testament Christianity.

People who thought they were saved get saved! People
who have only believed in a code now have placed their
faith and trust in Christ's person. It is not any deluxe
edition of Christianity—it is simply New Testament
Christianity having its place!

# THE CONDITIONS OF PEACE

*He came trembling and fell down before Paul and Silas . . .*
*and said, Sirs, what must I do to be saved? (Acts 16:29–30)*

In a world like ours, with conditions being what they are, what should a serious-minded man or woman do?

First, accept the truth concerning yourself. You do not go to a doctor to seek consolation, but to find out what is wrong and what to do about it.

Then seek the kingdom of God and His righteousness. Seek through Jesus Christ a right relationship to God and then insist upon maintaining a right relation to your fellow man.

Set about reverently and honestly to amend your doings. Magnify God, mortify the flesh, simplify your life. Take up your cross and learn of Jesus Christ to die to this world that He may raise you up in due time.

If you will do these things in faith and love, you will know peace; the peace of God that passes all understanding.

You will know joy; the joy of resurrection. You will know, too, the comfort of the indwelling Spirit of God, for you have sought to do the will of God at any price!

*June 19* _____

# OUR WILLS MUST SURRENDER

*His servants ye are to whom ye obey; whether of sin unto death, or of obedience unto righteousness. (Romans 6:16)*

The Christian doctrine of obedience to God and to His will is now largely neglected in modern religious circles, and many in our own congregations seem to feel that our obligation to obey has been discharged by the act of believing on Jesus Christ at the beginning of our Christian lives.

We need to remember that "the will is the seat of true religion in the soul." Nothing genuine has been done in a man or woman's life until his or her will has been surrendered in active obedience. It was disobedience that brought about the ruin of the race. It is the obedience of faith that brings us back again into the divine favor!

It needs to be said that a world of confusion results from trying to believe without obeying!

A mere passive surrender may be no surrender at all. Any real submission to the will of God must include willingness to take orders from Him from that time on.

I keep wondering whether the Lord's ministers will again give to obedience the place of prominence it occupies in the Scriptures.

# GOD UNDERSTANDS US

*God is love; and he that dwelleth in love dwelleth in God, and God in him. (1 John 4:16)*

We should revel in the joy of believing that God is the sum of all patience and the true essence of kindly good will!

Because He is what He is, we please Him most, not by frantically trying to make ourselves good, but by throwing ourselves into His arms with all our imperfections and believing that He understands everything—and loves us still!

The God who desires our fellowship and communion is not hard to please, although He may be hard to satisfy. He expects from us only what He has Himself supplied. When He must chasten us, He even does this with a smile—the proud, tender smile of a Father who is bursting with pleasure over an imperfect son who is coming every day to look more and more like the One whose child he is!

This is the best of good news: God loves us for ourselves. He values our love more than He values galaxies of newly created worlds.

He remembers our frame and knows that we are dust!

*June 21*

# OUR SOVEREIGN LORD

*The most High dwelleth not in temples made with hands . . .*
*Heaven is my throne, and earth is my footstool.*
*(Acts 7:48–49)*

How can you be a Christian and not be aware of the sovereignty of the God who has loved us to the death?

To be sovereign, God must be the absolute, infinite, unqualified ruler in all realms in heaven and earth and sea. To be Lord over all the creation, He must be omnipotent. He must be omniscient. He must be omnipresent.

With all that is within me, I believe that the crucified and risen and glorified Savior, Jesus Christ, is the sovereign Lord. He takes no orders from anyone. He has no counselors and no advisers. He has no secretary to the throne. He knows in the one effortless act all that can be known and He has already lived out our tomorrows and holds the world in the palm of His hand.

That is the Lord I serve! I gladly own that I am His; glory to God! The Christ we know and serve is infinitely beyond all men and all angels and all archangels; above all principalities and powers and dominions, visible and invisible—for He is the origin of them all!

# BEHIND THE MASK

*But wilt thou know, O vain man, that faith without works is dead? (James 2:20)*

I think it is pitiful and rather sad that about the only time you can find a fellow citizen who is not a "phony" is when he is mad. In our kind of society, most people feel that they must always be pretending, continually "putting on a front."

So, they are never their real selves until they get mad!

When Jesus faced His bitter religious enemies as recorded in John 8, there was no pretending, nothing staged for dramatic effect. Jesus confronted them with the words: "He that is of God heareth God's words. You, therefore, hear them not, because you are not of God!"

These were firm and severe words; His enemies answered with angry and insulting words. These men were mad; they were letting go. They had given up pretense. They were acting naturally now, showing what they were within.

As humans, we are what we do! If what we do proves us to be wrong, then it is either despair or obtaining the help we need. Jesus came to change our natures. He came to break old habits of sin, to break and conquer them!

*June 23* _____

# THE SPIRIT'S GIFTS

*But the manifestation of the Spirit is given to every man to profit withal. (1 Corinthians 12:7)*

In our Christian fellowship, we must recognize that the blessed Holy Spirit of God desires to take men and women and control them, and use them as instruments through which He can express Himself in the body of Christ.

Someone may try to give me credit for something they think I have done for God—but in actuality, God is doing it through His Holy Spirit—and using me as an instrument. There is no real sense in which we are able to do spiritual work of any kind without the Holy Spirit.

We do know that the Apostle Paul said: "If any man have not the Spirit of Christ he is none of his" (Romans 8:9b). But he also exhorted those early believers not to ignore the Spirit's gifts and to "covet earnestly the best gifts." It is still important for us to fulfill the Spirit-given functions and capabilities which are the spiritual birthright of every regenerated believer.

We should not be looking around for some other way. God has given us in His Holy Spirit every gift and power and help that we need to serve Him!

# CHRIST RECEIVES SINNERS

*Him hath God exalted with his right hand to be a Prince and a Saviour, for to give repentance . . . and forgiveness of sins. (Acts 5:31)*

What a gracious thing for us that Jesus Christ never thinks about what we have been. He always thinks about what we are going to be!

The Savior who is our Lord cares absolutely nothing about your moral case history. He forgives it and starts from there as though you had been born one minute before.

The woman of Samaria met our Lord at the well and we ask, "Why was Jesus willing to reveal so much more about Himself in this setting than He did in other encounters during His ministry?"

You and I would never have chosen this woman with such a shadow lying across her life, but Jesus is the Christ of God, and He could sense the potential within her innermost being. He gave her the secret of His Messiahship and the secret of the nature of God. Her frankness and her humility appealed to the Savior as they talked of man's need and the true worship of God by the Spirit of God.

In Jesus' day, His critics said in scorn: "This man receives sinners!" They were right—and He lived and died and rose again to prove it. The blessed part is this: He is still receiving sinners!

*June 25* _____

# LORD OF OUR LIVING

*Who died for us, that whether we wake or sleep, we should live together with him. (1 Thessalonians 5:10)*

I have studied the New Testament enough to know that our Lord Jesus Christ never made the sharp distinctions between "secular" and "sacred" that we do!

I think it is wrong to place our physical necessities on one side, and put praying and singing and giving and Bible reading and testifying on the other.

When we are living for the Lord and living to please and honor Him, eating our breakfast can be just as spiritual as having our family prayers. There is no reason for a committed Christian to apologize: "Lord, I am awfully sorry but you know I have to eat now. I will be with you again just as soon as I am through."

Well, we have a better way than that in our living for God, and we see as we consider His feeding of the 5,000 the meaning of His Lordship. Jesus Christ is Lord—Lord of our bread and Lord of our eating and Lord of our sleeping, and Lord of our working!

Brethren, our Lord is with us, sanctifying everything we do, provided it is honest and good.

# CHRIST GLORIFIED IN US

*Eye hath not seen, nor ear heard . . . the things which God hath prepared for them that love him. (1 Corinthians 2:9)*

The Bible tells us that eye has not seen nor ear heard, neither has it entered into the heart of men, the things that God has laid up for those who love Him!

That is why the apostle goes on to remind us that God has revealed these mysteries to us by the Holy Spirit.

Oh, if we would only stop trying to make the Holy Spirit our servant and begin to live in His life as the fish lives in the sea, we would enter into the riches of glory about which we know nothing now. Too many of us want the Holy Spirit in order to have some gift—healing or tongues or preaching or prophecy.

Yes, these have their place in that total pattern of the New Testament, but let us ever pray that we may be filled with the Spirit for a secondary purpose!

Remember, God wants to fill you with His Spirit as an end in your moral life. God's purpose is that we should know Him first of all, and be lost in Him; and that we should enter into the fullness of the Spirit that the eternal Son, Jesus Christ, may be glorified in us!

*June 27* _____

# THE SPIRITUAL ESSENCE

*By the renewing of the Holy Ghost, which he shed on us abundantly through Jesus Christ. (Titus 3:5–6)*

We who are the disciples of Jesus Christ often need to be reminded that God is allowing us to live on two planes at the same time.

He lets us live in this religious plane where there are preachers and songleaders and choirs, teachers and evangelists—and that is religion. It is actually "religion in overalls"—it is the external part of religion and it has its own place in God's work and plan.

But beyond that and superior to all of the externals in our religious experience is the spiritual essence of it all! It is that spiritual essence that I want to see enthroned in our communion and fellowship in the Church of Jesus Christ!

We need the caution that much theology, much Bible teaching and many Bible conferences begin and end in themselves. They circle fully around themselves—but when everyone goes home no one is any better than he was before. We sorely need this caution about holding truth that begins and ends in itself. The danger is that we teach and live so that truth is given no opportunity of moral expression!

# ETERNITY IN OUR HEARTS

*The high and lofty One that inhabiteth eternity . . . with him also that is of a contrite and humble spirit. (Isaiah 57:15)*

The only reason that men and women can be saved is the fact that God has put eternity in our hearts!

Man is fallen—yes! Man is lost, a sinner and needs to be born again—yes!

But God made man in His own image and He keeps the longing after eternity and a desire after everlasting life there within the hearts of men.

What, then, is the matter with man? Like the lion in the cage, he paces back and forth and roars to the heavens before he dies.

I think this is the truth—we are disturbed because God has put everlastingness in our hearts. He has put a longing for immortality in our beings, something that demands God and heaven. Yet, we are too blind and sinful to find Him or even to look for Him!

As Christian witnesses, we must be faithful and timely in our preaching and teaching. There is a note of warning in this—telling men and women why they are lost and that if they will not repent they will certainly perish!

*June 29* _____

# PRAYER FOR HUMILITY

Now, O Lord of heaven and earth, I consecrate my remaining days to Thee; let them be many or few, as Thou wilt.

I accept hard work and small rewards in this life. I ask for no easy place. I shall try to be blind to the little ways that could make life easier. If others seek the smoother path I will try to take the hard way without judging them too harshly.

I shall expect opposition and try to take it quietly when it comes. Or if, as sometimes it falleth out to Thy servants, I should have grateful gifts pressed upon me by Thy kindly people, stand by me then and save me from the blight that often follows. Teach me to use whatever I receive in such manner that will not injure my soul nor diminish my spiritual power. Let me never forget that I am a man with all the natural faults and passions that plague the race of men.

And if in Thy permissive providence honor should come to me from Thy Church, let me not forget that I am unworthy of the least of Thy mercies.

*June 30*

# WARNING IN THE GOSPEL

*He that believeth not is condemned already. (John 3:18)*

When God warns a nation or a city, a church or a person, it is a grievous sin to ignore such warning. In conservative Christianity, we believe that the Christian message does indeed contain an element of alarm, but not all Christians believe this.

Some have been taught that the Christian gospel is "good news exclusively." They believe that the only way to explain the full meaning of the Christian gospel is to quote one verse: "Believe on the Lord Jesus, and you will be saved."

"That is it! That is all there is to it," they say.

They surely need to be reminded that in the use of language, it is impossible to make certain definite statements without bringing to mind that which is exactly opposite. So, when the Scriptures admonish us to believe on the Lord Jesus Christ to be saved, there comes to our mind the fact of mankind's lost condition and the starkly plain message to those who do not believe: "He that believeth not is condemned already, because he hath not believed in the name of the only begotten Son of God" (John 3:18).

*July 1* _____

# CRITICAL DECISIONS

*The Lord had said unto Abram, Get thee out of thy country
. . . So Abram departed, as the Lord had spoken unto him.
(Genesis 12:1, 4)*

People have many different ideas about the most important moment of their lives on this earth. We know of many who have testified to the great importance of their own spiritual decision—the act of faith whereby they committed themselves and their entire futures to God!

I believe the Bible makes it plain that the single most critical, most important time in the life of Abraham was when he heard and answered the call of God. Unexpectedly and dramatically, God revealed Himself to Abraham and call him to be a pilgrim. It is a lesson to us that when Abraham was called, he by faith obeyed and went, even though he did not know where he was going!

I have found comfort in the doctrine of prevenient grace, which, simply stated, is the belief that before a sinner can seek God, God must first have sought him.

In Abraham's case, I believe that if he had been insensitive, he would never have heard God's voice calling him, and if Abraham had rejected God's overtures, the whole history of the world would have been vastly different—and different for the worse!

# FREE TO BE A SERVANT

*Understanding what the will of the Lord is. (Ephesians 5:17)*

Every man in a free society must decide whether he will exploit his liberty, or curtail it for moral and intelligent ends. He may take upon him the responsibility of business and a family, or he may shun all obligations and end on Skid Row. The tramp is freer than president or king, but his freedom is undoing. While he lives he remains socially sterile and when he dies he leaves nothing to make the world glad he lived.

The Christian cannot escape the peril of too much liberty. He is indeed free, but his very freedom may prove a source of real temptation to him. He is free from the chains of sin, free from the moral consequences of evil acts now forgiven, free from the curse of the law and the displeasure of God.

The ideal Christian is one who knows he is free to do as he will—and wills to be a servant. This is the path Christ took: blessed is the man who follows Him!

*July 3* _____

# ONLY GOD IS FREE

*Stand fast in the liberty wherewith Christ hath made us free. (Galatians 5:1)*

To any human who bothers to think a bit, it should be evident that there is in our society no such thing as absolute freedom—for only God is free!

It is inherent in creaturehood that its freedom must be limited by the will of the Creator and the nature of the thing created. Freedom is liberty within bounds, liberty to obey holy laws, liberty to keep the commandments of Christ, to serve mankind, to develop to the full all the latent possibilities within our redeemed natures. True Christian liberty never sets us free to indulge our lusts or to follow our fallen impulses.

On earth, a healthy society requires that its members accept a limited freedom. Each must curtail his own liberty that all may be free, and this law runs throughout all of the created universe, including the kingdom of God.

The glory of heaven itself lies in the character of the freedom enjoyed by those who dwell therein!

# GOD TOUCHES OUR EMOTIONS

*Set your affection on things above, not on things on the earth.* *(Colossians 3:2)*

I have heard people say that "Only doctrine is important."

Would they leave no room for Christian experience?

Consider the preaching and the example of the famed Jonathan Edwards, used so mightily by God in the Great Awakening throughout New England in the 18th century.

But, you say, "Jonathan Edwards was a Calvinist!"

I know—and that is my point. Edwards was acknowledged by society to have been one of the greatest intellects of his time. Yet he believed in genuine Christian experience so positively that he wrote a well-accepted book, *Religious Affections*, in defense of Christian emotion.

Charged by some that his revivals had too much emotion, Edwards stood forth and proclaimed that when men and women meet God, accepting His terms, they experience an awareness that lifts their hearts to rapture.

What higher privilege is granted to mankind on earth than to be admitted into the circle of the friends of God!

*July 5* _____

# GOD'S WILL: "OBEY!"

*If ye will not obey . . . then shall the hand of the Lord be against you. (1 Samuel 12:18)*

Independence is a strong human trait, so men and women everywhere bristle when anyone says, "You owe obedience!" In the natural sense, we do not take kindly to the prospect of yielding obedience to anyone.

Both Old and New Testaments of the Bible make it plain that sin is disobedience to the Law of God. Paul's picture of sinners in Ephesians concludes that the wrath of God will come upon those who are "the children of disobedience."

So, we live in a generation of men and women alienated from God, and who make a great case for individualism and "the right of self-determination." The individual's strong statement is this: "I belong to myself. No one has the authority to require my obedience!"

Now, if God had made us to be mere machines, we would not have the power of self-determination. He made us in His image, to be moral creatures with the power, but not the right, to choose evil. We have the right to be good. We never have the right to be bad because God, the Creator, is good. If we choose to be unholy, we are using a right that is not ours!

# DISCIPLINE IS DISMISSED

*Follow me, and I will make you fishers of men. And they straightway left their nets, and followed him.*
*(Matthew 4:19–20)*

We live in a land noted and favored for its freedom; a country where Protestant Christianity is popular and well accepted.

I noted this to speak of one of the great spiritual dangers inherent in Protestantism, the fact that there is no discipline involved. Anyone in our churches is pretty much free to do anything he wants to do. If he does not like one church he has only to cross the street and go to another. If he does not like the preacher, he can leave and soon be attending a church where he is quite pleased with the preacher and with the music and with the atmosphere.

You see, he is demanding Christianity without discipline. He is refusing to acknowledge that the Christian faith makes its own demands of obedience to God and humility of spirit.

When his personal desires take the upper hand, the voice of the Spirit of God is stifled and silenced. There can be only one result—the human soul will become starved and deformed!

*July 7* _____

# CHRISTIANS INDEED

*They . . . are choked with cares and riches and pleasures of this life, and bring no fruit to perfection. (Luke 8:14)*

I believe we are mistaken in Christian life and theology when we try to add the "deeper life" to an imperfect salvation, obtained through an imperfect concept of the entire matter.

Under the working of the Spirit of God through men like Finney and Wesley, no one would ever have dared to say, "I am a Christian" if he had not surrendered his whole being, taking Jesus Christ as his Lord and Savior!

Today, we let them say they are saved no matter how imperfect and incomplete the transaction, with the proviso that the deeper Christian life can be "tacked on" at some time in the future.

Brethren, I believe we must put the blame on faulty teaching—teaching that is filled with self-deception.

Let us look unto Jesus our Lord—high and holy, wearing the crown, Lord of Lords and King of all, having a perfect right to command full obedience from all of His saved people!

# TOO TIMID TO RESIST

*Speak every man truth with his neighbor; for we are members one of another. (Ephesians 4:25)*

The clever proponents of evil political ideologies are spending millions to make us Americans ashamed to love our country. They use every means possible to persuade our own people that there is little left worth defending and certainly nothing worth dying for.

They are building in the public mind a picture of an American as a generous, tolerant, smiling chap who loves baseball and babies, and who subscribes wholly to the doctrine of the brotherhood of man—so everything is going to be all right!

From our point of view, these concepts are having their effects on the nation's religious life, especially among Protestants.

Let a man rise to declare the unique Lordship of Jesus Christ and the absolute necessity of obedience to Him, and he is at once branded as a hate-monger and a divider of men.

The devil has brainwashed large numbers of religious leaders so successfully that they are now too timid to resist him! And he, being the kind of devil he is, takes swift advantage of their cowardice, erecting altars to Baal everywhere!

*July 9* _____

# THE CREATOR'S HANDIWORK

*The heavens declare the glory of God; and the firmament sheweth his handywork. (Psalm 19:1)*

Reading my Bible, I am greatly impressed by the manner in which godly men of old revealed in their writings an intense love for every natural beauty around them. They saw nature as the handiwork of an all-powerful and all-glorious Creator!

The Old Testament is a marvelous rhapsody on the creation. Start with Moses, and when you get beyond the Levitical order you will find him soaring in his acute consciousness of the presence of God in all creation.

Go to the book of Job. In the closing section you will be amazed at the sublimity of the language describing the world around us. Then go to the Psalms, with David literally dancing with ecstatic delight as he gazes out upon the wonders of God's world. Go to Isaiah, where imagery is neither fanciful nor flighty but a presentation of the wonders of creation.

In our generation, how rarely we get into a situation where we can feel the impulses of nature communicated to us. We seldom have time to lift our eyes to look at God's heaven—except when we are wondering if we should wear our boots!

# GOD'S SAVING GRACE

*Noah found grace in the eyes of the Lord. (Genesis 6:8)*

Grace is the goodness of God confronting human demerit. So, grace is what God is—unchanging, infinite, eternal!

This throws light on God's dealings with men and women throughout the Old Testament dispensations and history. It is certainly the truth, and a proper concept for us to hold, that no one was ever saved, no one is now saved, and no one will ever be saved except by the grace of God.

Before Moses came with the Law, men were saved only by grace. During the time of Moses, no one was saved except by grace. After Moses, before the cross, and after the cross, and during all of the dispensations, anywhere, anytime, no one was ever saved by anything but the grace of God!

We can say this with assurance because God dealt in grace with mankind looking forward to the Incarnation and the atoning death of Christ.

If God had not always operated in grace, He would have swept the sinning human race away. This, then, is the good news: God is gracious all the time, and when His grace becomes operative through our faith in Jesus Christ, then there is the new birth from above!

*July 11* _____

# WE ARE TOO COMFORTABLE

*And others were tortured, not accepting deliverance; that they might obtain a better resurrection. (Hebrews 11:35)*

Is the fact that millions of Americans refuse to attend our church services only another symptom of original sin and love of moral darkness?

No, I believe that explanation is too "pat" to be wholly true.

Churches cannot deny they are too comfortable, too rich, too contented! We hold the faith of our fathers, but it does not hold us. God is trying to interest us in a glorious tomorrow and we are settling for an inglorious today. God has set eternity in our hearts and we have chosen time instead. We are bogged down in local interests and have lost sight of eternal purposes.

It was the knowledge that they were part of God's eternal plan that imparted unquenchable enthusiasm to the early Christians. They burned with holy zeal for Christ, and felt they were part of an army which the Lord was leading to ultimate conquest over all the powers of darkness!

# OUT OF BALANCE

*If ye continue in my word, then are ye my disciples indeed.*
*(John 8:31)*

We must admit that in the evangelical Christian churches of our day, almost all of us are guilty of a lop-sided view of the Christian life—all is made to depend upon the initial act of believing. At a given moment a decision is made for Christ, and after that everything is "automatic."

This is because of our failure to lay a scriptural emphasis in our evangelical preaching.

In our eagerness to make converts we allow our believers to absorb the idea that they can deal with their entire responsibility once and for all by an act of believing. This is in some vague way supposed to honor grace and glorify God, whereas actually it is to make Christ the author of a grotesque, unworkable system that has no counterpart in the Scriptures of Truth.

In the New Testament accounts, faith was for each believer a beginning, not an end. Believing was not a once-done act; it was more than an act. It was an attitude of heart and mind which inspired and enabled the believer to take up his cross and follow the Lamb whithersoever He went!

*July 13* _____

# SELFISH PERSONAL INTEREST

*Chiefly them that walk after the flesh . . . and despise*
*government. Presumptuous are they, self-willed.*
*(2 Peter 2:10)*

Throughout history, the philosophers have pretty well
agreed on the conclusion that selfish personal interest is
the motive behind all human conduct.

The philosopher Epictetus illustrated his understanding
with the fact that two dogs may romp on the lawn with
every appearance of friendship until someone tosses a
piece of raw meat between them. Instantly, their play
turns into savage fight as each struggles to get the meat
for himself. Let us not condemn the old thinker for
comparing the conduct of men to animals. The Bible
frequently does and, humbling as it may be to us, we
humans often look bad by comparison.

If we would be wise in the wisdom of God we must face
up to the truth that men and women are not basically
good: they are basically evil and the essence of sin lies in
their selfishness! Putting our own interests before the
glory of God is sin in its Godward aspects, and the
putting of our own interests before those of our fellow
man is sin as it relates to society. By the Cross, Jesus
Christ demonstrated pure, selfless love in its fullest
perfection. When He died, He set a crown of beauty upon
a God-centered and an others-centered life!

# REPENTANCE IS RARE

*There is joy in the presence of the angels of God over one sinner that repenteth. (Luke 15:10)*

Humans, deceived by the devil and charmed by their own pride and abilities, deny that our world is a rebel province in God's universe. They deny that human society has willfully pulled loose from God's rule and the rest of God's domain.

In fact, they deny that men and women are the creation of God. They deny even that they owe any allegiance to God, their Creator!

The Bible is the record of how God deals with mankind and we can draw but one conclusion: all people are morally obligated to repent and to ask forgiveness of God. Failing to do so, they will perish.

How rare it is in our day to hear of genuine repentance. We live amid a proud, selfish and self-sufficient people. Even in our Christian churches there are those who want nothing more than to be known as "respectable church members!" When repentance is real and faith is genuine, the atoning death of Jesus Christ is effective for pardon and forgiveness and regeneration.

*July 15* _____

# GOD NEEDS NO PITY

*Who would not fear thee, O King of nations? . . . there is*
*none like unto thee. (Jeremiah 10:7)*

I do not think I could ever worship a God who was
suddenly caught off guard, unaware of circumstances in
His world around me!

I could never offer myself to a God that actually needed
me, brethren. If He needed me, I could not respect Him,
and if I could not respect Him, I could not worship Him!

Some of our missionary appeals are getting close to that
same error: that we should engage in missionary work
because God needs us so badly!

The fact is that God is riding above this world and the
clouds are the dust of His feet and if you do not follow
Him, you will lose all and God will lose nothing. He will
still be glorified in His saints and admired of all those
who fear Him. To bring ourselves into a place where God
will be eternally pleased with us should be the first
responsible act of every man!

All of these considerations are based upon the character
and worthiness of God. Not a man or woman anywhere
should ever try to come to God as a gesture of pity
because poor God needs you!

# LOSING THE MYSTERY

*If any man will do his will, he shall know . . . whether it be of God. (John 17:7)*

We may be sure we are gaining spiritually when we discover there is a sense of divine mystery running throughout all of the kingdom of God!

I am aware that there are teachers in various Christian circles who pretend to know everything about God. They will quickly answer any question you may have about God, His creation, His judgments. They end up taking the mystery out of life and the mystery out of worship. When they have done that, they have taken God out as well!

Their cleverness and glibness may well betray a lack of the divine awe within the human spirit—awe and adoration, silent and wonderful, that breathes a whisper, "Oh Lord God, Thou knowest!"

In Isaiah we see clearly what happens to a person in the mystery of the Presence. Overpowered within His own being, Isaiah can only confess, "I am a man of unclean lips!" A person who has sensed what Isaiah sensed will never be able to joke again about "The Someone up there who likes me."

*July 17* _____

# OLD THINGS PASS AWAY

*If any man be in Christ . . . old things are passed away;*
*behold, all things are become new.* (2 Corinthians 5:17)

The New Testament is, among others things, a record of the struggle of twice-born men and women to live in a world run by the once-born! That should indicate that we are not being as helpful as we ought to be when we fail to instruct the new Christian, that one who is "a babe in Christ," that our Lord told his earliest disciples, "In this world you will have tribulation."

The Apostle Paul knew what he was talking about when he told Christian believers, "All that will live godly in Christ Jesus will suffer persecution."

Take the example of a person recently converted to Christ. His inner witness is clear and up to the light he has, he is beginning to live as he believes a Christian should. But this new world is altogether different from the one he has just left. Standards, values, objectives, methods—all are different. Many solid pillars upon which he had previously leaned without question are now seen to be made of chalk and ready to crumble.

There will be tears but there will be joy and peace with the continuing discovery that in Christ, indeed, "old things pass away and all things become new."

# OBEDIENCE IS BETTER

*Leaving the principles of the doctrine of Christ, let us go on unto perfection. (Hebrews 6:1)*

The writer to the Hebrews long ago pointed out that some professed Christians were marking time and getting nowhere! They had had opportunity to grow—but they had not grown. They had had sufficient time to mature, yet they were still babes.

So, he plainly exhorted them to leave their meaningless religious round and press on to perfection.

It is possible to have motion without progress, and this describes much of the activity among Christians today. It is simply lost motion! It boils down to this—it is possible that we may attend church for a lifetime and be none the better for it. I think we can say that most Christians have no clear end toward which they are striving. On the endless religious merry-go-round they continue to waste time and energy.

A Christian cannot hope for the true manifestation of God while he lives in a state of disobedience. Let a man refuse to obey God on some clear point, and the rest of his religious activity will be wasted. The instructed and obedient Christian will yield to God as the clay yields to the potter, and will relish every moment in church!

*July 19* _____

# THE FAMILY OF GOD

*I bow my knees unto the Father of our Lord Jesus Christ, of whom the whole family in heaven and earth is named.*
*(Ephesians 3:14–15)*

There is an important message for the believing family of God in the Bible: next to God Himself we need each other most!

God's ideal is a fellowship of faith, a Christian community. He never intended that salvation should be received and enjoyed by the individual apart from the larger company of believers. With that, it also needs to be said that to live within the religious family does not mean that we must approve everything that is done there.

But God has so created us that we need each other. We may and should go into our closet and pray in secret, but when the prayer is ended we should go back to our people. That is where we belong.

No one is wise enough to live alone, nor good enough nor strong enough. From our brethren we can learn how to do things and sometimes also we can learn how not to do them!

Our Lord who is the Great Shepherd has said that we are the sheep of His pasture and it is in our nature to live with the flock. Best of all, the Shepherd always stays with His flock!

# IS YOUR LINE BUSY?

*I heard the voice of the Lord saying, Whom shall I send. . . .*
*Then said I, Here am I; send me. (Isaiah 6:8)*

The gospel invitation is offered freely to one and all, but many are too preoccupied to hear or heed. They never allow God's call to become a reason for decision. As a result, they live out their entire lives insisting that they never heard any call from God!

The answer to that is plain. God has been trying to get through to them, but engrossed in a host of worldly pursuits, their line is always busy.

The world around us wants to put us in the same straitjacket that would have kept Abraham in Ur of the Chaldees.

"We will talk to you about religion" is the seemingly kindly offer people give us today. But then they add the disclaimer: "Just do not make religion personal." Most people seem to have come to terms with an acceptance of religion if it does not have the Cross of Christ within it!

But when God calls men and women to the belief that Christ has given us the only way to God through His death and atonement, their faith will be an offense to the world. It was so in Abraham's day, and it is so in our day!

*July 21* _____

# OUR GODLY CONVERSATION

*Then they that feared the Lord spake often one to another; and the Lord hearkened and heard it.* (Malachi 3:16)

I have met Christians who were so intent upon winning souls to Christ that they would not talk to you about anything but God and His goodness!

Such a man was the Canadian, Robert Jaffray, one of our early pioneer missionaries. His family owned the *Toronto Globe and Mail* and as a young Christian he was disinherited because he chose to follow God's call to China rather than join the family business.

That good godly man spent his lifetime in China and the south Pacific, searching for the lost—and winning them! He was always reading maps and daring to go to the most difficult places, in spite of physical weaknesses and diabetic handicap. He sought out and lived among the poor and miserable, always praying to God, "Let my people go!"

When on furlough, he could not sit and talk about common things. Always his thoughts went back to God and missions and winning the lost. I am reminded of Malachi who said, "They that feared the Lord spoke often one to another; and the Lord hearkened."

# THE REALITY OF PRIDE

*The fear of the Lord is to hate evil: pride, and arrogancy,
and the evil way, . . . do I hate. (Proverbs 8:13)*

Let me warn you of the danger and the bigotry of
human pride. You will find it everywhere in the world
and it will feast on almost anything that will make it fat!

I have come to the conclusion that many people I have
met are not ever going to get right with God because they
have determined that they simply will not humble
themselves, ever!

Pride is an awesome quality in mankind, not only in
Jesus' day, but in ours as well.

I heard a newscast in which one of India's highest
officials was trying to deny a report that Christian
missionaries were being hindered in their work in India.
He said, "We are not hindering the propagation of the
Christian doctrine in India. In fact, we understand that
there have actually been a few people of low caste who
have believed the Christian teaching."

Oh, the rising pride in his voice as he made the
statement. The helpless and the hopeless in the lowest
caste—he was not going to get in their way if they wanted
to believe in Christ.

Yes, the bigotry of human pride is everywhere!

*July 23* _____

# TWO-WAY TRAFFIC

*Straightway the father of the child cried, and said with tears, Lord, I believe; help thou my unbelief.* (Mark 9:24)

In the uncertainty of our times, the traffic between faith and unbelief is tragically heavy, as the Scriptures declared it would be. But we may encourage our hearts with the knowledge that the traffic does not always move in the direction of unbelief—sometimes it moves the other way!

Every now and then the cheering news comes of some "liberal" who gets sick to his stomach of the mixture of applied psychology and cheap poetry, and comes home like the prodigal to the Father's house. It is true that the movement from orthodoxy to liberalism is usually slow; almost too slow to be perceived. I have never heard of a single instance where any person accepted modernism as a result of a spiritual experience.

But the movement back to faith is likely to be sudden, often explosive. A man or woman is converted to Christ by a sudden encounter with God and spiritual things!

The simple fact that the believer always experiences something and the unbeliever never does should tell us a great deal. Only the true Christian is sure the sun has risen!

# "UNFAIR! UNFAIR!"

*He was oppressed, and he was afflicted, yet he opened not
his mouth . . . neither was any deceit in his mouth.*
*(Isaiah 53:7, 9)*

Christians who understand the true meaning of Christ's
cross will never whine about being treated unfairly.
Whether or not they are given fair treatment will never
enter their heads. They know they have been called to
follow Christ, and certainly the Savior did not receive
anything approaching fair treatment from mankind.

In language the word "unfair" seems altogether
innocent but it indicates an inner attitude that has no
place among Christians.

The man who cries "Unfair!" is not a victorious man.
He is inwardly defeated and in self-defense appeals to the
referee to note that he has been fouled. This gives him an
alibi when they carry him out on a stretcher and saves his
face while his bruises heal.

It is a certainty that Christians will suffer wrongs; but if
they take them in good spirit and without complaint, they
have conquered their enemy. They remember that Jesus
was reviled—but any thought of His shouting for fair play
simply cannot be entertained by the reverent heart!

*July 25* _____

# THE PROPHETIC VOICE

*Speak every man truth . . . that which is good to the use of edifying, that it may minister grace unto the hearers.*
*(Ephesians 4:25, 29)*

The Christian minister cannot deny that God has called him to be a prophet to his own generation, for the Church is God's witness to each generation and its ministers are its voice. Through them, the voice of God becomes vocal!

The true minister, therefore, should know what he means when he says that he preaches "the truth." It is not enough that the man of God preach truth—suppose he recites the multiplication table? That is also truth. A church can wither as surely under the ministry of soulless Bible exposition as it can where no Bible is given at all. To be effective, the message must be alive—it must alarm, arouse, challenge; it must be God's present voice to a particular people.

To preach the truth, the prophet must be under the constant sway of the Holy Spirit. He must be driven to God for wisdom. Otherwise, he will not pierce the conscience of each listener as if the message had been directed to him or her alone. Further, it is necessary that the man of God know the people's hearts better than they themselves do!

# GOD NEEDS NO ADJECTIVES

*I will mention the loving kindness of the Lord, and the praises of the Lord, according to all that the Lord hath bestowed on us. (Isaiah 6:7)*

We do not need any enlarging adjectives when we speak of God, or of His love or mercy. God Almighty fills the universe and overfills it because it is His character—infinite and unlimited!

We do not need to say God's "great" love, although we do say it. We do not need to say God's "abundant" mercy, although we do say it. I expect we say it to cheer and elevate our own thoughts of God, not to infer that there is any degree in the mercy of God.

Our adjectives can be useful only when we talk about earthly things—when we refer to the great love of a man for his family, or of a man's fabulous wealth.

But when we are speaking of God there can be no such measuring point. When we speak of the riches of God we must include all the riches there are! God is not less rich or more rich—He is rich! He holds all things in His being!

So it is with mercy. God is not less merciful or more merciful. Thankfully, He is full of mercy. Whatever God is, He is that in the fullness of unlimited grace!

*July 27* _____

# A WORLDWIDE BODY

*For the body is not one member, but many . . . Now ye are*
*the body of Christ, and members in particular.*
*(1 Corinthians 12:14, 27)*

Stating it in the most simple terms, the Christian Church, called to be the Body of Christ on earth, is the assembly of redeemed saints.

We meet in local congregations and assemblies, yet we know that we are not an end in ourselves. If we are going to be what we ought to be in the local church, we must come to think of ourselves as a part of something more expansive, something larger that God is doing throughout the world.

There is an important sense here in which we find that we "belong"—belonging to something that is worthy and valuable, and something that is going to last forever!

These are considerations concerning the whole Church, the Body of Christ, and the fact that in our local congregation we have the joyful sense of belonging to an amazing fellowship throughout the world. Every believing church has a part with us and we a part with them.

Brethren, the Church must have the enabling and the power of the Holy Spirit and the glow of the Shekinah glory—God within us. For then, even lacking everything else, you still have a true church!

# MAKING CHRIST WAIT

*If any man . . . consent not to wholesome words, even the words of our Lord Jesus Christ, he is proud, knowing nothing. (1 Timothy 6:3–4)*

First I become indignant and then I become sad when a person to whom I am trying to give spiritual counsel tells me: "Well, I am trying to make up my mind whether or not I should accept Christ."

This scene is taking place in our society over and over again, as proud adamic sinners argue within themselves: "I don't know whether I should accept Christ or not." So, in this view, our poor Lord Christ stands hat-in-hand, shifting from one foot to the other, looking for a job—wondering whether He will be accepted!

Is it possible that we proud humans do not know that the Christ we are putting off is the eternal Son; the Lord who made the heavens and the earth and all things that are therein? He is indeed the One, the Mighty One!

Thankfully, He has promised to receive us, poor and sinful though we be. But the idea that we can make Him stand while we render the verdict of whether He is worthy is a frightful calumny—and we ought to get rid of it!

*July 29* _____

# OUR LOVE FOR GOD

*Let us not love in word, neither in tongue; but in deed and in truth. (1 John 3:18)*

The taking over of the romantic love ideal into our relation to God has been extremely injurious to our Christian lives. The idea that we should "fall in love" with God is ignoble, unscriptural, unworthy of us and certainly does no honor to the Most High God!

We do not come to love God by a sudden emotional visitation. Love for God results from repentance, amendment of life and a fixed determination to love Him. Then as God moves more perfectly into the focus of our hearts, our love for Him may indeed rise and swell within us till like a flood it sweeps everything before it.

But we should not wait for this intensity of feeling. We are not responsible to feel but we are responsible to love, and true spiritual love begins in the will.

We should set our hearts to love God supremely, however cold or hard they may seem to be, and go on to confirm our love by happy and careful obedience to His Word.

Enjoyable emotions are sure to follow!

# JESUS WILL COME

*And sware by him that liveth forever and ever, that there should be time no longer. (Revelation 10:6)*

We are living in a period when God waits in grace and mercy. In His faithfulness, God is calling out a people for His name—those who will in faith cast their lot with Jesus Christ! Then, at a time known only to God, the end of this age will come, and Jesus Christ will return to earth for His own believing people—His Church.

The event is certain—the timing is uncertain. When the mighty angel of Revelation shouts his signal and raises his hand heavenward, it will be eternally too late for unrepentant sinners.

When the time comes in heaven for that announcement, three worlds will hear it. Heaven will hear it, with full agreement that the time of judgment has indeed come. The underworld of hell will hear the shout, and there will be fright. And on earth, the saints, the believing Body of Christ, will hear it and be glad! Meanwhile, the Church is not simply a religious institution. It is an assembly of redeemed sinners, men and women called and commissioned to spread Christ's gospel to the ends of the earth.

*July 31* _____

# JUST PLAIN FAITHFUL

*The things that thou hast heard . . . commit them to faithful men.* (2 Timothy 2:2)

I realize that faithfulness is not a very dramatic subject and that many among us in the Christian faith would like to do something with more dash and more flair than just being faithful. While some are just concerned about getting their picture in the paper, I thank God for every loyal and faithful Christian who has only one recognition in mind, and that is to hear their Lord say in that Great Day to come: "Well done, faithful servant . . . enter into the joy of thy Lord!"

It is plain truth that faithfulness and goodness are at the root of much of the consistent fruit-bearing among the witnessing children of God! Throughout the Bible, the Lord has always placed a great premium on the faithfulness of those who love Him and serve Him.

Noah was faithful in his day. Abraham was faithful in his day. Moses was faithful in his day. And what do we need to say about the faithfulness of our Savior, Jesus Christ? The devil was there with his lies. The world threatened Him all around. But Christ was faithful to His Father and to us!

Are we willing to learn from the Holy Spirit how to be faithful and loving, unselfish and Christ-like?

# GOD WOULD STIR US

*Blessed are they which hunger and thirst after righteousness. (Matthew 5:6)*

There is no way that any of us can talk ourselves into getting a "longing for God." Spiritual desire and hunger must come from God Himself! It cannot be whipped up.

As a grown boy, I tried selling peanuts, popcorn, chewing gum, candy and books on the old Vicksburg and Pacific railroad. I did not sell enough to become any great success, but I recall that we often tried to stir up some desire for our wares among the passengers. We would go through the coaches and give each person a few salted peanuts. No one seemed to want to buy on the first trip through, but when we came back, nearly everyone who had tasted was ready to buy. This was a common trick on the trains.

But it is a different story when we consider the spiritual life. No one but God through His Spirit is able to stir up spiritual desire among us. Those who have accepted a common state of spiritual living and have no deep desire for Him will never be stirred by human means.

*August 2* _____

# THANK GOD FOR CONVICTION

*A man hath joy by the answer of his mouth; and a word spoken in due season, how good is it!* (Proverbs 15:23)

Modern mankind can go anywhere, do everything and be completely curious about the universe. But only a rare person now and then is curious enough to want to know God.

We do not thank God enough for seeking us and finding us and making it possible for us to say to His invitation: "Jesus, I come!"

I have meditated often on the Holy Spirit's quiet dealing with the heart of this untaught lad when I was only 17. We had a neighbor—I only knew him as "Mr. Holman"—and I had heard that he was a Christian.

One day we happened to be walking on the sidewalk together, and he said, "I am glad to have a chance to talk with you. I have been wondering if you are a Christian?"

I told him, "No, I am not a Christian. But I thank you for asking and I am going to give it some serious thought."

After that, I heard a man preaching on a street corner. He quoted Jesus' invitation, "Come unto Me," and the sinner's prayer, "Lord have mercy on me!" Those were the two things that bumped me into the kingdom of God. Sometimes it takes a very little word to stir an unnoticed desire for God and His truth!

# ENJOYING GOD FOREVER

*My sheep hear my voice . . . and they shall never perish.*
*(John 10:27)*

It should be illuminating to us that the difference between unbelief and faith, between man's point of view and God's often comes to light as the believer faces death.

We are told that when John Wesley was dying, he tried to sing but his voice was nearly gone. Although his own theology was Arminian, he was trying to sing the words of an old Calvinist hymn:

> I will praise my Maker while I've breath,
> And when my soul is lost in death,
> Praise shall employ my nobler powers.

That is at least one reason why I cannot get all heated up about contending for one theological position over another.

If Isaac Watts, a Calvinist, could write such praise to God and John Wesley, an Arminian, could sing it with yearning in his last moments, why should I allow anyone to force me to confess, "I don't know which I am!"

I was created and redeemed that I should worship Him and enjoy Him forever. That is the primary issue in our Christian walk!

*August 4*

# GIVING CHRIST HIS PLACE

*That every tongue should confess that Jesus Christ is Lord, to the glory of God the Father. (Philippians 2:11)*

Christianity at large and the Church, generally speaking, are afflicted with a dread, lingering illness that shows itself daily in the apathy and spiritual paralysis of its members.

How can it be otherwise when 20th-century Christians refuse to acknowledge the sharp moral antithesis that God Himself has set between the Church, as the Body of Christ, and this present world with its own human systems?

The differences between the churchly world and the followers of the Lamb are so basic that they can never be reconciled or negotiated. God has never promised His believing people that they would become a popular majority in this earthly scene.

I wonder how many believers would join me in a clear-cut manifesto to our times? I want it to be a declaration of our intentions to restore Christ to the place that is rightfully His in our personal lives, in our family situations and in the fellowship of the churches that bear His name.

Are we willing to demonstrate the standards of godliness and biblical holiness as a rebuke to this wicked and perverse generation?

# CHRIST DOES NOT CHANGE

*Jesus came and spake unto them . . . All power is given unto me in heaven and in earth. (Matthew 28:18)*

You will have to prove it to me if you are among those who claim that Jesus Christ refuses to do for you something that He has done for any other of His disciples!

I address this to all of those who insist that the gifts of the Spirit ended when the last apostle died. They have never furnished chapter and verse for their position.

When some men beat the cover off their Bible to demonstrate how they stand for the Word of God, they should be reminded that they are only standing by their own interpretation!

I find nothing in the Bible that says the Lord has changed. He has the same love, the same grace, the same mercy, the same power, the same desires for the blessings of His children.

Why can we not claim all that God has promised for His redeemed people? What a sad condition for Christians who are in the Church of the mighty Redeemer and Deliverer, who is eternally the Victor, the Rock of Ages. Let us never forget that Jesus Christ is the same yesterday, today and forever!

*August 6*_____

# CHRIST, THE BLESSED ONE

*Take my yoke upon you . . . For my yoke is easy, and my burden is light. (Matthew 11:29–30)*

I feel great sorrow for those who read the Sermon on the Mount and then conclude that Jesus was providing a word picture of men and women comprising the human race. In this world, we find nothing approaching the virtues of which Jesus spoke in the Beatitudes.

Instead of poverty of spirit, we find the rankest kind of pride. Instead of mourners, we find pleasure seekers.

Instead of meekness, we find only arrogance, and instead of hunger after righteousness, we hear men saying, "I am rich and increased with goods and have need of nothing!"

Instead of mercy, we find cruelty. Instead of purity of heart, we encounter corrupt imaginings. Instead of peacemakers, we find men quarrelsome and resentful, fighting back with every weapon at their command.

Jesus said He came to release us from our sad heritage of sin. Blessed is the sinner who finds that Christ's words are the Truth itself; that He is the Blessed One who came from above to confer blessedness upon mankind!

# GOD—ACTING LIKE GOD

*The only begotten Son, which is in the bosom of the Father,*
*he hath declared him. (John 1:18)*

When Jesus walked and taught in Galilee 2,000 years ago, many asked, "Who is that Man?"

The Bible's answer is clear: that Man walking in Galilee was God, acting like God! It was God, limited deliberately, having crossed the wide, mysterious gulf between God and not God, between God and creature. No man had seen God at any time.

In John 1:18, the English translators have said, "The only begotten Son hath declared him." Other versions skirt around it, doing everything to try to say what the Holy Spirit said, but when we have used up our words and synonyms, we still have not said all that God revealed when He said, "Nobody has ever looked at God, but when Jesus Christ came He showed us what God is like" (paraphrase of John 1:18).

He has revealed Him—He has shown us what God is like!

He has declared Him! He has set Him forth! He has revealed Him!

He is in the Father's bosom. It is stated in present, perpetual tense; the language of continuation. Therefore, when Jesus hung on the cross, He did not leave the bosom of the Father!

*August 8* _____

# A HEAVENLY FRAGRANCE

*To the end he may stablish your hearts unblameable in*
*holiness . . . at the coming of our Lord Jesus Christ.*
*(1 Thessalonians 3:13)*

I have been affected in my own heart and life by reading
the testimonies and commentaries of humble men of God
whom I consider to be among the great souls of Christian
church history. From them I have learned that the word
and idea of "holiness" as originally used in the Hebrew
did not have, first of all, the moral connotation.

The original root of the word "holy" was of something
beyond, something strange and mysterious and
awe-inspiring. When we consider the holiness of God, we
talk about something heavenly, full of awe, mysterious
and fear-inspiring. This is supreme when it relates to
God, but it is also marked in men of God and deepens as
men become more like God.

It is a sense of awareness of the other world, a
mysterious quality and difference that has come to rest
upon some men and women—that is a holiness. When
those persons with this special quality and mysterious
Presence are morally right and walking in all the holy
ways of God, and carrying without even knowing it the
fragrance of a kingdom that is supreme above the
kingdoms of this world, I am ready to accept that as being
of God and from God!

# CHOSEN IN HIM

*He hath chosen us in him before the foundation of the world, that we should be holy and without blame. (Ephesians 1:4)*

I have been told that sometimes when I preach I really worry the Calvinists, but I want to make a point here, and I take the chance of worrying my brethren in the Arminian persuasion.

The recorded acts of Creation in the beginning were not God's first activity. God had been occupied before that, for He must have been engaged in choosing and fore-ordaining before the foundation of the world!

Paul told the Ephesian Christians: "God has chosen us in Him before the foundation of the world; that we should be holy and without blame before Him in love."

Can I explain how God could have chosen us before the creation of the world? Can I explain the eternal nature of God, the uncreated Being? Can I explain a time when there was only God—no matter, no law, no motion, no relation and no space, no time and no beings, only God?

God was there, and God is not a void! He is the triune God and He is all there is. Before the Creation, He was already busy with eternal mercies and a redemptive plan for a mankind not yet created!

*August 10*

# SPIRITUAL SUFFOCATION

*Where sin abounded, grace did much more abound.*
*(Romans 5:20)*

How can I illustrate man's proneness to spiritual suffocation?

I have read that mining companies used to take live caged birds deep into the mines to detect the presence of dangerous gases. If there was a high concentration of poison, the bird would quickly fall down and die in the bottom of the cage.

I consider a bird a miracle created by God; a wonder with wings, created to soar over green meadows and breathe the sweet air of the heavens. But take him underground where there is blackdamp and pollution and he quickly dies of suffocation!

You can apply that also to the soul of man!

God created man a living soul and intended him to rise and mount up into the eternities and live with God. There is in each of us a longing after immortality. But sin has ruined us. We have listened to that serpent, the devil. We have gone down into the isolated, dark poison-infested pockets of the world, and lost men are dying everywhere of spiritual suffocation!

# WE CAN AFFORD TO DIE

*For here we have no continuing city, but we seek one to come. (Hebrews 13:14)*

Brethren, it is a fact indeed, that we will never fully realize in our earthly life what it means to be co-heirs with Christ!

The apostles have made it quite plain that all of the eternal implications of our heavenly inheritance will not be known to us until we see Christ face to face in a future time.

I have said that only a Christian has the right and can afford to die! But if we believers were as spiritual as we ought to be, we might be looking to our "home-going" with a great deal more pleasure and anticipation than we do.

I say also that if we are true believers in the second advent of our Savior, we will be anticipating His return with yearning. Common sense, the perspective of history, the testimony of the saints, reason and the Bible—all agree with one voice that He may come before we die.

The Christian believer whose faith and hope are in Jesus Christ alone knows that he may die before the Lord comes. If he dies, he is better off, for Paul said, "It is far better that I go to be with the Lord!"

# HOW DO WE KNOW HIM?

*I know whom I have believed. (2 Timothy 1:12)*

I must ask this question in the context of today's modern Christianity: "Is it not true that for most of us who call ourselves Christians there is no real experience?"

We have substituted theological ideas for an arresting encounter; we are full of religious notions, but our great weakness is that for our hearts there is no one there!

Whatever else it embraces, true Christian experience must always include a genuine encounter with God. Without this, religion is but a shadow, a reflection of reality, a cheap copy of an original once enjoyed by someone else of whom we have heard.

It cannot but be a major tragedy in the life of any man or woman to live in a church from childhood to old age and know nothing more real than some synthetic god compounded of theology and logic, but having no eyes to see, no ears to hear—and no heart to love!

# OUR INNER SIGHT

*The eyes of your understanding being enlightened; that ye*
*may know what is the hope of his calling. (Ephesians 1:18)*

Revival and blessing come to the church when we stop
looking at a picture of God and look at God Himself!
Revival comes when, no longer satisfied to know about a
God in history, we meet the conditions of finding Him in
living, personal experience.

Conversely, revival cannot come if we are far removed
from God. It cannot come if, instead of hearing His voice,
we are content with only an echo!

Put those deficiencies together and you have the reason
why we are dissatisfied and empty. You have the reason
why there is so little of vivid, vibrant joy in the things of
God.

I hold fast to the opinion that our God is ever trying to
reveal Himself to us. There is no way for sinful men and
women to find their way into God's presence unless He
reveals Himself and appears to us. I do not mean that God
is trying to appear to our physical eyesight. Rather, He is
trying to appear to the eye of our soul through an inner
consciousness. Never apologize for your inner eyes! They
are the real eyes for discerning the nature of issues
important to God.

*August 14*_____

# BLESSEDNESS TO COME

*We have a building of God, a house not made with hands,*
*eternal in the heavens. (2 Corinthians 5:1)*

A lot of people talk about going to heaven in spite of the feeble hope popular religion affords.

Any valid hope of a state of blessedness beyond the incident of death must be in the goodness of God and in the work of atonement accomplished for us by Jesus Christ on the Cross.

The deep, deep love of God is the fountain out of which flows our future beatitude; and the grace of God in Christ is the channel by which it reaches us. The Cross of Christ creates a moral situation where every attribute of God is on the side of the returning sinner.

The true Christian may safely look forward to a future state that is as happy as perfect love wills it to be. Since love cannot desire for its object anything less than the fullest possible measure of enjoyment for the longest possible time, it is virtually beyond our power to conceive of a future as consistently delightful as that which Christ is preparing for us.

And who is to say what is possible with God?

# "FROZEN" UNBELIEF

*Take heed, brethren, lest there be in any of you an evil heart of unbelief. (Hebrews 3:12)*

Study the life of faithful Noah and you will know what he would say if he could come and counsel you today: "Whenever you hear God's truth," he would say, "you will go either in the direction you are moved, or you will just wait.

"If you wait, you will find that the next time you hear the truth, it will not move you quite as much. The next time, it will move you less—and the time will come when that truth will not move you at all!"

We need that message in our generation, for there is a distressing kind of "frozen" unbelief all around us. Men and women are paying little heed to any of God's warning signals.

As a farm boy, I learned the lesson of little chicks—an easy prey for hawks overhead. The mother hen heard the high-pitched cry of the soaring hawk and gave her own special "cluck-cluck" of warning. Her chicks scampered to her side and soon she had them all tucked safely under her feathers.

Thank God, there is a true faith that is not ashamed to move in the direction of the Ark of Safety!

*August 16*_____

# LET US MOVE FORWARD

*That ye might be filled with all the fullness of God.*
*(Ephesians 3:19)*

The Apostle Paul's greatest desire was to always move forward in the knowledge and blessing of God. But some modern Bible teachers now call that kind of hunger and thirsting fanaticism, instead of desire for spiritual maturity.

These teachers assure the new Christian: "You are now complete in Christ. Just relax and be glad that there is nothing more you will ever need."

With great desire, Paul wrote: "That I may win Christ"—and yet he already had Christ! With obvious longing he said: "That I may be found in Him"—and yet he was already in Him!

Paul humbly and intensely breathed his great desire: "That I may know Him"—even though he already knew Him!

Because he did not want to stand still, Paul testified: "I follow after; I press toward the mark. I am striving to lay hold of that for which Christ laid hold on me!"

It is very plain that the apostle had no other desire than to be completely available to God. Many of us refuse to follow his example!

# GOD'S ETERNAL WORK

*The creature itself also shall be delivered from the bondage of corruption. (Romans 8:21)*

Is it possible that some of our brothers and sisters in Christ have forgotten that even though we are Christians, we live day by day in unredeemed physical bodies?

Yes, brethren, this is orthodox Christian theology, given us by the Apostle Paul in these words: "Even though we have the firstfruits of the Spirit, we groan within ourselves, waiting for the redemption of the body." These bodies of ours will be redeemed, for that is the promise of God. But in this life they are not yet actually redeemed. That is why we cannot do God's eternal work ourselves, for only the Holy Spirit of God can bring about His eternal purposes.

If we are to successfully engage in the Christian witness God expects of us while we are here on this earth, we must consciously know and experience the indwelling illumination of the Holy Spirit of God. We must depend upon His gifts and His enduement and His anointing if we hope to cope with the universal blight which is upon mankind.

*August 18* _____

# GOD FAR AWAY

*Am I a God at hand, saith the Lord, and not a God afar off?*
*. . . Do not I fill heaven and earth? (Jeremiah 23:24)*

I remember the words of a little song I heard when I was young about God's presence "Far Away Beyond the Star-lit Sky."

That is really where mankind has placed God. He is far away, out there somewhere beyond the star-lit sky.

As men and women in this world, we are prone to think of God's presence in terms of space, as we understand it. We think in terms of light years or meters or miles or fathoms. We think of God as dwelling in space—which He does not! God is not contained in heaven and earth as some seem to think.

God in His person and His attributes fills heaven and earth exactly as the ocean fills a bucket which is submerged in the ocean depths.

Why, then, does man say "God is far, far away!"? Because of the complete dissimilarity between the nature of the holy God and the perverted nature of sinful man!

# CHRISTIAN "SHRINKAGE"

*Be ye followers of God, as dear children; and walk in love as Christ also hath loved us. (Ephesians 5:1–2)*

Why should we have to accept the idea held in some Christian circles that new converts will soon lose their first zeal and settle down to a life of dull religious routine? I believe that I carry the welfare of the saints in my heart and it disturbs me that some Christians are satisfied to accept the title of "dead average."

What happens? Can it be that the person who has held a joyful conversion becomes enamored of his experience, failing to keep his eyes fixed on the Lord?

Only engrossment with God can maintain perpetual spiritual enthusiasm because only God can supply everlasting novelty. In God every moment is new and nothing ever gets old. Of things religious we may become tired, even prayer may weary us; but God never!

Brothers and sisters, nothing can preserve the sweet savor of our first experience except to be preoccupied with God Himself! Let the new convert know that if he would grow instead of shrink, he must spend his nights and his days in communion with the triune God!

*August 20*

# TESTING OUR FAITH

*That ye may be sincere and without offense until the day of Christ. (Philippians 1:10)*

Any belief that does not command the daily walk of the one who holds it is not a real belief: it is a pseudo-belief only!

I think it might shock some of us profoundly if we were suddenly brought face to face with our beliefs and forced to test them in the fores of practical living. How many professing Christians boast in the Lord but watch carefully that they never get caught fully depending on Him? Pseudo-faith always arranges a way out to serve in case God "fails."

What we need very badly these days is a company of Christians prepared to trust God as completely now as they must do at the last day! For each of us, the time is surely coming when we shall all have nothing but God! To the men of pseudo-faith, that is a terrifying thought!

For true faith, it is either God or total collapse, and not since Adam first stood up on the earth has God failed anyone who trusted Him! We can prove our faith by our committal to it—and in no other way!

# GOD GIVES ASSURANCE

*But ye, beloved, building up yourselves on your most holy faith . . . keep yourselves in the love of God. (Jude 20–21)*

Moral sanity requires that we settle this most important matter first of all: settling our personal and saving relation with God!

In some Christian groups, there are believers who actually make fun of Christians in other groups who occasionally arise and sing the words of an old hymn, "Do I love the Lord, or no?" No serious-minded person should ever laugh at any man or woman who, knowing that death is only three jumps ahead, contemplates: "My God, do I really know Thee or not? Have I been mistaken in meaningless religious connection? My God, what must I do to be saved?"

Many of us better start asking questions today. We know that we had better not try to stand on our own reputation.

There is nothing in the whole world of greater meaning than to come back into the family of God by faith and through His grace! There is no joy that can be compared to that which God gives when He forgives us, cleanses us, restores and saves us, and assures us that the gift of God is indeed eternal life, to as many as will believe!

*August 22* _____

# CHRIST'S ETERNAL GLORY

*We beheld his glory, the glory as of the only begotten of the Father. (John 1:14)*

The Apostle John speaks for all when he writes of the eternal Son and reminds us that "we beheld His glory." John was speaking of much more than the glory of Christ's wondrous works. Every part of nature had to yield to Him and His authority. Everything our Lord did was meaningful in the display of His eternal glory.

But we may be sure that John had a much greater glory in mind than the gracious and wonderful acts of healing and help.

It was the very person and character of Jesus that was glorious. It was not only what He did—but what He was. What He was in His person primary!

Brethren, there can be no argument about Jesus Christ's glory—it lay in the fact that He was perfect love in a loveless world; that He was perfect purity in an impure world; and that He was perfect meekness in a harsh and quarrelsome world. Patience in suffering, unquenchable life and God's grace and truth were in the eternal Word, as well.

This is the divine and eternal glory that earth's most famous and capable personalities can never attain!

# HEIR TO ALL CREATION

*God . . . hath spoken unto us by his Son, whom he hath appointed heir of all things. (Hebrews 1:1–2)*

In this life, we are experiencing only unfinished segments of God's great eternal plan. Certainly we are not able to comprehend fully the glory that will be ours in that future day when leaning on the arm of our heavenly Bridegroom we are led into the presence of the Father in heaven with exceeding joy!

The writer to the Hebrews has tried to help us in the proper exercise of our faith, with the amazing statement that our Lord Jesus Christ is the heir of all things in God's far-flung creation. All things created have been ordered and laid out so they become the garment of deity and the universal living expression of Himself to this world!

What does "heir of all things" really mean? It includes angels, seraphim, cherubim, ransomed men and women of all ages, matter, mind, law, spirit, value, meaning. It includes life and events on varied levels of being—and God's great interest embraces them all!

Surely God has left nothing to chance in His creative scheme—whether it be the tiniest blade of grass or the mightiest galaxy in the distant heavens above!

*August 24* _____

# SATAN'S STRATAGEM

*For we have not followed cunningly devised fables.*
*(2 Peter 1:16)*

It is amazing that Satan's wiliest stratagem against Christian believers is to use our virtues against us! Perhaps it is more amazing that he often does this with great success.

By means of temptation to sin he strikes at our personal lives; by working through our virtues he gets at the whole community of believers and unfits it for its own defense.

To capture a city an enemy must first weaken or destroy its resistance. The Church will never fall as long as she resists. This the devil knows; consequently he uses any stratagem to neutralize her resistance.

Satan first creates a maudlin, inaccurate concept of Christ as soft, smiling and tolerant. He reminds us that when Christ, as a lamb brought to slaughter, opened not His mouth—and suggests that we do likewise. Then if we notice his foot in the door and rise to oppose him, he appeals to our desire to be Christlike. "Love everybody and all will be well," he urges.

The shepherd, taken in by this sweet talk, is afraid to use his club, and the wolf gets the sheep!

# PRAYER—AND GOD'S SPIRIT

*We know not what we should pray for as we ought: but the Spirit maketh intercession for us. (Romans 8:26)*

Probably none of us really know as much about prayer as we should—but as students of the Word of God we may agree that only the Spirit can pray effectively.

The idea has been expressed that "wrestling in prayer" is always a good thing, but that is by no means true. Extreme religious "exercises" may be undergone with no higher motive than to get our own way!

The spiritual quality of a prayer is determined not by its intensity but by its origin. In evaluating prayer we should inquire who is doing the praying—our determined hearts, or the Holy Spirit? If the prayer originates with the Spirit, then the wrestling can be beautiful and wonderful; but if we are the victims of our own overheated desires, our praying can be as carnal as any other act.

Consider Jacob's wrestling: "a man wrestled with him till daybreak." But when Jacob had been beaten upon, he cried, "I will not let you go unless you bless me!" That wrestling was of divine origin, and the blessed results are known to every Bible student!

*August 26* _____

# MEN WHO DO NOT PRAY

*The fire shall try every man's work of what sort it is.*
*(1 Corinthians 3:13)*

The indications are all around us in Christianity that we are greatly in need of worshipers.

We have a lot of men who are willing to sit on our church boards but have no desire for spiritual joy and radiance and who never show up for the church prayer meeting!

It has always seemed to me to be a frightful incongruity that men who do not pray and do not worship are nevertheless running many of the churches and ultimately determining the direction they will take.

It hits very close to our own situation, perhaps, but we should confess that in many "good churches," we let the women do the praying and let the men do the voting!

God calls us to worship, but in many instances we are majoring in entertainment, just running a poor second to the theater. This is where we are, even in evangelical churches. Yet God's first call to us is for the offering of true worship!

# TRUST—NOT ADJUST

*Your life is hid with Christ in God. (Colossians 3:3)*

We ought to recognize one of the great problems in our modern Christianity: those who come to Christ probably have their minds made up that to stay sane they must remain "adjusted" to society around them.

This notion has been drilled into them from their playpen, and it never occurs to them to question it. There is a "norm" out there somewhere to which they must conform, and that norm is above criticism. Their success and happiness depend upon how well they adjust to it; and Christianity, though it may add something to it, must never disagree with the main idea!

This is the popular notion in the world: "To be happy, adjust to the social norm!" The problem is that the idea will not hold up under examination. The world does not know where it is going; it has not found life's highest good; it is instead puzzled, frightened and frustrated.

Thankfully, it was to this kind of world Jesus came. He died for its sin and now lives for the salvation of all who will repudiate it!

*August 28* _____

# MORE THAN CONSOLATION

*Blessed is the man . . . his delight is in the law of the Lord.*
*(Psalm 1:1–2)*

It is my judgment that too many of us go to church on Sunday for the same reason that a child climbs into its mother's arms after a fall or a bump or a fright—the child wants consolation!

We have fallen upon times when religion is mostly for consolation—for we are in the grip of the cult of peace. We want to relax and have the great God Almighty pat our heads and comfort us with peace of mind, peace of heart, peace of soul. This has become religion!

According to my Bible, there should be a people of God, a people called of God and subjected to a spiritual experience by God. Then they are to learn to walk in the way of Truth and the way of the Scripture, producing the righteous fruit of the child of God no matter what world conditions may be.

But there is a great misunderstanding among us. Too many tend to think that we get the flower and the fragrance and the fruit of the Spirit by some kind of magical shortcut, instead of by cultivation. Meanwhile, our neighbors are waiting to see the likeness of Christ in our daily lives!

# HUMAN PSYCHOLOGY

*God hath chosen the weak things of the world to confound the things which are mighty. (1 Corinthians 1:27)*

To meet the kind of temptations and enemies confronting us in this world, it is not enough for us to stick out our chins, inflate our chests and mutter the old refrain, "Never Say Die!"

Since I have been a Christian, I have had a negative reaction to that kind of human psychology. I do not mind saying that my favorite hymns are not those that exhort me to flex my biceps and tell the world where to get off! That is not my philosophy because it would put my confidence in the wrong place. If my faith, my belief, my confidence are in myself, then they cannot at the same time be resting in God!

The Bible tells us to believe in God and put our trust in Him. It warns us against having any confidence in the flesh. So I do not want some voice exhorting me to "Rise up, O man of God; go forth to face the foe"—and all of that. I would rather go to a place of prayer, meet God there and then let Him face the world for me.

We rest our case completely on God—then our experiences proceed by faith, through faith and in faith! Our victory must be God's victory first!

*August 30*_____

# PRAYER FOR GOD'S WILL

Well do I know, Thou God of the prophets and the apostles, that as long as I honor Thee, Thou wilt honor me. Help me therefore to take this solemn vow to honor Thee in all my future life and labors, whether by gain or by loss, by life or by death, and then to keep that vow unbroken while I live.

I beseech Thee, give me sharp eyes to detect the presence of the enemy; give me understanding to see—and the courage to report what I see faithfully.

Make my voice so like Thine own that even the sick sheep will recognize it and follow Thee.

O Lord, I am Thy servant to do Thy will, and that will is sweeter to me than position or riches or fame, and I choose it above all things on earth or in heaven.

I pray Thee, my Lord and Redeemer, fill me with Thy power by the Holy Spirit, and I will go daily in His strength. Then, when I am old and weary, have a place ready for me above and make me to be numbered with Thy saints in everlasting glory. Amen.

# CONFIDENCE IN GOD

*If our heart condemn us not, then have we confidence in God. (1 John 3:21)*

This is surely one of the great realizations that can come to us in the Christian life—we can put our complete confidence in the God who has revealed Himself to us!

It was a gracious day in my early Christian experience when I realized that it was not in God's character to pounce upon me in judgment. He knows that we are dust and as our God He is loving and patient towards us.

If it were true that the Lord would put the Christian on the shelf every time he failed or blundered or did something wrong, I would have been a piece of statuary by this time!

It is surely true that God will bring judgment when judgment is necessary, but the Scriptures say that judgment is God's strange work. Where there is a lifetime of rebellion, hardened unbelief and love of sin, judgment will come.

But God watches over us for spiritual growth and maturity, trying to teach us the necessity for fully trusting Him and coming to the place of complete distrust of ourselves. We have met God, and can now say with Paul, "That the excellency of the power may be of God and not of us."

*September 1* _____

# ATTRIBUTES OF GOD

*And there appeared unto them cloven tongues like as of fire, and it sat upon each of them. (Acts 2:3)*

What a broad world in which to roam; what an expansive sea in which to swim—and I speak of the God and Father of our Lord Jesus Christ!

He is eternal, which means He is wholly independent of time. Time began in Him and will end in Him.

He is immutable, which means that He has never changed and can never change in any smallest measure. Being perfect, He cannot become more perfect. If He were to become less perfect, He would be less than God.

He is omniscient, which means that He knows in one free and effortless act all matter, all spirit, all relationships, all events. He is; and none of the limiting terms of creatures can apply to Him. Love and mercy and righteousness are His, and holiness so ineffable that no comparisons or figures will avail to express it.

In the pillar of fire He dwelt. The fire that glowed in the "holy place" was called the Shekinah, the Presence. Then when the Old gave way to the New, He came at Pentecost as a fiery flame and rested upon each disciple!

*September 2*

# HOLINESS NOT AN OPTION

*He that in these things serveth Christ is acceptable to God, and approved of men. (Romans 14:18)*

Many believers in our day seem to consider the expression of true Christian holiness to be just a matter of personal option: "I have looked it over and considered it, but I don't buy it!"

But the Apostle Peter clearly exhorts every Christian to holiness of life and conversation: God's children ought to be holy because God Himself is holy! I am of the opinion that New Testament Christians do not have the privilege of ignoring such apostolic injunctions.

There is something basically wrong with our Christianity and our spirituality if we can carelessly presume that if we do not like a biblical doctrine and choose to ignore it, there is no harm done. God has never instructed us that we should weigh His desires for us and His commandments to us in the balance of our own judgments—and then decide what we want to do about them.

We have the power within us to reject God's instruction—but where else shall we go? If we turn away from the authority of God's Word, to whose authority do we yield?

*September 3* _____

# "BE THOU EXALTED"

*Be thou exalted, O God, above the heavens; let thy glory be above all the earth.* (Psalm 57:5)

Essentially, God's gracious plan of salvation was wrought to bring about the restoration of a right relationship between men and women and their Creator.

The disobedience and fall of Adam and Eve destroyed the proper Creator-creature relation, in which, unknown to them, their true happiness lay.

Many of us are interested in walking with God and pleasing God and resting in the promises of God. We have discovered that such a life on this earth begins with a complete change in relationship between God and the sinner; a conscious and experienced change affecting the sinner's whole nature.

The atonement in Jesus' blood makes such a change judicially possible, and the working of the Holy Spirit makes it emotionally satisfying.

We must begin with God—and God must be the center of all we are and all we do. "Be Thou exalted" is plainly the language of victorious spiritual experience and central to the life of God in the soul!

# MEEKNESS AND REST

*Blessed are the meek, for they shall inherit the earth.*
*(Matthew 5:5)*

Jesus calls us to His rest, and meekness in His method!

But, we may be assured, the meek man is not a human mouse afflicted with a sense of his own inferiority.

Rather, he may be in his moral life as bold as a lion and as strong as Samson, but he has stopped being fooled about himself. He has accepted God's estimate of his own life.

He knows that he is as weak and helpless as God has declared him to be. Paradoxically, he knows at the same time that he is, in the sight of God, of more importance than angels. In himself, nothing! In God, everything!

The truly meek man rests perfectly content to allow God to place His own values. He will be patient to wait for the day when everything will get its proper price tag and real worth will come into its own—when the righteous shall shine forth in the kingdom of their Father!

Having attained a place of soul rest, he is willing to wait for the coming of that day!

*September 5* _____

# WEAK IN DISCIPLESHIP

*Let us go forth therefore unto him without the camp,*
*bearing his reproach. (Hebrews 13:13)*

The absence of the concept of discipleship from present-day Christianity leaves a vacuum which men and women instinctively try to fill with a variety of substitutes.

One is a kind of pietism—an enjoyable feeling of affection for the person of our Lord, which is valued for itself and is wholly unrelated to cross-bearing.

Another substitute is literalism—which manifests itself among us by insisting on keeping the letter of the Word while ignoring its spirit. It habitually fails to apprehend the inward meaning of Christ's words and contents itself with external compliance with the text.

A third substitute surely is zealous religious activity. "Working for Christ" has today been accepted as the ultimate test of godliness among all but a few evangelical Christians. Christ has become a project to be promoted or a cause to be served, instead of a Lord to be obeyed! To avoid the snare of unauthorized substitution, I recommend careful and prayerful study of the Lordship of Christ and the discipleship of the believer!

# A LOWER LEVEL

*O God, thou hast taught me from my youth: and hitherto have I declared thy wondrous works. (Psalm 71:17)*

There are leaders and there are churches within the Christianity of our day who will surely answer for their failure to apply the disciplines of the New Testament to the present generation of young people.

Much of Christianity today does not hold to the necessity for disciplines in the Christian life. If we have any of God's concerns in our hearts, we must grieve over the lack of spirituality in the lives of great segments of professing Christian young people.

It is not my calling to assess blame. It is part of my Christian calling to proclaim the fact that no one, young or old, has the right to come to Jesus Christ and stake out their own conditions and terms.

Segments of Christianity have made every possible concession in efforts to win young people to Christ; but instead of converting them to Christ they have "converted" Christianity to them. Too often they have come down to the modern level—playing, teasing, coaxing and entertaining. In essence, they have been saying to them, "We will do everything as you want it," instead of giving them Christ's insistent word, "Take up your cross!"

*September 7*

# WHAT DO WE LOVE?

*But we all . . . are changed into the same image from glory to glory, even as by the Spirit of the Lord.*
*(2 Corinthians 3:18)*

God wants us to recognize that human nature is in a formative state and that it is being changed into the image of the thing it loves.

Men and women are being molded by their affinities, shaped by their affections and powerfully transformed by the artistry of their loves. In the unregenerate world of Adam this produces day by day tragedies of cosmic proportions!

For His own children, our heavenly Father has provided right moral objects for admiration and love. They are not God but they are nearest to God; we cannot love Him without loving them.

I speak of His righteousness; and the heart drawn to righteousness will be repulsed in the same degree by iniquity. I speak of wisdom, and we admire the Hebrew prophets, who refused to divorce wisdom from righteousness.

I speak also of truth as another object of our Christian love. Our Lord Jesus Christ said, "I am the truth" and in so saying He joined truth to the Deity in inseparable union. Thus, to love God is to love the truth!

# THE WORLD IS SCARED

*Look up, and lift up your heads; for your redemption
draweth nigh. (Luke 21:28)*

A fear-stricken church cannot help a scared world; and
it needs to be said that surely a fear-ridden Christian has
never examined his or her defense!

No one can blame humans for being afraid. Beyond the
continuing times of crisis and terror and violence, God
has also warned that the world is in a baptism of fire,
sooner or later. God has declared this by the voice of all
of the holy prophets since time began—there is no
escaping it!

Bible-reading Christians should be the last persons on
earth to give way to hysteria. We have been given a
prophetic preview of all those things that are to come to
pass upon the earth. Can anything take us unaware?

We who are in God's secret place of safety must begin
to talk and act like it! We, above all who dwell on the
earth, should be calm, hopeful, buoyant and cheerful. We
will never convince the scared world that there is peace
and assurance at the Cross if we continue to exhibit the
same fears as those who make no profession of
Christianity!

*September 9* _____

# GOD'S EXHORTATION

*As he which hath called you is holy, so be ye holy in all manner of conversation. (1 Peter 1:15)*

What is the Apostle Peter saying to us in relaying to us God's exhortation: "Be ye holy as I am holy, and because I am holy"?

First is our own responsibility to bring our spiritual lives into line so that God may settle upon us with the Holy Spirit—with that quality of the Wonderful and the Mysterious and the Divine.

This is not something that can be humanly cultivated. This is something that we will not even be conscious we have. It is this quality of humility invaded by the Presence of God which the church of our day lacks.

Oh, that we might yearn for the knowledge and Presence of God in our lives from moment to moment, so that without human cultivation and without toilsome seeking there would come upon us this enduement, this sweet and radiant fragrance that gives meaning to our witness!

I am willing to confess in humility that we need this in our day.

# GOD'S VALIDATION

*Our gospel came not unto you in word only, but also in power, and in the Holy Ghost, and in much assurance.*
*(1 Thessalonians 1:5)*

One marked characteristic of modern evangelicalism is its lack of assurance, resulting in a pathetic search for external evidence to corroborate its faith. It sets out bravely to declare its trust in Christ, but is shortly overawed by the counter declarations of science and philosophy and before long it is looking about for some collateral evidence to restore its confidence.

The faith of the Christian must rest upon Christ Himself. He is the mystery of Godliness, a miracle, and emergence of the Deity into time and space for a reason and a purpose. He is complete in Himself, and gains nothing from any human philosophy.

The New Testament points to Christ and says God now commands all men everywhere to repent: because He has appointed a day in which He will judge the world in righteousness by that Man He has ordained! Our assurance is the fact that He raised Him from the dead. In that, God validated forever the claims of Christ. He is who He said He was and what He said He was. So, Christ is enough! To have Him and nothing else is to be rich beyond all conceiving.

*September 11* _____

# OUR UNWORTHY ATTITUDES

*God is greatly to be feared in the assembly of the saints, and
to be had in reverence of all them that are about him.
(Psalm 89:7)*

Being a Christian does not exempt any of us from the
necessity of self-examination, the necessity of dealing
with injuries and unworthy mental attitudes.

I speak particularly of the attitudes and habits of many
men and women who gather with us regularly as we
come into the house of God to worship and pray.

Actually, as Christian men and women, we do have an
appointment to meet with the King of kings and the Lord
of lords. Just think of the preparations we would make if
we suddenly had in invitation to meet the president of the
United States in the White House.

But how many of us are lacking in respect and
reverence when we come into the Christian church?
Among us there are thoughtless tendencies to tell jokes
on the way into church; to sit in the pews and let our
minds rove about like sparrows; to daydream about where
we have been and where we are going.

There is a great need for us to pray for grace that will
improve our mental attitudes when we gather to honor
our Savior and God!

# GOD-HUNGRY SOULS

*But we preach Christ crucified, unto the Jews a*
*stumblingblock, but unto the Greeks foolishness.*
*(1 Corinthians 1:23)*

The Greek philosopher Pythagoras divided men into three classes: 1. Seekers after knowledge; 2. Seekers after honor; 3. Seekers after gain.

I wonder why he failed to notice two other classes: those who are not seeking anything and those who are seekers after God.

Let us add them to his list:

4. Seekers after nothing. These are the human vegetables who live by their glands and their instincts. I refer to the millions of normal persons who have allowed their magnificent intellectual equipment to wither away from lack of exercise. Their reading matter is the sports page and the comic section; their music is whatever is popular and handy—and loud!

5. Seekers after God. I am thinking of men and women who are God-hungry souls though their numbers may not be large. By nature they are no better than the rest of mankind, and by practice they have sometimes been worse. The one sign of their divine election is their insatiable thirst after the Source of their being. Thank the Lord for seekers after God and their destiny lies in the hand of the One who gave His only begotten Son to die for the life of the world!

*September 13* _____

# LONGING TO SEE JESUS

*Behold, I come quickly; hold fast that which thou hast, that no man take thy crown. (Revelation 3:11)*

There is no doubt in my mind that millions of Christians in our day yearn within themselves to be ready to see the Lord Jesus when He appears. These are the saints of God who have a real understanding that what our Lord Jesus Christ is to us in our personal lives, moment by moment, is more important than merely dwelling on "what He did for us!"

I say this because a great segment of Christian theology emphasizes the "utility" of the cross on which Jesus died, rather than the Person who died on that cross for our sins.

Because of that view, many really have no emotional yearning for the return of Jesus. The best hope they know is a kind of intellectual, theological hope. But an intellectual knowledge of what the New Testament teaches about the return of Christ is surely a poor substitute for a love-inflamed desire to look on His face!

While we await Him, our Lord expects us to love one another, to worship Him together and to send this gracious gospel to the ends of the earth.

*September 14*

# HUMILITY—AND WORSHIP

*Humble yourselves, therefore, under the mighty hand of God. (1 Peter 5:6)*

Real worship is, among other things, a feeling about the Lord God! It is in our hearts, and we must be willing to express it in an appropriate manner.

We can express our worship to God in many ways. But if we love the Lord and are led by His Holy Spirit, our worship will always bring a delighted sense of admiring awe and a sincere humility on our part.

There must be humility in the heart of the person who would worship God in spirit and in truth. So, the proud and lofty man or woman cannot worship God any more acceptably than can the proud devil himself!

Unfortunately, many of us are strictly "Santa Claus Christians." We need to go on from an elementary kind of love, in which we think of God as putting up a kind of Christmas tree and putting all our gifts underneath. We need, rather, to be delighted in the presence of utter, infinite excellence!

Such worship will have the ingredient of fascination, the personality captured by the Presence of God!

*September 15* _____

# HEAVENLY WISDOM

*For the Lord giveth wisdom: out of his mouth cometh knowledge and understanding. (Proverbs 2:6)*

The writer of the Proverbs in the Old Testament taught that true spiritual knowledge is the result of a visitation of heavenly wisdom. It is a kind of baptism of the Spirit of Truth that comes to God-fearing men and women. This wisdom is always associated with righteousness and humility; it is never found apart from godliness and true holiness of life.

We need to learn and declare again the ministry of wisdom from above. It is apparent that we cannot know God by the logic of reason. Through reason we can only know about God. The deeper mysteries of God remain hidden to us until we have received illumination from above. We were created with a capacity to know spiritual things—that potential died when Adam and Eve sinned. Thus, "dead in sin" is a description of that part of our being in which we should be able to know God in conscious awareness.

Christ's atoning death enabled our Lord and Savior to take God the Father with one hand and man with the other and introduce us. Jesus enables us to find God very quickly!

*September 16*

# GUILTY SILENCE

*Peter and John answered . . . We cannot but speak the things we have seen and heard. (Acts 4:19–20)*

In this unfriendly world, is our Christian deportment too fearful and cowardly? Is this generation guilty of the sin of silence?

The Bible has much to say in praise of prudence but it has nothing but condemnation for the coward! It is also plainly taught in the New Testament that the soul that is too timid to own and confess Christ before men will be denied before the Father in heaven.

It is apparent that Christian men and women are not speaking out as they should when the enemy stalks into the very sanctuary and pollutes the holy place! Fun and frolic, films and fiction, Hollywood ideals and religious entertainment, big business techniques and cheap worldly philosophies now overrun the sanctuary. The grieved Holy Spirit broods over the chaos but no light breaks forth.

Could it be that too many of God's true children—and especially the preachers—are sinning against God by guilty silence? Those who do speak up on the side of Truth will pay a price for their boldness but the results will be worth it!

*September 17* _____

# FUN AND RELIGION

*Thou therefore endure hardness . . . if we suffer, we shall also reign with him. (2 Timothy 2:3, 12)*

History reveals that times of suffering for the Christian Church have also been times of looking upward. Tribulation has always sobered God's people and encouraged them to look for and yearn after the return of their Lord.

Our present preoccupation with the world may be a warning of bitter days to come. God will wean us from the earth some way—the easy way if possible, the hard way if necessary. It is up to us!

It is apparent that many now think Christianity is jolly good fun—another and higher form of entertainment; because Christ has done all the suffering. He has shed all the tears. He has carried all the crosses. So, we have but to enjoy the benefits of His heartbreak!

The "work of Christ" has been stressed until it has eclipsed the Person of Christ. We need to reexamine much of popular fundamentalist theology which emphasizes the utility of the cross, rather than the beauty of the One who died on that cross.

*September 18*

# HE IS OUR VICTORY

*Therefore glorify God in your body, and in your spirit,*
*which are God's. (1 Corinthians 6:20)*

We will never be delivered from the pride of our own selfish condition until we allow the Holy Spirit of God to demonstrate God's own victory within us.

I have had disobedient believers assure me: "But, Mr. Tozer, I already know that I am bad. I am a believer in total depravity!" My reply: it is possible to be a confirmed believer in total depravity and still be as proud as Lucifer; to still trust in yourself in such a way that the face of God is hidden and you are kept from spiritual victory.

Our concern here is not with theological depravity. There is no argument with the fact that as soon as we are big enough to sin, we go directly into the business of sinning! But God is trying to reveal by His Holy Spirit the utter weakness of the child of God who is still putting his trust in himself.

Why does it take us so long to put our complete trust in God? He has made it so simple, so rewarding to yield what we are to Him!

*September 19* _____

# GOD HAS THE ANSWERS

*Lord, make me to know the measure of my days, that I may know how frail I am. (Psalm 39:4)*

We can all learn something from David's prayer—for none of us have all of the answers! David had come through the trying experiences of life and was now unsure about the things he once thought he knew. In the autumn of his life, I think David was a more relaxed man and more dependent on the divine answers.

I found a lesson in this for myself and I pass it on.

Some time ago I preached for a week in Rochester, New York. At the conclusion and before the benediction, the chairman of the congregation told the audience: "We have enough time for questions. Mr. Tozer will answer any question you have."

This was news to me, so I got up and said: "Mr. Chairman, you are 25 years too late! Twenty-five years ago I could have answered questions on almost any subject, but now I beg to be excused!"

In our Christian life and experience, it is a blessed thing to find out that we do not have to know everything after all!

# LOVE NOT THIS WORLD

*The god of this world hath blinded the minds of them that believe not. (2 Corinthians 4:4)*

Our Lord Jesus Christ drew a sharp line between the kingdom of God and this present world. He has instructed us that no one can be at the same time a lover of both!

The apostles stood together in the New Testament teachings that it is necessary for a person to turn the back upon the world and have not fellowship with it.

What, then, is this world against which we are warned?

It is the familiar world of human society. No Christian need fail to recognize it, providing he wants to know what it is. Here are a few of its marks of identification:

1. Unbelief. To have fellowship with those who live in unbelief is the love of the world. Religion without the Son of God is worldly religion.

2. Impenitence. The worldling shrugs off his sin and continues in it. The Christian mourns over his sin and is comforted.

3. Godless philosophies. Men and women of this world accept the sufficiency of this world and make no provision for any other, esteeming earth above heaven.

4. Externalism. The man of the earth lives only for the world around him—he has no kingdom within him!

*September 21* _____

# GOD'S BENEFICIARY

*To an inheritance incorruptible and undefiled, and that
fadeth not away. (1 Peter 1:4)*

The Holy Spirit has made it plain throughout the
Scriptures, that generally whatever God does becomes a
means toward something else that He is planning to do.

Therefore, when God elects a man or woman it does not
mean that he or she can sit down and at ease announce: "I
have arrived! Put a period there and write 'finis' across
my experience!"

No, of course not! God begets us into His provision and
that which is still before us always is greater than that
which is behind us.

Peter was not using figures of speech. He said plainly
his persecuted brethren were believers in Jesus Christ,
elect and begotten! The electing and the begetting were
means leading into a hope and an inheritance—the true
Christian believer is actually the beneficiary of God!

This is not a figure—not just a poetic phrase. It is
openly taught from Genesis to Revelation that God being
who He is, His beneficences are infinite and limitless!

# DECISION! DECISION!

*We then, as workers together with him, beseech you also*
*that ye receive not the grace of God in vain.*
*(2 Corinthians 6:1)*

I believe there must be great throngs of men and
women who keep on assuring themselves that they will
"make it" into the kingdom of God by a kind of heavenly
osmosis! They have a fond hope that there is a kind of
unconscious "leaking through" of their personalities into
the walls of the kingdom.

That is a vain hope. No one ever comes to God by an
automatic or unconscious process; it does not happen
that way at all!

The individual man or woman must make the
choice—and on that point we must be dogmatic. We have
the Book, the Word of God. We know that God has
revealed Himself through the giving of Jesus Christ, the
eternal Son. We know that the saving message is the
gospel—the good news of our Lord Jesus Christ.

There is no way that God can come to us and forgive us
and restore us to the position of son or daughter until we
consciously let Him! This is an authentic experience of
the grace and mercy of God—we have made our decision!

*September 23* _____

# OUR DAILY PROBLEMS

*There hath no temptation taken you but such as is common to man: but God is faithful. (1 Corinthians 10:13)*

Christian believers are wrongly taught if they believe that the Christian life is a guarantee against human trials and problems. If they believe that, they have mistaken earth for heaven and expect conditions here below which can never be realized until we reach the better world above.

There is a sense in which God makes no difference between the saint and the sinner. He makes His sun to rise on the evil and on the good, and He sends rain on the just and the unjust. It is strange that we rarely notice the other side of this truth: that God also visits His children with the usual problems common to all the sons of men.

If we cannot remove our problems, then we must pray for grace to endure them without murmuring. We will learn, too, that problems patiently endured will work for our spiritual perfecting. Think of our Lord and Savior—He was surrounded by enemies from the moment of His birth. They constituted a real and lasting problem which He simply had to endure for the period of His earthly life. He escaped it only by dying!

# WE TRUST GOD'S PLAN

*And cried with a loud voice, saying, Salvation to our God,*
*which sitteth upon the throne, and unto the Lamb.*
*(Revelation 7:10)*

We who believe in God's faithfulness and in the inspired Scriptures are certain that the world's redemption does not lie in the hands of mankind. I cannot tell you how glad I am that this is at least one thing that we humans cannot bungle!

The plan of salvation and the day of consummation that is coming are in God's eternal plan. The power in redemption is God's power. Only the worthy Lamb of God could die in our place. This is God's way of doing things, not our way!

Millions have feared the threat of world-wide communism with silly, frightened people declaring they would "rather be Red than dead!" But communism cannot prevail because it is raised in a materialism teaching that there is no God, no Christ, no heaven and no hell. Communism cannot prevail because our God in heaven has His plan and program, not just for this earth, but for all of His vast created universe.

There is no human being and no human philosophy or force able to wrest dominion from our living God. Are we being faithful in our witness and warning of the wrath of the Lamb—the crucified, resurrected, outraged Lamb of God?

*September 25* _____

# ROOT OF BITTERNESS

*Looking diligently . . . lest any root of bitterness springing up trouble you. (Hebrews 12:15)*

It is on record that Charles Spurgeon made this comment about a man who was well-known for his bitter and resentful spirit: "May the grass grow green on his grave when he dies, for nothing ever grew around him while he lived!"

The sad and depressing bitter soul will compile a list of slights at which it takes offense and will watch over itself like a mother bear over her cubs. And the figure is apt, for the resentful heart is always surly and suspicious like a she-bear!

In our Christian fellowship, what can be more depressing than to find a professed Christian defending his or her supposed rights and bitterly resisting any attempt to violate them? Such a Christian has never accepted the way of the Cross. The sweet graces of meekness and humility are unknown to that person. Every day he or she grows harder and more acrimonious, trying to defend reputation, right, ministry, against imagined foes.

Is there a cure for this? Yes! The cure is to die to self and rise with Christ into newness of life!

# NO PLACE FOR FANTASY

*I am persuaded that he is able to keep that which I have committed unto him against that day. (2 Timothy 1:12)*

Let me tell you about the true Christian, the Bible Christian, and his view of this troubled and uncertain world in which he lives.

He is not the worldly-wise, smiling optimist who draws his comfort from a denial of the facts; or bases his hopes on false expectation of peaceful intentions among nations.

Rather, he is of all men the truest realist. He will have nothing to do with fantasy—he wants to know the facts—and he does not hesitate to face up to any truth wherever he finds it.

He knows the world is lost on a wide area, and that the Christian alone knows the way to the desired haven. For in the Bible and there only, is found the chart to tell us where we are in this rough and unknown ocean.

He knows that the day when Christians should meekly apologize is over; that they can get the world's attention not by trying to compromise and please, but by boldly declaring the truth of divine revelation with the affirmative signature, "Thus saith the Lord!"

*September 27* _____

# WHY BE ARTIFICIAL?

*Except ye become as little children, ye shall not enter into the kingdom of heaven. (Matthew 18:3)*

Christian men and women who have sincerely knelt at the feet of Jesus and have surrendered themselves to His meekness have found a comforting and satisfying place of rest.

They have discovered that we do not have to worry about what people think of us—as long as God is pleased!

We are no longer plagued with the heavy burden of artificiality. Think of the millions who live in secret fear that some day they will be careless and by chance an enemy or a friend will be allowed to peep into their poor, empty souls. Bright people are tense and alert in fear that they may be trapped into saying something common or stupid.

It is plain to see that the heart of the artificial worldling is breaking under the burden, under the weight of pretense and pride.

To men and women everywhere Jesus says, "Come unto Me, and I will give you rest!" He offers His grace and His mercy—blessed relief that comes when we accept ourselves for what we are and cease to pretend!

*September 28*

# WHAT WE SHALL BE

*For whom he did foreknow, he also did predestinate to be
conformed to the image of his Son. (Romans 8:29)*

We must take a high view of what God has done for us
in consummating the plan of salvation for a lost race!

The supreme work of Christ in redemption is not just
to save us from hell, but to restore us to God-likeness
again. Paul has confirmed this in Romans 8:29, "Whom
he did foreknow, he also did predestinate to be
conformed to the image of his Son."

While perfect restoration to the divine image awaits the
day of Christ's appearing, the work of restoration is going
on now. There is a slow but steady transmutation of the
base metal of human nature into the gold of God-likeness
effected by the faith-filled gaze of the soul at the glory of
God—the face of Jesus Christ!

We have already moved from what we were to what we
are, and we are now moving toward what we shall be. To
become like God is and must be the supreme goal of all
moral creatures!

*September 29* _____

# WHY DO BIRDS SING?

*And God created . . . every winged fowl after his kind: and God saw that it was good. (Genesis 1:21)*

I am thankful I have found a promise from the God of all grace that deals with the "long term" and the eternal. I belong to a body of plain people who believe the truth revealed in the Bible. These are the people who believe that God in the beginning made the heavens and the earth and all things that are therein.

Yes, these plain believing people will tell you that God created the flowers to be beautiful and the birds to sing, so that men and women could enjoy them. We believe that God made the birds to warble and harmonize as though they were tuned to a harp.

But the scientist disagrees, saying, "It is simply biological. The bird sings only to attract a mate."

Actually, the God who made the birds is the Chief Musician of the universe. He made the harps in those little throats and said, "Go and sing!" Thankfully, the birds obeyed and they have been singing and praising God ever since they were created!

*September 30*

# "I WILL ARISE AND GO"

*I will arise and go to my father, and will say unto him,
Father, I have sinned. (Luke 15:18)*

When Jesus told the story of the Prodigal Son, He was
giving our lost society a graphic picture of more than a
willful son or a backslidden man.

Years ago I spent time alone with God, in prayer and
supplication, asking the Spirit of God to aid me in the
comprehension of the parable of the Prodigal Son. I have
relied upon the understanding which I believe God gave
me.

I believe the Prodigal Son is God's clear-cut picture to
us of the entire human race that went out to the pig-sty in
Adam—and came back to the Father in Christ!

The most telling part of the parable is the fact that the
errant son "came to himself"—and that speaks to us of
the reality and necessity of repentance. He could repent
and turn and seek forgiveness because he knew that his
Father had not changed. He knew the character of his
Father. Except for that knowledge, he could never have
said: "I will arise and go to my Father!"

Brethren, all of us who have come back to God by faith
in our Lord Jesus Christ have found, as did the prodigal,
that the Father in heaven has not changed at all!

*October 1* _____

# UNWILLING TO YIELD

*Yield yourselves to God, as those that are alive from the dead. (Romans 6:13)*

I know there are people who hear me preach regularly who will never consider changing their way of living. They will go "underground" before they will do that!

Our situation is not an isolated case. There are millions of men and women with an understanding of the revelation of God in Jesus Christ, who are still not willing to receive and commit themselves to Him whom the very angels and stars and rivers receive. They hesitate and they delay because they know God is asking the abdication of their own selfish little kingdom and interests.

This is the tragedy of mankind, my brethren! We have rejected Him from our lives because we must have our own way. But until Jesus Christ is sincerely received, there can be no knowledge of salvation, nor any understanding of the things of God.

The little, selfish, sinful man rejects the Son of God. While he is still enumerating the things he deserves, the Son of God stands outside.

My brethren, I repeat: this is the great tragedy of mankind!

# A CHRISTIAN VIRTUE

*Let brotherly love continue. (Hebrews 13:1)*

I am being very frank about this and I hope I am being helpful: do not ever say you are not right with God because you like some people better than others!

I believe you can be right with God and still not like the way some people behave. It is easy to love those who are the friendly; others rub us the wrong way or perhaps they cut us down.

The writer to the Hebrews has appealed to us as Christian believers to "let brotherly love continue"—in other words, "never stop loving one another in the Lord."

Here is what I have found: it is possible to love people in the Lord even though you may not like their boorish or distasteful human traits. We still love them for Jesus' sake!

Yes, I believe you can be right with God and still not like the way some people behave. Our admonition is to love them in a larger and more comprehensive way because we are all one in Christ Jesus. This kind of love is indeed a Christian virtue!

*October 3* _____

# "TOWARD THE MARK"

*Forgetting things which are behind . . . I press toward the mark. (Philippians 3:13–14)*

It is one of the devil's oldest tricks to discourage Christian believers by causing them to look back at what they once were. It is indeed the enemy of our souls who makes us forget that we are never at the end of God's love.

No one will make progress with God until the eyes are lifted to the faithfulness of God and we stop looking at ourselves!

Our instructions in the New Testament all add up to the necessity of looking forward in faith—and not spending our time looking back or just looking within.

Brethren, our Lord is more than able to take care of our past. He pardons instantly and forgives completely, and his blood makes us worthy!

The goodness of God is infinitely more wonderful than we will ever be able to comprehend. If the "root of the matter" is in you and you are born again, God is prepared to start with you where you are!

# THE WINSOME SAINTS

*Being filled with the fruits of righteousness, which are by Christ Jesus. (Philippians 1:11)*

Much of Christianity overlooks the fact that if we are led by the Spirit of God and if we show forth the love of God this world needs, we become the "winsome saints."

The strange and wonderful thing about it is that truly winsome and loving saints do not even know about their attractiveness. The great saints of the past did not know they were great saints. If someone had told them, they would not have believed it, but those around then knew that Jesus was living His life in them.

I think we join the winsome saints when God's purposes in Christ become clear to us. We join them when we begin to worship God because He is who He is! Brethren, God is not a charity case—He is not some frustrated foreman who cannot find enough help.

Let us remember that God has never actually needed any of us—not one! But we pretend that He does and we make a big thing of it when someone agrees "to work for the Lord."

God is trying to call us back to that for which He created us—to worship and to enjoy Him forever!

*October 5* _____

# FAILURE OF RELIGION

*Having a form of godliness, but denying the power thereof.*
*(2 Timothy 3:5)*

Millions of men and women refuse to face up to the fact that religion, in and of itself, is not enough for the sinner's need.

It is amazing how many things religious people want to do to you. They can start with infant baptism and end up with the last rites when you are 108 years old—and all of that time they will manipulate you, maul you and sweet-message your soul. When it is all done you are just what you were. You are just a decorated and massaged sinner—a sinner who did not eat meat, or on the other hand, a sinner who did eat fish!

When religion has done all it can, you are still a sinner who either went to church or did not go to church. Religion can put us on the roll and educate us and train us and instruct us. But after all that, there is still something within our beings that cries, "Eternity is in my heart and I have not found anything to satisfy it!"

Only our Lord Jesus Christ is enough to satisfy the eternal longing in our souls.

# STRIVING FOR NUMBERS

*Whatsoever things are true, whatsoever things are honest*
*. . . think on these things. (Philippians 4:8)*

In Christian circles today, the church that can show an impressive quantitative growth is frankly envied and imitated by other ambitious churches.

Numbers, size and amounts seem to be very nearly all that matters—with a corresponding lack of emphasis on quality!

This is the age of the Laodiceans. The great goddess, Numbers, is worshiped with fervent devotion and all things religious are brought before her for examination. Her Old Testament is the financial report and her New Testament is the membership roll. To these she appeals as the test of spiritual growth and the proof of success or failure in most Christian endeavors.

A little acquaintance with the Bible should show this up for the heresy it is. To judge anything spiritual by statistics is to judge by another than scriptural judgment. Yet this is being done every day by ministers, church boards and denominational leaders. And hardly anyone seems to notice the deep and dangerous error!

*October 7* _____

# "SOMEONE" IS THERE

*Seek the Lord, and his strength: seek his face evermore.*
*(Psalm 105:4)*

Wherever faith has proved itself to be real, it has inevitably had upon it a sense of the "present" God. The holy Scriptures possess in marked degree this feeling of actual encounter with a real Person.

The men and women of the Bible talked with God. They spoke to Him and heard Him speak in words they could understand. With Him they held person-to-person converse, and a sense of shining reality is upon their words and deeds.

This sense of "Someone there" filled the members of the early Christian church with abiding wonder. The solemn delight which those early disciples knew sprang straight from the conviction that there was One in the midst of them—they were in the very Presence of God!

This sense of "Someone" there makes religion invulnerable to critical attack. It secures the mind against collapse under the battering of the enemy. Those who worship the God who is present may ignore the objection of unbelieving men!

# EVERYDAY WORSHIP

*Their heart is far from me . . . in vain they do worship me.*
*(Matthew 15:8–9)*

It is my experience that the totality of our Christian lives—our entire attitude as persons—must be towards the worship of God!

If you do not know the presence of God in your office, your factory, your home—then God is not in the church you attend, either!

I became a Christian when I was a young man working in a tire factory in Akron, Ohio. I remember my work there—but I remember my worship there, too! I had plenty of worshipful tears in my eyes. No one ever asked me about them, but I would not have hesitated to explain them.

You can learn to use certain skills until they are automatic. I became so skillful that I could do my work and then I could worship God even while my hands were busy.

If the love of God is in us and the Spirit of God is breathing praise within us, all the musical instruments in heaven are suddenly playing in full support! Even our thoughts become a sanctuary in which God can dwell.

*October 9* _____

# MISUSING THE BIBLE

*Which they . . . wrest, as they do also the other scriptures,*
*unto their own destruction. (2 Peter 3:16)*

I believe that everything in the Bible is true, but to attempt to make the Bible a textbook for science is to misunderstand it completely and tragically!

It has become a fairly popular practice for Bible teachers to claim to find in the Scriptures confirmation of almost every recent discovery made by science. Apparently no one noticed that the scientist had to find it before the Bible teacher could, and it never seemed to occur to anyone to wonder why, if it was there in the Bible in such plain sight, it took several thousand years and the help of science before anyone saw it.

In recent years, the Bible has been "recommended" for many other purposes from the one for which it was written. The purpose of the Bible is to bring men to Christ, to make them holy and prepare them for heaven. Any manipulation of the Scriptures to make them speak peace to the natural man is evil and can only lead to ruin!

# GAME OF PIOUS WORDS

*If any man offend not in word, the same is a perfect man, and able also to bridle the whole body. (James 3:2)*

Do you realize that most men play at religion as they play at games? Religion itself being of all games the one most universally played.

The Church has its "fields" and its "rules" and its equipment for playing the game of pious words. It has its devotees, both laymen and professionals, who support the game with their money and encourage it with their presence, but who are no different in life or character from many who take no interest in religion at all.

As an athlete uses a ball so do many of us use words: words spoken and words sung, words written and words uttered in prayer. We throw them swiftly across the field; we learn to handle them with dexterity and grace—and gain as our reward the applause of those who have enjoyed the game. In the games men play there are no moral roots. It is a pleasant activity which changes nothing and settles nothing, at last.

Sadly, in the religious game of pious words, after the pleasant meeting no one is basically any different from what he had been before!

*October 11* _____

# LIGHT—AND SHADOWS

*Charity suffereth long, and is kind. (1 Corinthians 13:4)*

A person once called me to ask this question: "Mr. Tozer, do you think a person who is really a Christian can hurt another Christian?"

There is no easy answer—but I had to reply: "Yes, I think so."

Why is it that a man can be on his knees one day, praying earnestly, and the next day be guilty of offending or injuring another Christian? I think it is because we are halfway between heaven and hell. It is because the light—and the shadows—fall upon us.

The best answer is that we are being saved out of all these contradictions we find in our lifetime. Perhaps on this earth we will never be able to comprehend fully the awful, terrible price the Lord of all beauty paid to gain our redemption; to save His people from the ugliness of sin.

If you do not know Him and worship Him, if you do not long to reside where He is, if you have never known wonder and ecstasy in your soul because of His crucifixion and resurrection, your claim of Christianity has little foundation!

# THE REALITIES OF HEAVEN

*Let not your heart be troubled . . . I go to prepare a place for you. (John 14:1–2)*

Much of the secularism and rationalism of our times dismisses the Christian view and teaching about heaven as "nothing more than hopeful thinking."

But the Christian's promised hope of future blessedness is founded upon the fullest and plainest revelations of the Old and New Testaments. That it accords with the most sacred yearnings of the human breast does not weaken it, but serves rather to confirm the truth of it, since the One who made the heart might be expected also to make provision for the fulfillment of its deepest longings.

God's promises are made to the Christian believer, who generally has difficulty picturing himself as inheriting such bliss as the Scriptures describe. The reason is not hard to discover, for the most godly Christian is the one who knows himself best, and no one who knows himself will believe that he deserves anything better than hell. But even justice is on his side, for it is written, "If we confess our sins, God is faithful and just to forgive us our sins, and to cleanse us from all unrighteousness" (1 John 1:9).

*October 13* _____

# GOD AT THE CENTER

*He built there an altar, and called the place El-beth-el:*
*because there God appeared unto him. (Genesis 35:7)*

After Jacob's first memorable encounter with God in the wilderness, he called the place Beth-el, which means "the house of God." Many years later, after he had suffered and sinned and repented, and discovered the worthlessness of all earthly things, he renamed the place, El-beth-el; literally "the God of the house of God."

Thus Jacob had shifted his emphasis from the sacred place to the God he had met there. God Himself now took the center of his interest.

We need to consider that many Christians never get beyond Beth-el. God is in their thoughts but He has not been given first place. Faithfulness to the local church is a good thing; but when the church becomes so large and important that it hides God from our eyes, it may become a good thing wrongly used.

Always God must be first—and we ought never forget that the church was never intended to substitute for God! What is our primary interest? Is it Beth-el or El-beth-el? Is it my church or my Lord? Is it my creed or my Christ?

# RESOURCES THAT ENDURE

*I wish above all things that thou mayest prosper and be in health, even as thy soul prospereth.* (3 John 2)

The people of this world have always fussed and argued over this world's resources—hope for life, health, financial prosperity, international peace and a set of favorable circumstances. These resources are good in their own way, but they have a fatal defect—they are uncertain and transitory! Today we have them; tomorrow they are gone.

It is this way with all earthly things since sin came to upset the beautiful order of nature and made the human race victims of chance and change.

We desire for all of God's children a full measure of every safe and pure blessing that the earth and sky might unite to bring them. But if in the sovereign will of God things go against us, what do we have left? If life and health are placed in jeopardy, what about our everlasting resources?

If the world's foundations crumble, we still have God and in Him we have everything essential to our ransomed beings forever! We have Christ, who died for us; we have the Scriptures, which can never fail; we have the faithful Holy Spirit. If worst comes to worst here below, we have our Father's house and our Father's welcome!

*October 15* _____

# CHILD OF TWO WORLDS

*Jesus answered, My kingdom is not of this world.*
*(John 18:36)*

In the kingdom of God, the surest way to lose something is to try to protect it, and the best way to keep it is to let it go. This was the word of our Lord Jesus Christ: "If any man will come after me, let him deny himself and take up his cross!"

Christ turned from the fallen world of Adam and spoke about another world altogether, a world where Adam's philosophy is invalid and his technique inoperative. He spoke of the kingdom of God whose laws are exactly opposite to those of the kingdom of men.

So, the true Christian is a child of two worlds. He lives among fallen men, but when he is regenerated, he is called to live according to the laws and principles that underlie the new kingdom. He may, then, find himself trying to live a heavenly life after an earthly pattern—and this is what Paul called "carnal" living. That is why it is vitally important to move up into the life of the Spirit of God. Give up your earthly "treasures" and the Lord will keep them for you unto life eternal!

*October 16*

# A SACRED GIFT OF SEEING

*Your young men shall see visions, and your old men shall dream dreams. (Acts 2:17)*

As God created us, we all have to some degree the power to imagine. That imagination is of great value in the service of God may be denied by some persons who have erroneously confused the word "imagination" with the word "imaginary."

The gospel of Jesus Christ has no truck with things imaginary. The most realistic book in the world is the Bible. God is real. Men are real and so is sin and so are death and hell! The presence of God is not imaginary; neither is prayer the indulgence of a delightful fancy.

The value of the cleansed imagination in the sphere of religion lies in its power to perceive in natural things shadows of things spiritual. A purified and Spirit-controlled imagination is the sacred gift of seeing; the ability to peer beyond the veil and gaze with astonished wonder upon the beauties and mysteries of things holy and eternal.

The stodgy pedestrian mind does no credit to Christianity!

*October 17* _____

# MAN'S EMPTY PROMISES

*For when they shall say, peace and safety; then sudden*
*destruction cometh upon them. (1 Thessalonians 5:3)*

We have listened throughout our lifetime to the
continuing promises of peace and progress made by the
educators and the legislators and the scientists, but so far
they have failed to make good on any of them.

Perhaps it is an ironic thought that fallen men, though
they cannot fulfill their promises, are always able to make
good on their threats!

Well, true peace is a gift of God and today it is found
only in the minds of innocent children and in the hearts
of trustful Christian believers. Only Jesus could say: "My
peace I give unto you. Let not your heart be troubled;
neither let it be afraid!"

Surely the "great" of this world have underestimated the
wisdom of the Christian, after all. When the Day of The
Lord comes, he may stand like Abraham above the
burning plain and watch the smoke rising from the cities
that forgot God. The Christian will steal a quick look at
Calvary and know that this judgment is past!

# A LIBEL AGAINST GOD

*He that believeth not God hath made him a liar.*
*(1 John 5:10)*

Human sin began with loss of faith in God! When our mother Eve listened to Satan's sly innuendoes against the character of God, she began to entertain a doubt of His integrity—and right there the doors were opened to the incoming of every possible evil, and darkness settled upon the world.

Relationship between moral beings is by confidence, and confidence rests upon character which is a guarantee of conduct. God is a being of supreme moral excellence, possessing in infinite perfection all the qualities that constitute holy character. He deserves and invites the unreserved confidence of every moral creature, including man. Any proper relation to Him must be by confidence, that is, faith.

Idolatry is the supreme sin and unbelief is the child of idolatry. Both are libels on the Most High and Most Holy. John wrote: "He that believeth not God hath made Him a liar." A God who would lie is a God without character.

Repentance is a man's sincere apology for distrusting God for so long, and faith is throwing oneself upon Christ in complete confidence. Thus by faith reconciliation is achieved between God and man!

*October 19* _____

# DOTING ON THE PAST

*In an acceptable time have I heard thee, and in a day of salvation have I helped thee. (Isaiah 49:8)*

I always get an uneasy feeling when I find myself with people who have nothing to discuss but the glories of the days that are past!

Why are we not willing to believe what the Bible tells us? The Christian's great future is before him. Therefore, the whole direction of the Christian's look should be forward.

It is a fact that we should ponder soberly that so many Christians seem to have their future already behind them! Their glory is behind them. The only future they have is their past. They are always bringing around the cold ashes of yesterday's burned-out campfire!

Even their testimony, if they give it, reveals their backward look. Their downcast look betrays that they are facing in the wrong direction.

We should take Paul for an example here. I think he occasionally took a quick, happy backward look just to remind himself of the grace and goodness of God enjoyed by the maturing believers in their Savior, Jesus Christ!

# FAITH AND PRAYER

*The effectual fervent prayer of a righteous man availeth much. (James 5:16)*

In Hebrews we find a long list of benefits which faith brings to its possessor: justification, deliverance, fruitfulness, endurance, victory over enemies, courage, strength and even resurrection from the dead.

Then, everything that is attributed thus to faith might with equal truth be attributed to prayer; for faith and true prayer are like two sides of the same coin—they are inseparable!

Men may, and often do, pray without faith (though this is not true prayer), but it is not thinkable that men should have faith and not pray.

Whatever God can do faith can do, and whatever faith can do prayer can do when it is offered in faith.

It should not be considered strange, then, that an invitation to prayer is an invitation to omnipotence, for prayer engages the Omnipresent God and brings Him into our human affairs. According to the Bible, we have because we ask or we have not because we ask not. It does not take much wisdom to discover our next move. Is it not to pray and pray again and again until the answer comes? Let us not fail the world and disappoint God by failing to pray!

*October 21* _____

# PROBLEMS AND PRESSURES

*Who shall separate us from the love of Christ? Shall*
*tribulation, or distress, or persecution, or famine, or*
*nakedness, or peril, or sword? (Romans 8:35)*

Jesus did not promise any of us that consistent
Christian living would be easy!

He did not promise a release from daily problems and
pressures. He did not promise to take us to our heavenly
home on a fluffy pink cloud!

We live our lives in the knowledge of the grace of God,
but we dare not forget that our Lord came to die for us
and to express the never-changing moral and redemptive
will of God for His people.

Before we condemn the Jews of Bible history for their
failures, we must be sure that we are not overlooking
spiritual and moral shortcomings of our own!

As Christian believers, you and I must be careful about
the reasons we give for not heeding God's Word and
God's warning from heaven.

Have we taken His grace seriously enough that we have
sought forgiveness for spiritual carelessness, indifference
and apathy?

# THE LONELY HUMAN

*The joy of our heart is ceased; woe unto us that we have sinned! (Lamentations 5:15–16)*

There is a strange contradiction in human nature all around us: the fact that a person can reek with pride, display a swollen ego and strut like a peacock—and yet be the loneliest and most miserable person in the world!

We find these people everywhere—pretending and playing a game. Deep within their beings, they are almost overwhelmed by their great loneliness, by their sense of being orphans in the final scheme of things.

The result of this strange, aching human sense of loneliness and cosmic orphanage is the inward, groping question: "What good is it to be a human being? No one cares about me!"

In the garden, Eve believed Satan's lie—the lie that God was not concerned about her and that God had no emotional connection with her life and being. This is where the unregenerate person is in today's world.

It is only sin and defeat that can bring this sense of orphanage, this sense of having been put out of the father's house, and the feeling that follows when the house is burned down and the father is dead.

*October 23* _____

# POSTPONING OBEDIENCE

*Believe on the Lord Jesus Christ, and thou shalt be saved.*
(Acts 16:31)

A notable heresy has come into being throughout our evangelical Christian circles—the widely accepted concept that we humans can choose to accept Christ only because we need Him as Savior, and that we have the right to postpone our obedience to Him as long as we want to!

The truth is that salvation apart from obedience is unknown in the sacred Scriptures. Peter makes it plain that we are "elect according to the foreknowledge of God the Father, through sanctification of the Spirit unto obedience."

It seems most important to me that Peter speaks of his fellow Christians as "obedient children." He knew their spirituality—he was not just giving them an exhortation to be obedient.

The entire Bible teaches that true obedience to God and His Christ is one of the toughest requirements in the Christian life. Actually, salvation without obedience is a self-contradicting impossibility!

Humans do not want to admit it, but the Apostle Paul wrote to the Romans long ago that "by one man's disobedience" came the downfall of the human race!

# HUMANS JUDGE THE LORD?

*But in vain they do worship me, teaching for doctrines the commandments of men. (Matthew 15:9)*

It is a fact that God made us to worship Him, and if we had not fallen with Adam and Eve, worship would have been the most natural thing for us.

Sinning was not the natural thing for Adam and Eve, but they disobeyed and fell, losing their privilege of perfect fellowship with God, the Creator. Sin is the unnatural thing; it was never intended by God to be our nature.

Men and women who are out of fellowship with God, the Creator, still have an instinct towards some practice of worship. In most of our "civilized" circles, the practice of picking out what we like to worship and rejecting what we do not like is widespread.

This has opened up an entire new field for applied psychology and humanism under a variety of religious disguises. Thus men and women set themselves as judges of what the Lord has said—and so they stand with pride and judge the Lord.

In the Bible, God takes the matter of worship out of the hands of men and puts it in the hands of the Holy Spirit. It is impossible to worship God without the impartation of the Holy Spirit!

*October 25* _____

# CHEAP RELIGION

*Neither will I offer burnt offerings unto the Lord my God of that which doth cost me nothing. (2 Samuel 24:24)*

What passes for Christianity in our day is cheap religion!

To listen to the current concepts of Christianity, we would conclude it is little more than bits of beautiful poetry, a man-made bouquet of fragrant flowers, a kindly smile for our neighbor and a couple of good deeds on behalf of a brother or sister.

When I consider some of the elements now offered in Christianity as acceptable religion, I have to restrain myself lest I speak too disapprovingly. I fear my words would be so strong that I would have to repent of them! And I read in the Scriptures that there are some things God does not want us to say even about the devil.

What do we find surfacing in much of our Christian fellowship? The complaint that God takes a long time to work out His will. We do not want to take the time to plow and cultivate. We want the fruit and the harvest right away. We do not want to be engaged in any spiritual battle that takes us into the long night. We want the morning light right now!

We do not want the cross—we are more interested in the crown!

# BROTHERHOOD OF THE REDEEMED

*To them gave he power to become the sons of God.*
*(John 1:12)*

Anyone making even a quick review of Genesis will discover that God has told us more about His presence in creation and in history than about the details of human civilization.

We believe that eternity dwells in the Person of God and that the material universe came into being through God's creation.

The first man and woman in the human race were created. They failed in their initial encounter with Satan, our archenemy. Following that, the Genesis record becomes a narrative of human failure against the abiding backdrop of God's faithfulness.

God Himself, through the Holy Spirit, points out a universal problem: the natural brotherhood of human beings is a sinful brotherhood. It is the brotherhood of all who are spiritually lost.

But the Bible has good news. It is the revelation of a new brotherhood, the brotherhood of the redeemed! We know it in our time as the believing church of our Lord Jesus Christ in all nations. It is a new brotherhood among men based on regeneration—and restoration!

*October 27* _____

# GOD IS ON OUR SIDE

*Let them be confounded and consumed that are adversaries
to my soul. (Psalm 71:13)*

It was a gracious revelation to my human spirit when I
discovered that the Word of God was actually on my side,
operating in my behalf!

I was reading Psalm 71 and I came to this amazing
statement: "Thou hast given commandment to save me!"
My heart has been warmed with that realization ever
since. I believe that the Word of the living God has gone
throughout all the earth to save me and keep me! Let the
theological experts raise their eyebrows—I do not care!
The living Word has charged Himself with responsibility
to forgive, to cleanse and to keep me!

Let us not be guilty of underrating the Word of God
operating on our behalf. I dare to say that there is not an
uncontrolled stroke or force anywhere in all of God's
mighty universe that can take eternal life away from a
trusting, believing, obedient child of God.

Let us thank God for the Word! It is living and
powerful and sharper than any two-edged sword!

# "TOP SIDE OF THE SOUL"

*To open their eyes and to turn them from darkness to light, and from the power of Satan to God. (Acts 26:18)*

It is certainly a reality in our day that too few men and women are willing to keep the "top side" of their souls open to God and to His light from heaven.

You may wonder about such expression as the "top side" of the soul, but I do think it is in line with Bible teaching, and certainly in line with all Christian experience.

The heart and soul are open to God in some people's lives, but certainly not in others.

We should be aware that man's forgiveness is not always like God's. When a man makes a mistake and has to be forgiven, the shadow may still hang over him among his fellows.

But when God forgives, He begins the new page right away. Then when the devil runs up and says, "What about his past?" God replies, "What past? He has been forgiven!"

Now, I think that kind of forgiveness and justification and acceptance with God depends upon a person's willingness to keep the "top side" of the soul open to God and His saving grace!

*October 29* _____

# THE DAY OF THE LORD

*These shall make war with the Lamb, and the Lamb shall
overcome them. (Revelation 17:14)*

The human race has always been quick to blame the
world's disasters, floods, famines, plagues on natural
causes. But in the end of the age, when the final
judgments of God begin to fall, how long will it be until
people confess that there is another real, though invisible,
force in operation?

Truly the wrath of God will leave no hiding place for
sinning, alienated men and women!

John, in the Revelation, speaks of the mighty trumpets
that will sound and the woes that will descend upon the
earth. In my own view, I link these events to the dramatic
period throughout the earth when the antichrist has
prevailed by deception and force.

When God is finally ready to refine and restore the
earth, everyone in heaven and on earth and in hell will
know that no human laboratory could compound the fire
that will be poured out on the earth. God has promised
that He will not hide His wrath forever. He is prepared to
speak in supernatural manifestations in that coming Day
of The Lord!

# A PRAYER AT COMMUNION

*Ye do shew the Lord's death till he come.*
*(1 Corinthians 11:26)*

Dear Lord and Savior, we come to your table in faith, for you have told us, "As often as you do this, do it in memory of Me." Help us to celebrate this remembrance of death and resurrection in the very best way we know how.

Do then, we pray Thee, overshadow us with Thy very breathing Presence. Breathe on us, O Breath of God; quicken and heal and purify and cleanse. Strengthen and perfect that which is wanting in us.

Bless the strangers and the friends who happen to be within our gates today. Dear Lord, make them sense that they have found a home among us as we worship, and to realize that they are just as much "owners" here as we are; for it is the Lord's house and the Lord's table—it is not ours.

We are all guests and children in the household—all of us! And we pray that we may love Thee acceptably, for we would not wound Thee again! Thou didst love us with such poured-out love that not even the blood in Thy veins was dear enough to Thee—we were dearer than that blood!

All of this we ask in Jesus Christ, our Lord. Amen.

*October 31* _____

# A CAREER—AND CHRIST

*A woman named Lydia, of the city of Thyatira . . . whose heart the Lord opened. (Acts 16:14)*

It is a beautiful New Testament story that tells us of Lydia of Philippi, a career woman in her own right, long before there were laws and proclamations to set women free.

A seller of purple, Lydia traveled to the market of her day, and undoubtedly she had found freedom and satisfaction in that era when women were not counted at all.

But Lydia heard the Apostle Paul tell of the death and resurrection of Jesus Christ, and the Lord opened her heart. In Christ she found an eternal answer, which career and position had never been able to give.

Now, about conditions today. Our society has set women free to be just as bad as the men—and just as miserable. We have set them free to swear and curse and to set their own morals. Politically, women are now free to vote just as blindly as the men do. But I hope women today will find what Lydia found: that their careers will lack the word "eternal" until they find their answer in the eternal Christ, our Lord Jesus!

# REJOICE—OR GRUMBLE

*Ye greatly rejoice . . . though you are in heaviness through manifold temptations. (1 Peter 1:6)*

I think all of us meet Christian men and women who always seem to look on the gloomy side and are never able to do anything with life's problems but grumble about them! I meet them often and when I do, I wonder: "Can these people be reading and trusting the same Bible I have been reading?"

The Apostle Peter wrote to the tempted, suffering and persecuted believers in his day and noted with thanksgiving that they could rejoice because they counted God's promises and provisions greater than their trials!

We do live in a sinful and imperfect world, and as believers in Christ we acknowledge that perfection is a relative thing now—and God has not really completed a thing with us, as yet!

Peter testified that the persecuted and suffering Christians of his day were looking, in faith, to a future state of things immeasurably better than that which they knew, and that state of things would be perfect and complete!

*November 2* _____

# IS THE CHURCH WEARY?

*In this, the children of God are manifest. (1 John 3:10)*

As Christian believers, we stand together in the evangelical faith—the historical faith of our fathers. Yet, we must confess that many congregations seem bogged down with moral boredom and life-weariness.

The church is tired, discouraged and unastonished—Christ seems to belong to yesterday.

The prophetic teachers have projected everything into the dim future where it is beyond our reach—unavailable! They have dispensationalized us into a state of spiritual poverty—and they have left us there!

But regardless of such teachers, the course of spiritual victory is clear; let us trust what the Word of God continues to say to us!

The Scriptures are open and plain. Jesus Christ is our Savior and Lord. He is our great High Priest, alive and ministering for us today. His person, His power and His grace are the same; without change, yesterday, today and forever!

# CLAIM YOUR INHERITANCE

*That thou mayest prosper and be in health, even as thy soul prospereth. (3 John 2)*

Did you know that it is possible for a Christian believer to live day after day, clutching the book of Ephesians, and still not realize that he is spiritually lean and hungry?

If a pastor or evangelist suggests that this person could be in a more prosperous spiritual state, his reaction may be bristling: "Am I not accepted in the Beloved? Is not God my Father and am I not an heir with God?"

Holding the text of the will is not enough. It is necessary to come into the possession of the riches. Suppose a rich man dies, leaving a will which passes on all of his millions to his only son. That boy borrows the text of the will from the attorney and carries it around with him. He is satisfied with the text of the will, but it has never been properly executed. Thus the son has never presented his legitimate claims to the inheritance.

He may be going around ragged, hungry and weak. In actual experience he has received nothing. He simply holds the text of his father's will!

*November 4* _____

# WORTHY—OR UNWORTHY?

*And to know the love of Christ, which passeth knowledge.*
*(Ephesians 3:19)*

The love of Jesus is so inclusive that it knows no boundaries. At the point where we stop loving and caring, Jesus is still there—loving and caring!

The question may be asked: "How does the living Christ feel today about the sinful men and women who walk our streets?"

There is only one answer: He loves them!

We may be righteously indignant about the things they do. We may be disgusted with their actions and their ways. We are often ready to condemn and turn away from them.

But Jesus keeps on loving them! It is His unchanging nature to love and seek the lost. He said many times when He was on earth, "I have come to help the needy. The well do not need a doctor—but the sick need attention and love."

We are prone to look at the needy and measure them: "Let us determine if they are worthy of our help." During all of His ministry, I do not think Jesus ever helped a "worthy" person. He only asked, "What is your need? Do you need My help?"

# I CHOOSE TO WORSHIP

*Not a novice, lest being lifted up with pride he fall into the condemnation of the devil. (1 Timothy 3:6)*

Strange things are happening all around us in Christian circles because we are not truly worshipers.

For instance, any untrained, unprepared, unspiritual empty rattletrap of a person can start something "religious" and find plenty of followers who will listen and promote it! Beyond that, it may become very evident that he or she had never heard from God in the first place.

All of the examples we have in the Bible illustrate that glad and devoted and reverent worship is the normal employment of human beings. Every glimpse that is given us of heaven and of God's created beings is always a glimpse of worship and rejoicing and praise—because God is who He is!

Because we are not truly worshipers, we spend a lot of time in the churches just spinning our wheels; making a noise but not getting anywhere.

What are we going to do about this awesome, beautiful worship that God calls for? I would rather worship God than do any other thing I know of in all this wide world!

*November 6* _____

# A MORAL PRONOUNCEMENT

*Thy word is a lamp unto my feet, and a light unto my path
. . . I will keep thy righteous judgments.*
*(Psalm 119:105–106)*

What is God saying to His human creation in our day
and time?

In brief, He is saying, "Jesus Christ is My beloved Son.
Hear Him!"

Why is there rejection? Why do men and women fail to
listen?

Because God's message in Jesus is a moral
pronouncement. Men and women do not wish to be
under the authority of the moral Word of God!

For centuries, God spoke in many ways. He inspired
holy men to write portions of the message in a book.
People do not like it so they try their best to avoid it
because God has made it the final test of all morality, the
final test of all Christian ethics.

God, being one in His nature, is always able to say the
same thing to everyone who hears Him. Christian
believers must know that any understanding of the Word
of God must come from the same Spirit who provided the
inspiration!

_____ *November 7*

# MYSTICISM PLUS THEOLOGY

*Holy men of God spake as they were moved by the Holy Ghost. (2 Peter 1:21)*

Christian preachers and ministers ought to acknowledge, publicly and with humility, their great indebtedness to the apostles John and Paul.

Study the Gospel of John and you will concur with me that John is surely the mystic of the New Testament!

Explore the epistles of the Apostle Paul and you will also concur with the assessment that Paul is surely the theologian of the New Testament!

John and Paul were completely immersed in love and adoration for Jesus, the Christ, the eternal Son and the Savior of the world. So we may say that Paul is the instrument and John is the music!

God Himself was able to pour into the great mind and spirit of Paul the basic doctrines of the New Testament. But in John, God found harp-like qualities to sound forth devotion and praise.

Paul, then, is the theologian who lays foundations. John does not really soar any higher than Paul—but he sings just a bit more sweetly! It is not amazing, really, that there is much mysticism in Paul's theology, and much theology in John's mysticism!

*November 8* _____

# PRAYERS: TOO LATE

*For the great day of his wrath is come; who shall be able to stand? (Revelation 6:17)*

John, in the sixth chapter of Revelation, describes the most tragic, unavailing prayer meeting in the world's history!

Cries and groans, shouts and demands, moans and whispers—all will be heard in that coming Day of the Lord when the forces of judgment are released. Even the mountains and the islands will be removed from their places.

But by then, the prayers and cries of sinful men and women will be too little and too late!

All of the great men of the earth, all the important people, all who have mistakenly put their trust and hope in purely human abilities will join those crying out in guilt. They will call on the crumbling rocks and mountains to fall on them to hide them from the wrath of God.

I am among those who believe that the judgments of God are certain. We do not know the day nor the hour. But God is indeed going to shake the earth as it has never been shaken before, and He will turn it over to the Worthy One to whom it belongs—Jesus Christ!

# MORAL DETERMINATION

*He was glad, and exhorted them all, that with purpose of heart they would cleave unto the Lord. (Acts 11:23)*

Though we do not have much of it in this age of spineless religion, there is nevertheless much in the Bible about the place of moral determination in the service of the Lord.

The Old Testament tells us that "Jacob vowed a vow," and Daniel "purposed in his heart." Paul determined "not to know anything among you, save Jesus Christ, and Him crucified." Above all, we have the example of the Lord Jesus "setting His face like a flint" and walking straight toward the Cross. These and many others have left us a record of spiritual greatness born out of a will firmly set to do the will of God!

They did not try to float to heaven on a perfumed cloud, but cheerfully accepted the fact that "with purpose of heart they must cleave to the Lord."

We must surrender—and in that terrible, wonderful moment we may feel that our will has been forever broken, but such is not the case. In His conquest of the soul, God purges the will and brings it into union with His own, but He never breaks it!

*November 10* _____

# GOD'S PLACE AS CREATOR

*Thou art worthy, O Lord, to receive glory and honour and power: for thou hast created all things. (Revelation 4:11)*

We make a mistake if we do not learn to admire God in all things, great and small; for a new rich mine would be opened in our consciousness if we could learn to recognize God in nature as well as in grace!

We do acknowledge that the God of nature is also the God of grace; and it is true that we glorify God's redeeming grace no less when we glorify His creating and sustaining power. When Christ came to redeem us, He stepped into the framework of an already existent nature.

If we will obey and believe, we can go on pushing back the narrow borders of our spiritual world until it takes in the whole creation of God!

At one time, the English merchant and renowned poet, William Blake, stood watching the sun come up out of the sea. The bright yellow disk of the sun emerged, gliding the water and painting the sky with a thousand colors. "Ah! I see gold!" the merchant said.

Blake answered, "I see the glory of God! And I hear a multitude of the heavenly host crying, 'The whole earth is full of His glory.'"

# WHAT REALLY MATTERS?

*For what hath man of all his labour . . . wherein he hath laboured under the sun? (Ecclesiastes 2:22)*

It is all but impossible these days to get people to pay any attention to things that really matter. The broad cynic in our modern civilization is likely to ask: "What really matters, after all?"

It is our personal relationship to God that really matters!

That takes priority over everything else; for no man can afford to live or die under the frowning displeasure of God. Yet, name one modern device that can save him from it. Where can a man find security? Can philosophy help him? or psychology? or science? or atoms or wonder drugs or vitamins?

Only Christ can help him, and His aid is as old as man's sin and man's need.

A few other things matter to be sure. We must trust Christ completely. We must carry our cross daily. We must love God and our fellow men. We must fulfill our commission as ambassadors of Christ among men. We must grow in grace and in the knowledge of God and come at last to our end like a ripe shock of corn at harvest time.

These are the things that really matter!

*November 12*

# FAITH MUST BE RESTORED

*Take heed, brethren, lest there be in any of you an evil heart of unbelief. (Hebrews 3:12)*

The Bible tells about man's being alienated from and an enemy to God. Should this sound harsh or extreme you have only to imagine your closest friend coming to you and stating in cold seriousness that he no longer has any confidence in you.

"I do not trust you. I have lost confidence in your character. I am forced to suspect every move you make"—such a declaration would instantly alienate friends by destroying the foundation upon which every friendship is built. Until your former friend's opinion of you had been reversed there could be no further communion.

People do not go boldly to God and profess that they have no confidence in Him and they usually do not witness publicly to their low view of God. The frightful thing, however, is that people everywhere act out their unbelief with a consistency that is more convincing than words.

Christianity provides a way back from this place of unbelief and alienation: "He that cometh to God must believe that He is and that He is a rewarder of them that diligently seek Him." God took the wrong upon Himself in order that the one who committed the wrong might be saved!

# TOO MUCH "AT HOME"

*These all died in faith . . . and confessed that they were*
*strangers and pilgrims on the earth. (Hebrews 11:13)*

One of the most telling indictments against many of us
who comprise our Christian churches is the almost
complete acceptance of the contemporary scene as our
permanent home!

We have been working and earning, getting and
spending, and now we are enjoying the creature comforts
known to human beings in this land. You may bristle a bit
and ask: "Is there anything wrong with being
comfortable?"

Let me answer in this way: if you are a Christian and
you are comfortably "at home" in Chicago or Toronto, in
Iowa or Alberta—or any other address on planet earth,
the signs are evident that you are in spiritual trouble.

The spiritual equation reads like this: the greater your
contentment with your daily circumstances in this world,
the greater your defection from the ranks of God's
pilgrims enroute to a city whose architect and builder is
God Himself!

If we can feel that we have put down our roots in this
present world, then our Lord still has much to teach us
about faith and attachment to our Savior!

*November 14* _____

# ANSWERING GOD'S CALL

*The Lord called as at other times, Samuel, Samuel. Then Samuel answered, Speak, for thy servant heareth.*
*(1 Samuel 3:10)*

When will men and women realize that when God calls us out He is completely faithful to call us into something better?

In his faith, Abraham was against idolatry and idol-making, but that was not his crusade. Because of his faith, God led him into a promised land, into possessions and into the lineage that brought forth the Messiah. The call of God is always to something better—keep that in mind!

God calls us into the joys and reality of eternal life. He calls us into purity of life and spirit, so that we may acceptably walk with Him. He calls us into a life of service and usefulness that brings glory to Himself as God. He calls us into the sweetest fellowship possible on this earth—the fellowship of the family of God!

If God takes away from us the old, wrinkled, beat-up dollar bill we clutch so desperately, it is only because He wants to exchange it for the whole federal mint, the entire treasury! He is saying, "I have in store for you all the resources of heaven. Help yourself!"

*November 15*

# AUTHORITY IN PREACHING

*Preach the word; be instant in season, out of season;*
*reprove, rebuke, exhort with all longsuffering and doctrine.*
*(2 Timothy 4:2)*

Because we are Christians who believe the inspired Word of God and because we believe that the Holy Spirit is the abiding third person of the Trinity, there should be more divine authority in our preaching ministries.

A preacher of this gospel of our Lord Jesus Christ should have the authority of God upon him, so that he makes the people responsible to listen to him. When they will not listen to him, they are accountable to God for turning away from the divine Word.

A preacher under God's unction should reign from his pulpit as a king from his throne. He should not reign by law or by regulation or by man's authority. He ought to reign by moral ascendancy!

The divine authority is missing from many pulpits. We have "tabby cats" with their claws carefully trimmed in the seminary, so they can paw over the congregations and never scratch them at all! The Holy Spirit will sharpen the arrows of the man of God who preaches the whole counsel of God!

*November 16* _____

# THE UNITY OF ALL THINGS

*For it pleased the Father . . . by him to reconcile all things unto himself . . . whether they be things in earth, or things in heaven. (Colossians 2:19–20)*

If we are humble and sincere Christians, this should be one of the most welcome thoughts we have ever considered: the work of Christ in redemption will achieve ultimately the expulsion of sin, the only divisive agent in the universe!

When that is accomplished, God's creation will once more realize the unification of all things. We who are men and women, though redeemed and regenerated, are submerged in time; therefore we properly say that prophecy is history foretold and history is prophecy fulfilled. But in God there is no "was" or "will be" but a continuous and unbroken "is." In Him, history and prophecy are one and the same. God contains past and future in His own Being.

It is sin that has brought diversity, separation, dissimilarity. Sin has introduced divisions into a universe essentially one. We do not understand this, but we must let our faith rest on the character of God.

The concept of the unity of all things is seen in the Scriptures. Paul said that God will reconcile all things unto Himself, whether they be things in earth or in heaven!

# CROSSING OVER JORDAN

*O death, where is thy sting? . . . thanks be to God, which giveth us the victory through our Lord Jesus Christ.*
*(1 Corinthians 15:55, 57)*

The prophets and the psalmists of the Old Testament wrestled as we do with the problem of evil in a divine universe, but their approach to God and nature was much more direct than ours. They did not interpose between God and His world that opaque web we moderns call the "laws of nature."

They could see God in a whirlwind and hear Him in a storm and they did not hesitate to say so! There was about their lives an immediate apprehension of the divine. Everything in heaven and on earth assured them that this is God's world and that He rules over all.

I heard a Methodist bishop tell of being called to the bedside of an elderly dying woman in his early ministry. He said he was frightened; but the old saint was radiantly happy. When he tried to express the sorrow he felt about her illness, she would not hear it.

"Why, God bless you young man," she said cheerfully, "there is nothing to be scared about. I am just going to cross over Jordan, where my Father owns the land on both sides of the river!" She understood about the unity of all things in God's creation.

*November 18* _____

# GOD AND THE INDIVIDUAL

*Blessed is the man to whom the Lord will not impute sin.*
*(Romans 4:8)*

When the eternal Son of God became the Son of Man and walked on this earth, He always called individuals to His side. Jesus did not come into the world to deal with statistics!

He deals with individuals and that is why the Christian message is and always has been: "God loves the world! He loves the masses and throngs only because they are made up of individuals. He loves every individual person in the world!"

In the great humanistic tide of our day, the individual is no longer the concern. We are pressed to think of the human race in a lump. We are schooled to think of the human race in terms of statistics. In many nations, the state is made to be everything and the individual means nothing at all.

Into the very face and strength of this kind of humanism comes the Christian evangel, the good news of salvation, wondrously alight with the assurance for all who will listen:

"You are an individual and you matter to God! His concern is not for genes and species but for the individuals He has created!"

# SAVED FROM IDOLATRY

*Thou shalt not bow down thyself to them, nor serve them:*
*for I the Lord thy God am a jealous God. (Exodus 20:5)*

It has been proven often in history that whoever entertains an unworthy conception of God is throwing his or her being wide open to the sin of idolatry, which is in essence, a defamation of the divine character.

It is vitally important that we think soundly about God. Since He is the foundation of all our religious belief, it follows that if we err in our ideas of God, we will go astray in everything else.

We would like to believe that there are no longer false gods in the world, but actually we recognize some of them in our own society. What about the glorified "Chairman of the Board" of the modern businessman? Or the story-telling, back-slapping god of some of the service clubs? Think of the dreamy-eyed god of the unregenerate poet—cozy, aesthetic and willing to fellowship with anybody who thinks high thoughts and believes in moral equality. We often encounter the tricky, unscrupulous god of the superstitious; and the list goes on!

Thankfully, we have found that to know and follow Christ is to be saved from all forms of idolatry!

*November 20* _____

# GLAMOR INSTEAD OF GLORY

*Therefore, brethren, stand fast, and hold the traditions*
*which ye have been taught, whether by word, or our epistle.*
*(2 Thessalonians 2:15)*

One ominous sign in the social structure that surrounds us is the false attitude toward anything that can be called "ordinary." There has grown up all around us an idea that the "commonplace" is old-fashioned and strictly for the birds!

This existing mania for glamor and contempt for the ordinary are signs and portents in American society. Even religion has gone glamorous!

In case you do not know what glamor is, I might explain that it is a compound of sex, paint, padding and artificial lights. It came to America by way of the honky-tonk and the movie lot; got accepted by the world first, and then strutted into the Church—vain, self-admiring and contemptuous. Instead of the Spirit of God in our midst, we now have the spirit of glamor, as artificial as painted death!

Say what you will, it is a new kind of Christianity, with new concepts that face us brazenly wherever we turn within the confines of evangelical Christianity. The new Christian no longer wants to be good or saintly or virtuous!

# GETTING GOD IN FOCUS

*But he, being full of the Holy Ghost, looked up steadfastly into heaven, and saw the glory of God. (Acts 7:55)*

While many are busy trying to set forth satisfactory definitions of the word "faith," we do well to simply consider that believing is directing the heart's attention to Jesus!

It is lifting the mind to "behold the Lamb of God," and never ceasing that beholding for the rest of our lives. At first this may be difficult, but it becomes easier as we look steadily at His wondrous Person, quietly and without strain.

Distractions may hinder, but once the heart is committed to Him the attention will return again and rest upon Him like a wandering bird coming back to its window.

I would emphasize this one great volitional act which establishes the heart intention to gaze forever upon Jesus. God takes this intention for our choice and makes what allowances He must for the thousand distractions which beset us in this evil world. So, faith is a redirecting of our sight, getting God in our focus, and when we lift our inward eyes upon God, we are sure to meet friendly eyes gazing back at us!

*November 22* _____

# "A CHEERFUL HEART"

*Singing and making melody . . . giving thanks always for all things. (Ephesians 5:19–20)*

The thankful Christian will turn with true delight to the expression of Joseph Addison in his Thanksgiving hymn, "When All Thy Mercies, O My God," found in many of the better hymnals. Addison gives a mental image that requires music for its expression:

> Ten thousand thousand precious gifts
> My daily thanks employ;
> Nor is the least a cheerful heart
> That tastes these gifts with joy!

Here is the spirit of thanksgiving. Here is the understanding of what pleases God in our acceptance and use of His gifts. "A cheerful heart that tastes these gifts with joy" is the only kind of heart that can taste them safely.

While Addison had in mind chiefly the gifts God showers upon us here below, he was too much of a Christian to think that God's gifts would cease at death. So he sang:

> Through every period of my life
> Thy goodness I'll pursue;
> And after death in distant worlds,
> The glorious theme renew!

# LET US BE THANKFUL

*Giving thanks always . . . in the name of our Lord Jesus Christ. (Ephesians 5:20)*

To be grateful to God's servants is to be grateful to God; and it follows that in a very real sense we thank God when we thank His people!

We will always have spiritual leaders, and I think we make two mistakes in our attitudes toward them. One is not being sufficiently grateful to them. The other is in following them too slavishly.

The first is a sin of omission, and because it is something that is not there, it is not likely to be noticed as a sin that is plainly present.

We do make a serious mistake when we become so attached to the preaching or writing of a great Christian leader that we accept his teaching without daring to examine it. We should follow men only as they follow the Lord. We should keep an open mind lest we become blind followers of a man whose breath is in his nostrils.

Learn from every holy man and his ministry. Be grateful to every one of them and thankful for them—and then follow Christ!

*November 24* _____

# GOD GIVES—AND GIVES

*Fight the good fight of faith, lay hold on eternal life,*
*whereunto thou art also called. (1 Timothy 6:12)*

We ought to spend more time remembering the blessings and the benefits God is continually giving us while we are alive—before we leave this vale of tears!

He gives us forgiveness—so we are to live for Him as forgiven sinners.

He gives us eternal life. This is not just a future reality—our life in Him is a present bestowment.

He gives us sonship: "Beloved, now are we the sons of God!" In this relationship there are many other gifts we receive from God, and if we do not possess them it is because we are not God's children in faith!

We ask God to help us, to meet some need, to do something for us—and the Lord mercifully does it. I consider these the little and the trifling things, yet we make a great deal of them. But they are really the passing things compared to the great present benefactions of forgiveness, reinstatement in favor with God, sonship and eternal life!

# FAITHFUL STEWARDSHIP

*Upon the first day of the week let every one of you lay by him in store, as God has prospered him.*
*(1 Corinthians 16:2)*

God has been pleased to deal with us in a most remarkable way concerning our Christian stewardship and responsibility of honoring Him with the things He has entrusted to us.

The Bible teaching is plain: you have the right to keep what you have all to yourself—but it will then rust and decay, and ultimately ruin you!

This may hurt some of you but I am obliged to tell you that God does not need anything you have!

He does not need a dime of your money!

What you need to understand is that it is your own spiritual welfare at stake in such matters as this.

There is a beautiful and enriching principle involved in our offering to God what we are and what we have, but none of us are giving because there is a depression in heaven!

A long time ago God said: "If I had need of anything, would I tell you?"

Brethren, if the living God had need of anything, He would no longer be God!

*November 26* _____

# LIVE FOR GOD'S GLORY

*That ye may with one mind and one mouth glorify God,*
*even the Father of our Lord Jesus Christ. (Romans 15:6)*

It may be difficult for the average Christian to get hold
of the idea that his daily labors can be performed as acts
of worship acceptable to God by Jesus Christ.

We must practice living to the glory of God actually and
determinedly. By one act of consecration of our total
selves to God we can make every subsequent act express
that consecration. By meditation upon this truth, by
talking it over with God often in our prayers, by recalling
it to our minds frequently as we move about among men,
a sense of its wondrous meaning will begin to take hold
of us.

The New Testament accepts as a matter of course that
in His incarnation, our Lord took upon Him a real human
body. He lived in that body here among men and never
once performed a non-sacred act!

Brethren, we must offer all our acts to God and believe
that He accepts them. We should then keep reminding
God in our times of private prayer that we mean every act
for His glory. We thus meet the temptations and trials by
the exercise of an aggressive faith in the sufficiency of
Christ!

# "WHY AM I HERE?"

*Who worshipped and served the creature more than the Creator; . . . God gave them over to a reprobate mind. (Romans 1:25, 28)*

Since the first fallen man got still long enough to think, fallen men have been asking these questions: "Whence came I? What am I? Why am I here? and Where am I going?"

The noblest minds of the race have struggled with these questions to no avail. Did the answer lie somewhere hidden like a jewel it would surely have been uncovered, for the most penetrating minds of the race have searched for it everywhere in the region of human experience. Yet the answers remain as securely hidden as if they did not exist.

Why is man lost philosophically? Because he is lost morally and spiritually. He cannot answer the questions life presents to his intellect because the light of God has gone out in his soul. The fearful indictment the Holy Ghost brings against mankind is summed up count by count in the opening chapters of Romans and the conduct of every man from earliest recorded history is evidence enough to sustain the indictment.

Apart from the Scriptures we have no sure philosophy: apart from Jesus Christ we have no true knowledge of God; apart from the inliving Spirit we have no ability to live lives morally pleasing to God!

*November 28* _____

# NOTHING BUT SWEETNESS

*It was in my mouth as sweet as honey: and as soon as I had eaten it, my belly was bitter. (Revelation 10:10)*

Let me caution you about the attitudes of some of the bubbly "happy! happy!" people in our congregations who will insist that the Word of God can never be anything but honey sweet!

Fellow believers, when we digest, absorb and soak up the Word of the Lord, it becomes part and parcel of our daily lives. It is our delight. It is indeed honey and sweetness. But as we share that same Word in our witness to lost men and women, we will know something of bitterness and hostility, even enmity.

It will follow then in experience, that Christian believers who are intent upon being faithful witnesses for Jesus Christ may not always find sweetness and light in their contacts with evil, rebellious people.

We need to pray for men and women in our churches who have determined to set their own agendas—to live their lives as they please! They have determined to manage the influences of the Word of God in their lives.

# THOUGHTS ON COMMUNION

*He took bread . . . and their eyes were opened, and they knew him. (Luke 24:30–31)*

What a sweet comfort to us that our Lord Jesus Christ was once known in the breaking of the bread.

In earlier Christian times, believers called the Communion "the medicine of immortality," and God gave them the desire to pray:

> Be known to us in breaking bread,
> But do not then depart;
> Savior, abide with us and spread
> Thy table in our heart.

Some churches have a teaching that you will find God only at their table—and that you leave God there when you leave. I am so glad that God has given us light. We may take the Presence of the table with us. We may take the Bread of life with us as we go.

> Then sup with us in love divine,
> Thy body and Thy blood;
> That living bread and heavenly wine
> Be our immortal food!

In approaching the table of our Lord, we dare not forget the cost to our elder Brother, the Man who was from heaven. He is our Savior; He is our Passover!

*November 30* _____

# THE BREATH OF GOD

*The word that I have spoken . . . shall judge him in the last day. (John 12:2)*

Two of the great realities in our midst are surely the promised Presence of God and the testimony of His eternal Word!

By the "Word of God" I do not refer only to the book you hold in your hand—paper and letters, pages and ink—sewed together with silk thread. By the Word of God I do mean the expression of the mind of God: the mighty, world-filling breath of God!

Most of the things men and women talk about cannot be counted among the great realities of life. In October, people talk a great deal about the World Series as a great reality, but by December they have forgotten who pitched and who struck out.

People spend their entire lives in the pursuit of those things that can only perish and fade away. But when it is all over, they are still going to be faced with the reality of the eternal Word of God, the revelation of Truth which God has given us!

Think of the changes that would come if humans would suddenly stop and hear the Word of God!

*December 1*

# LIFE FLOWS FROM GOD

*God saw everything that he had made, and, behold, it was very good. (Genesis 1:31)*

Without doubt, we have suffered the loss of many spiritual treasures because we have let slip the simple truth that the miracle of the perpetuation of life is in God!

Be assured that God did not create life and toss it from Him like some petulant artist disappointed with his work. All life is in Him and out of Him, flowing from Him and returning to Him again, a moving indivisible sea of which He is the fountainhead.

That eternal life which was with the Father is now the possession of believing men and women, and that life is not God's gift only—but His very Self! The regeneration of a believing soul is but a recapitulation of all His work done from the moment of creation.

So, redemption is not a strange work which God for a moment turned aside to do: rather it is His same work performed in a new field, the field of human catastrophe!

*December 2*_____

# LET US TAKE IT PERSONALLY

*Lord, thou wilt ordain peace for us: for thou also hast wrought all our works in us. (Isaiah 26:12)*

What a difference it makes when we humans cease being general and become pointed and personal in our approach to God! We then come to see that all that God did was for each of us.

It was for me that holy men spoke as they were moved by the Holy Spirit. For me Christ died—and when He arose on the third day it was for me. When the promised Holy Spirit came it was to continue in me the work He had been doing for me, since the morning of the Creation!

So, I have every right to claim all of the riches of the Godhead in mercy given. What a blessed thought—that an infinite God can give all of Himself to each of His children!

He does not distribute Himself that each may have a part, but to each one He gives all of Himself as fully as if there were no others.

All that He is and all that He has done is for us and for all who share the common salvation.

_____ *December 3*

# CONFUSED ABOUT WORSHIP

*For ye are the temple of the living God. (2 Corinthians 6:16)*

To really know Jesus Christ as Savior and Lord is to love and worship Him!

As God's people, we are so often confused that we could be known as God's poor, stumbling, bumbling people, for we are most prone to think of worship as something we do when we go to church on Sunday!

We call it God's house. We have dedicated it to Him. So, we continue with the confused idea that it must be the only place where we can worship Him.

We come to the Lord's house, made of brick and stone and wood. We are used to hearing the call to worship: "The Lord is in His holy temple—let us kneel before Him!" This is on Sunday and in church—very nice!

But on Monday, as we go about our different duties, are we aware of the continuing Presence of God? The Lord desires still to be in His holy temple, wherever we are; for each of us is a temple in whom dwells the Holy Spirit of God!

*December 4*_____

# LET THE DAY DAWN

*The path of the just . . . shineth more and more unto the perfect day. (Proverbs 4:18)*

The Bible tells us that when a person becomes a Christian, it is as though the sun has come up and the day has dawned. Then his experience along the path should be like the glowing light which shineth more and more unto the perfect day!

This brings us to a question: if all Christians are alike in standing and state, why did Jesus point out three distinctions in the Christian life—"some thirty, some sixty and some a hundred fold"?

If we are all alike and have all "arrived" at the same place and state, why did the Apostle Paul tell the Philippian Christians—"I have suffered the loss of all things, that I may know Him and if by any means, I might attain unto that superior resurrection"?

I am of the opinion that we cannot experience that which we have not believed. I still think we must instruct and urge men and women, toiling along in average and common Christian ways, to move forward and claim spiritual victory they have not yet known.

# EVERYONE MAY COME

*Whosoever will, let him take the water of life freely.*
*(Revelation 22:17)*

There is a strange beauty in the ways of God with men. He sends salvation to the world in the person of a Man and sends that Man to walk the byways, saying, "If any man will come after Me!" No fanfare; no tramp of marching feet!

A kindly Stranger walks through the earth, and so quiet is His voice that it is sometimes lost in the hurly-burly; but it is the last voice of God, and until we become quiet to hear it, we have no authentic message.

"If any man," He says, and teaches at once the universal inclusiveness of His invitation and the freedom of the human will. Everyone may come; no one need come, and whoever does come, comes because he chooses to.

Every man thus holds his future in his hand. Not the dominant world leader only, but the inarticulate man lost in anonymity is "a man of destiny!" He decides which way his soul shall go. He chooses, and destiny waits on the nod of his head. He decides, and hell enlarges itself, or heaven prepares another mansion!

So much of Himself has God given to man!

*December 6*_____

# WHERE IS THE RADIANCE?

*He that believeth on the Son of God hath the witness in himself. (1 John 5:10)*

I keep looking, but with little success, for a distinguishing radiance in life and testimony among our evangelical Christians.

Instead of an inner witness, too many professing Christians are depending upon logical conclusions drawn from Bible texts. They have no witness of an encounter with God, no awareness of inner change!

I believe that where there is a divine act within the soul, there will be a corresponding awareness. This act of God is its own evidence: it addresses itself directly to the spiritual consciousness.

Thankfully, there are elements that are always the same among men and women who have had a personal meeting with God.

There is the compelling sense of God Himself; of His Person and of His Presence. From there on, the permanent results will be evident in the life and walk of the person touched as long as he or she lives!

# MORE THAN PARDON

*For godly sorrow worketh repentance to salvation not to be repented of. (2 Corinthians 7:10)*

It is a fact that the New Testament message of good news, "Christ died for our sins according to the scriptures," embraces a great deal more than an offer of free pardon.

Surely it is a message of pardon—and for that may God be praised—but it is also a message of repentance!

It is a message of atonement—but it is also a message of temperance and righteousness and godliness in this present world!

It tells us that we must accept a Savior—but it tells us also that we must deny ungodliness and worldly lusts!

The gospel message includes the idea of amendment—of separation from the world, of cross-carrying and loyalty to the kingdom of God even unto death!

These are all corollaries of the gospel and not the gospel itself; but they are part and parcel of the total message which we are commissioned to declare. No man has authority to divide the truth and preach only a part of it. To do so is to weaken it and render it without effect!

*December 8*_____

# GIFTS AND GRACES

*. . . gifts of the Holy Ghost, according to his own will.*
*(Hebrews 2:4)*

I go back often to Genesis 24 for the illustration and the figure in the Old Testament reminding us of the adornments of grace and beauty that will mark the believing Body of Christ. Abraham sent his trusted servant to his former homeland to select a bride for Isaac.

The adornment of Rebekah's beauty consisted of jewels and the raiment that came as gifts of love from the bridegroom whom she had not yet seen.

It is a reminder of what God is doing in our midst right now. Abraham typifies God the Father; Isaac, our Lord Jesus Christ, the heavenly Bridegroom. The servant who went with the gifts into the far country to claim a bride for Isaac speaks well of the Holy Spirit, our Teacher and Comforter.

He gives us, one by one, the gifts and the graces of the Holy Spirit that will be our real beauty in His sight. Thus we are being prepared, and when we meet our coming Lord and King, our adornment will be our God-given graces!

# "THUS SAITH THE LORD"

*The Lord giveth wisdom: out of his mouth cometh knowledge and understanding. (Proverbs 2:6)*

In a time when everything in the world seems to be related to vanity, God is depending on His believing children to demonstrate that He is the great Reality; that we are made by God and for Him! The answer to the question, "Where did I come from?" can never be better answered than by the Christian mother who tells her child, "God made you!"

The great store of knowledge in today's world cannot improve on that simple answer! The scientist can tell us the secrets of how matter operates, but the origin of matter lies in deep silence, refusing to give an answer to man's question.

It is important for Christian believers to be able to stand firmly and positively in this declaration: "Thus saith the Lord!" Our chief business is not to argue or to persuade our generation. With our positive declaration of God's Word and revelation, we make God responsible for the outcome. No one can know enough to go beyond this!

*December 10*_____

# THE NEED FOR REVERENCE

*God is greatly to be feared . . . and to be had in reverence.*
*(Psalm 89:7)*

Many persons who have been raised in our churches no longer think in terms of reverence, which seems to indicate that they doubt God's presence is there! Much of the blame must be placed on the growing acceptance of a wordly secularism that seems much more appealing than any real desire for the spiritual life that is pleasing to God.

We secularize God; we secularize the gospel of Christ and we secularize worship!

No great and spiritually minded men of God are going to come out of such churches, nor any great spiritual movement of believing prayer and revival. If God is to be honored and revered and truly worshiped, He may have to sweep us away and start somewhere else!

Let us confess that there is a necessity for true worship among us. If God is who He says He is and if we are the believing people of God we claim to be, we must worship Him! In my own assessment, for men and women to lose the awareness of God in our midst is a loss too terrible ever to be appraised!

*December 11*

# MORE THAN A NAME

*Let every one that nameth the name of Christ depart from iniquity.* (2 Timothy 2:19)

There have always been professing Christians who argue and insist: "I am all right—I worship in the name of Jesus." They seem to believe that worship of God is based on a formula. They seem to think there is a kind of magic in saying the name of Jesus!

Study the Bible carefully with the help of the Holy Spirit and you will find that the name and the nature of Jesus are one. It is not enough to know how to spell Jesus' name!

If we have come to be like Him in nature, if we have come to the place of being able to ask in accordance with His will, He will give us the good things we desire and need.

We worship God as the result of a new birth from above in which God has been pleased to give us more than a name.

He has given us a nature transformed, and Peter expresses that truth in this way:

> Whereby are given unto us exceeding great and precious promises, that by these ye might be partakers of the divine nature, having escaped the corruption that is in the world through lust.
> (2 Peter 1:4)

*December 12*_____

# GLORY TO GOD

*The spirit of glory and of God resteth upon you.*
*(1 Peter 4:14)*

When the Holy Spirit comes among us with His anointing, we become a worshiping people!

Now, that does not mean that all Christians everywhere must all worship alike—but that under the guidance of the Holy Spirit believers everywhere are united in their praises to God.

When Jesus came into Jerusalem presenting Himself as Messiah there was a great multitude and there was a great noise. Very often our worship is audible, but I do not believe it is necessarily true that we are worshiping God when we are making a lot of racket. But I think there is a word for those who are cultured, quiet, self-possessed, poised and sophisticated. If they are embarrassed in church when some happy Christian says, "Amen!" they may actually be in need of some spiritual enlightenment.

If some believer's "Glory to God!" really bothers you, it may be because you do not know the kind of spiritual blessing and delight the Holy Spirit is waiting to provide among God's worshiping saints. I can only speak for myself, but I want to be among those who worship!

# BETTER FARTHER ON

*Then opened he their understanding, that they might understand the scriptures. (Luke 24:45)*

Truth that is not experienced is no better than error, and may be fully as dangerous.

Remember that the scribes who sat in Moses' seat were not the victims of error; they were the victims of failure to experience the truth they taught!

We should see that one of the greatest foes of the Christian is religious complacency. The man who believes that he has "arrived" will not go any further; and the present neat habit of quoting a text to prove we have arrived may be a dangerous one if in truth we have no actual inward experience of the text.

The great saints of the past have all had yearning hearts. Their longing after God all but consumed them; it propelled them onward and upward to heights toward which less ardent Christians look with languid eye and entertain no hope of reaching.

May we offer this word of exhortation: pray on, fight on, sing on! Press on into the deep things of God. Keep your feet on the ground, but let your heart soar as high as it will!

*December 14*_____

# OCCUPIED WITH PRAISE

*They rest not day and night, saying, Holy, holy, holy, Lord God almighty.* (Revelation 4:8)

It is surely an erroneous supposition for humans to think or to believe that death will transform our attitude and dispositions.

This is what I mean: if in this life we are not really comfortable talking and singing about heaven and its joy, I doubt that death will transform us into enthusiasts! If the worship and adoration of God are tedious now, they will be tedious also after the hour of death.

I do not know that God is going to force any of us into His heaven. I doubt that He will say to any of us, "You were never very interested in worshiping Me while you were on earth, but in heaven I am going to make that your greatest interest and your ceaseless occupation."

Controversial?

Perhaps, but in the heavenly scene John describes, the living creatures crying "Holy, holy, holy!" rest neither day nor night. My fear is that too many of God's professing people down here are resting far too often between their efforts to praise and glorify the living God!

# THE SECRET WORKING OF GOD

*That being justified by his grace, we should be made heirs according to the hope of eternal life. (Titus 3:7)*

I do believe in the secret and mysterious working of God in the human breast. I must believe it after finding the forgiving and converting grace of God in the Savior, Jesus Christ.

My father and mother held high human standards, but completely without any thought of God. My parents appeared to be without any spark of desire after God; attitudes that were cold, earthy, profane.

Can you tell me why, then, at the age of 17, as a boy surrounded by unbelief—100 percent—I could find my way to my mother's attic, kneel on my knees, and give my heart and life in committal to Jesus Christ?

I cannot tell you why. I can only say that I know there is such a thing as the secret workings of God within the human being who has a sensitivity to hear the call of God. In my own case, I do have the testimony that my conversion to Jesus Christ was as real as any man's conversion has ever been!

My fellow man, if the Spirit of God is still tugging at your heart, thank God—and follow the light!

*December 16*_____

# MERCY: A BOUNDLESS SEA

*God, who is rich in mercy . . . even when we were dead in sins. (Ephesians 2:4–5)*

A human being is never really aware of the great boundless sea of the mercy of God until by faith he comes across the threshold of the kingdom of God and recognizes it and identifies it!

My father was 60 years old when he bowed before Jesus Christ and was born again. That was a near lifetime in which he had sinned and lied and cursed. But to him, the mercy of God that took him to heaven was no greater than the mercy of God that had endured and kept him for 60 years.

I recall the story of an ancient rabbi who consented to take a weary old traveler into his house for a night of rest. In conversation, the rabbi discovered the visitor was almost 100 years old and a confirmed atheist. Infuriated, the rabbi arose, opened the door and ordered the man out into the night.

Then, sitting down by his candle and Old Testament, it seemed he heard a voice, God's voice: "I have endured that sinner for almost a century. Could you not endure him for a night?" The rabbi ran out and overtaking the old man, brought him back to the hospitality of his home for the night.

*December 17*

# GIVE GOD THE CONTROL

*Make me to go in the path of thy commandments, for*
*therein do I delight. (Psalm 119:35)*

I know that I am being repetitious—but this needs to be
said again and again: our Lord will not save those whom
He cannot command!

The lifetime God has given us down here is a lifetime of
decisions. Each person makes his own decisions as to the
eternal world he is going to inhabit. We must decide to
take Jesus for what He is—the anointed Savior and Lord
who is King of kings and Lord of all lords! He would not
be who He is if He saved us and called us without the
understanding that He can also guide us and control our
lives.

The root of sin is rebellion against God, and hell is the
Alcatraz for the unconstituted rebels who refuse to
surrender to the will of God.

There are many arguments about the reality of hell. A
man might endure fire and brimstone and worms—but
the essence of hell and judgment for a moral creature is to
know and be conscious that he is where he is because he
is a rebel!

Hell will be the eternal domain of all the disobedient
rebels who have said, "I owe God nothing!"

*December 18*_____

# REVIVAL—AND RENEWAL

*Though our outward man perish yet the inward man is renewed day by day.* *(2 Corinthians 4:16)*

I hope some of you will agree with me that it is of far greater importance that we have better Christians than that we have more of them!

If we have any spiritual concerns, our most pressing obligation is to do all in our power to obtain a revival that will result in a reformed, revitalized, purified church.

Each generation of Christians is the seed of the next, and degenerate seed is sure to produce a degenerate harvest; not a little better than but worse than the seed from which it sprang. Thus the direction will be down until vigorous, effective means are taken to improve the seed.

Why is it easier to talk about revival than to experience it? Because followers of Christ must become personally and vitally involved in the death and resurrection of Christ. And this requires repentance, prayer, watchfulness, self-denial, detachment from the world, humility, obedience and cross-carrying!

# DO YOU LOVE BEAUTY?

*There shall in no wise enter into it any thing that defileth,*
*neither whatsoever worketh abomination. (Revelation 21:27)*

When we look closely at this world system and society,
we see the terrible and ugly scars of sin. Sin has obscenely
scarred and defaced this world, taking away its harmony
and symmetry and beauty.

That is the negative picture. Thank God for the positive
promise and prospect that heaven is the place of all
loveliness, all harmony and beauty.

These are not idle words. If you love beautiful things,
you had better stay out of hell, for hell will be the
quintessence of all that is morally ugly and obscene. Hell
will be the ugliest place in all of creation!

It is a fact that earth lies between all that is ugly in hell
and all that is beautiful in heaven. As long as we are living
here, we will have to consider the extreme—much that is
good and much that is bad!

As believers, we are held firm in the knowledge that the
eternal Son came to save us and deliver us to a beautiful
heaven and everlasting fellowship with God!

*December 20*_____

# IF JESUS CAME TODAY

*We will not have this man to reign over us. (Luke 19:14)*

People have asked me if our present generation would gladly accept Jesus if He came at this time, instead of 2,000 years ago. I have to believe that history does repeat itself!

In our own day, many who want to follow the Christian traditions still balk and reject a thorough-going spiritual housecleaning within their own lives.

When Jesus came, many realized that it would mean probable financial loss for them to step out and follow Christ. Also, many of those men and women who considered the claims of Christ in His day knew that following Him would call for abrupt and drastic changes in their patterns of living. The proud and selfish aspects of their lives would have been disturbed.

Beyond that, there was an almost complete disdain for the inward spiritual life which Jesus taught as a necessity for mankind; that it is the pure in heart who will see God!

I am afraid that humanity's choice would still be the same today. People are still more in love with money and pride and pleasure than they are with God and His salvation!

*December 21*

# THE WORD MADE FLESH

*And lo, a voice from heaven saying, this is my beloved Son, in whom I am well pleased. (Matthew 3:17)*

I have given much thought and contemplation to the sweetest and tenderest of all of the mysteries in God's revelation to man—the Incarnation! Jesus, the Christ, is the Eternal One, for in the fullness of time He humbles Himself. John's description is plain: the Word was made flesh and dwelt among us.

I confess that I would have liked to have seen the baby Jesus. But the glorified Jesus yonder at the right hand of the Majesty on high, was the baby Jesus once cradled in the manger straw. Taking a body of humiliation, He was still the Creator who made the wood of that manger, made the straw, and was Creator of all the beasts that were there.

In truth, He made the little town of Bethlehem and all that it was. He also made the star that lingered over the scene that night. He had come into His own world, His Father's world. Everything we touch and handle belongs to Him. So we have come to love Him and adore Him and honor Him!

*December 22*_____

# CHRISTMAS IS REAL

*Great is the mystery . . . God was manifest in the flesh.*
*(1 Timothy 3:16)*

The birth of Christ was a divine declaration, an eternal statement to a race of fallen men and women.

The Advent of Christ clearly established:

First, that God is real. The heavens were opened and another world than this came into view.

Second, that human life is essentially spiritual. With the emergence into human flesh of the Eternal Word of the Father, the fact of man's divine origin is confirmed.

Third, that God indeed had spoken by the prophets. The coming of the Messiah-Savior into the world confirmed the veracity of the Old Testament Scripture.

Fourth, that man is lost but not abandoned. Had men not been lost no Savior would have been required. Had they been abandoned no Savior would have come.

Finally, that this world is not the end. We are made for two worlds and as surely as we now inhabit the one we shall also inhabit the other!

*December 23*

# JOY AND WONDER

*Fear not: for, behold, I bring you good tidings of great joy.*
*(Luke 2:10)*

It is tragic that men and women everywhere are losing the sense of wonder, confessing now only one interest in life—and that is utility! Even Christmas Day has been degraded.

We ignore the beautiful and the majestic, asking only "How can I use it? How much profit will it bring?"

The believing children of God once upon a time saw God in everything. They were enraptured with everything before them. There was no common hill—they were all the hills of God! There was no common cloud—they were the chariots of God! They saw God in everything: in our day we never look up in happy surprise!

But let me tell you that it has been a never-failing delight throughout my years to watch little children on Christmas morning. The gifts may be humble, but the child's burst of spontaneous delight and wonder is genuine and rewarding. That incredulous look in the child's face—everything is full of wonder and beauty!

Sad, indeed, for adults to lose the wonder in worship—for worship is wonder and wonder is worship!

*December 24*_____

# THE HAPPY MORN

*For unto you is born this day in the city of David a Saviour.*
*(Luke 2:11)*

When we sing, "The Light of the world is Jesus," there should be a glow on our faces that would make the world believe indeed that we really mean it! The Incarnation meant something vast and beautiful for John Milton—and he celebrated the coming of Jesus into the world with one of the most beautiful and moving expressions ever written by a man:

This is the month, and this the happy morn,
Wherein the Son of Heaven's eternal King,
Of wedded maid, and Virgin mother born,
Our great redemption from above did bring.

That glorious form, that Light insufferable,
And that far-beaming blaze of majesty,
He laid aside, and here with us to be,
Forsook the courts of everlasting Day,
And chose with us a darksome house of mortal clay.

Oh! run; prevent them with thy humble ode,
And lay it lowly at His blessed feet,
Have thou the honor first thy Lord to greet
And join thy voices with the Angel quire,
From out His secret altar touched with hallowed
    fire!

*December 25*

# CHRIST'S WORLD OF NATURE

*Then the devil leaveth him, and, behold, angels came and ministered unto him. (Matthew 4:11)*

Jesus Christ came into our world in the fullness of time, and His own world, the world of nature, received Him, even though His own people received Him not!

It is my own feeling that when Jesus came, all of nature went out to greet Him. The star led the wise men from the East. The cattle in the stable stall in Bethlehem did not bother Him. His own things in created nature received Him.

Dr. G. Campbell Morgan believed that when Jesus went into the wilderness to be tempted of the devil, He was there with the wild beasts for 40 days and nights. Dr. Morgan held that there had been a wrong conception, as if Jesus needed angelic protection from the animals.

Jesus was perfectly safe there. He was nature's Creator and Lord. Jesus was in total harmony with nature and I am of the opinion that the deeper our Christian commitment becomes, the more likely we will find ourselves in tune and in harmony with the natural world around us!

*December 26*_____

# BETTER THAN GOLD

*That ye might know the things that are freely given to us of God. (1 Corinthians 3:12)*

Every Christian believer should be aware that our God has given us definite promises of an amazing inheritance to be realized in the eternal!

The blessings and riches of our divine inheritance are not riches that will come to us for anything that is worthy or superior in ourselves; but will come because of our relationship in faith to the One who is the fount of every blessing.

We must remember that an inheritance has not actually been earned. Such bequests come from One who owns everything and gives to another whom He delights to honor and who can establish his rightful claim.

Inheritance is a right resulting from a relationship. In this case, the right belongs to the children of God by virtue of the fact that their identification as children of God by faith in the eternal Son of God has been established and is in the heavenly records! The apostle said of us: "Men and women cannot imagine or even dream of all the things which God has prepared for those who love Him!"

# CHRIST'S PICTURE EVERYWHERE

*Thou art worthy, O Lord, to receive honor and glory and power. (Revelation 4:11)*

We try to sympathize with the writer John as he attempts to describe heavenly creatures in human terms in the book of Revelation. He knew and we know that it was impossible for God to fully reveal Himself and the heavenly glories to a man.

John tries to describe for us the four "living creatures" in Revelation 4. The first was like a lion; the second was like an ox; the third had the face of a man; the fourth was like a soaring eagle. Did you know that for centuries Christians have seen those same "faces" in the four gospels of the New Testament?

God has put Jesus Christ's picture everywhere! Matthew's is the gospel of the King. Mark's, the gospel of the suffering Servant. Luke's, the gospel of the Son of Man. John's, the gospel of the Son of God. Four loving, adoring, worshiping beings, faithfully and forever devoted to praising God!

Make no mistake about it: the imagery is plainly the gospel of Christ. He is what Christianity is all about!

*December 28*_____

# THE LORD OF ALL BEAUTY

*They shall see the glory of the Lord; and the excellency of our God. (Isaiah 35:2)*

Think with me about beauty—and about this matchless One who is the Lord of all beauty, our Savior!

God has surely deposited something within our human beings that is capable of understanding and appreciating beauty—the love of harmonious forms, appreciation of colors and beautiful sounds.

Brother, these are only the external counterparts of a deeper and more enduring beauty—that which we call moral beauty. It has been the uniqueness and the perfection of Christ's moral beauty that have charmed even those who claimed to be His enemies throughout the centuries of history.

We do not have any record of Hitler saying anything against the moral perfection of Jesus. One of the great philosophers, Nietzsche, objected to Paul's theology of justification by faith, but he was strangely moved within himself by the perfection of moral beauty found in the life and character of Jesus, the Christ.

We should thank God for the promise of heaven being the place of supreme beauty—and the One who is all-beautiful is there!

# GOD'S SOVEREIGN PLAN

*Then cometh the end, when he shall have delivered up the Kingdom to God . . . for he must reign.*
*(1 Corinthians 15:24–25)*

Many people continue to live in daily fear that the world "is coming to an end."

Only in the Scriptures do we have the description and prediction of the age-ending heavenly and earthly events when our Lord and Savior will be universally acknowledged as King of kings and Lord of lords.

God's revelation makes it plain that in "that day" all will acclaim Him "victor!"

Human society, generally, refuses to recognize God's sovereignty or His plan for His redeemed people. But no human being or world government will have any control in that fiery day of judgment yet to come.

John's vision of things to come tells us clearly and openly that at the appropriate time this world will be taken away from men and placed in the hands of the only Man who has the wisdom and authority to rightly govern.

That Man is the eternal Son of God, the worthy Lamb, our Lord Jesus Christ!

*December 30*_____

# THE PERFECTIONS OF GOD

*Give unto the Lord the glory due unto his name; worship the Lord in the beauty of holiness. (Psalm 29:2)*

I hope that if I am remembered at all it will be for this reason: I have spent my efforts and my energies trying to turn the direction of the people away from the external elements of religion to those that are internal and spiritual.

I have tried to take away some of the clouds in the hope that men and women would be able to view God in His glory. I would like to see this sense of glory recaptured throughout the church—too many Christians do not expect to experience any of the glory until they see Him face to face!

Within our Christian fellowship and worship, we must recapture the Bible concepts of the perfection of our God Most High! We have lost the sense and the wonder of His awe-fullness, His perfection, His beauty.

Oh, I feel that we should preach it, sing it, write about it, talk about it and tell it until we have recaptured the concept of the Majesty of God!

Only that can be beautiful ultimately which is holy—and we who belong to Jesus Christ should know the true delight of worshiping God in the beauty of His holiness!

# Subject Index

Since dates rather than page numbers designate each devotional selection, the subject and Scripture indexes use the number of the month rather than the name of the month; therefore, 1/2 means January 2.

## January
Yes, Everything Is Wrong . . . until Jesus Makes It Right     1/1
In the Beginning     1/2
Man Has Lost God     1/3
Savior and Lord     1/4
Our Charter Is from God     1/5
Yes, God Loves Us     1/6
Riches of Grace     1/7
Benefits of Grace     1/8
God's Gracious Act     1/9
Grace Can Be Costly     1/10
United with Christ     1/11
Dealing with Sin     1/12
Love without Measure     1/13
The Wonder of Redemption     1/14
Our Life Is in Christ     1/15
God Sets No Limit     1/16
Explore God's Word     1/17
Faith and Obedience     1/18
Salvation's Price     1/19
God's Faithful Voice     1/20
The True Son of Man     1/21
Guidance Is by the Spirit     1/22
Majesty—and Meekness     1/23
Bringing Us to Glory     1/24
Spiritual Readiness     1/25
Journey of the Heart     1/26
We Get around It     1/27
Ministry of the Church     1/28
A Believing Remnant     1/29
Christ Will Rule     1/30
A Prayer of Concern     1/31

## February

Our God: All Sufficient — 2/1
Sharing God's Nature — 2/2
God Reveals Himself — 2/3
Jesus Said He Was God — 2/4
Both Lord and Christ — 2/5
Truth Is a Person — 2/6
Christ Is Not Divided — 2/7
Who Hears the Call of God? — 2/8
Who Will Come to Jesus? — 2/9
Christ Came to Save — 2/10
We Are Not Orphans — 2/11
Think Like God Thinks — 2/12
Our Highest Happiness — 2/13
Activity Is Not Enough — 2/14
Playing at Religion — 2/15
We See God's Purpose — 2/16
Man's Wasted Potential — 2/17
We Were Outcasts, Too — 2/18
God's Highest Will — 2/19
Every Hindrance Removed — 2/20
We Have It All — 2/21
Our Individual Worth — 2/22
The Spirit Illuminates — 2/23
Give Time to God — 2/24
"Now It Is the Lord" — 2/25
"Be Still and Know" — 2/26
The End of the Age — 2/27
Prayer for Anointing — 2/28

## March

Begin with God — 3/1
The Godhead—Forever One — 3/2
Glory of the Trinity — 3/3
Preach a Whole Christ — 3/4
Lord of Righteousness — 3/5
The Gospel Warning — 3/6
The Eternal Verity — 3/7
We Know What We Believe — 3/8

"Automatic" Saints?                3/9
Normal—or Nominal?                3/10
The Great Physician                3/11
Wisdom from God                    3/12
The Image We Project               3/13
Worship—and Work                  3/14
"Tears of Joy—Amen!"              3/15
Except Ye Repent                   3/16
Response to the Word               3/17
The Crowd Turns Back               3/18
Money Is Not Truth                 3/19
Tell the Whole Truth               3/20
Pour Yourself Out                  3/21
God's Overcomers                   3/22
Here for Our Time                  3/23
"Born of God"                      3/24
Conviction and Pain                3/25
Break with This World              3/26
The Wordly "Virus"                 3/27
Let Fear Become Trust              3/28
Our Future Rewards                 3/29
Which Cross Do We Carry?           3/30
Power of the Cross                 3/31

## April

The Presence of God                4/1
God Has a Remedy                   4/2
Spiritual Unanimity                4/3
Hope—or Despair?                  4/4
The Easter Triumph                 4/5
Resurrection Power                 4/6
Resurrection: A Fact               4/7
Easter—and Missions               4/8
"I Will Not Forsake You!"          4/9
Leaning Toward Heresy              4/10
To Sin Is to Rebel                 4/11
The Transformed Life               4/12
Running Life's Race                4/13
Are We Mired Down?                 4/14

Mediocre Christianity                4/15
Instruct—Then Exhort                 4/16
Not Ready for Heaven?                 4/17
Knowing His Presence                 4/18
Come as You Are                      4/19
Seeking after Truth                  4/20
Spiritual Testing                    4/21
Glorious Contradictions              4/22
Rejoicing in Trials                  4/23
Confessing Our Love                  4/24
"As I Was, So I Will Be!"            4/25
The Walk of Faith                    4/26
Enoch Escaped Death                  4/27
A Man Sent from God                  4/28
Demonstrate Your Faith               4/29
Prayer of a Servant                  4/30

## May

Your Devotional Life                 5/1
Practicing the Truth                 5/2
An Exclusive Attachment              5/3
A Birth from Above                   5/4
Spiritual Confirmation               5/5
The Ethics of Jesus                  5/6
Faith and Experience                 5/7
We Are Not All Alike                 5/8
Questions We Ask                     5/9
Beyond Empty Profession              5/10
Confess Christ's Lordship            5/11
How Do We Listen?                    5/12
Unclean by Comparison                5/13
God Knows the Hypocrites             5/14
More Than Religion                   5/15
Holy Spirit, All Divine              5/16
Honor God's Spirit                   5/17
Responding to the Spirit             5/18
When Pentecost Came                  5/19
The Promise of the Spirit            5/20
Geared into Things Eternal           5/21

God Is Sovereign                              5/22
Blame Someone Else                            5/23
Unholy, Unrighteous, Unhappy                  5/24
Bragging about God                            5/25
Man's View of This World                      5/26
The Humble Place                              5/27
Ashamed of Sin                                5/28
A Great Moral Blunder                         5/29
Astonished Reverence                          5/30
God Knows My Prayer                           5/31

## June
God's Grace Is Eternal                        6/1
His Cross Is My Cross                          6/2
New Testament Roots                           6/3
Spectator Christians                          6/4
Do Things Possess Us?                         6/5
Without Feeling?                              6/6
Who Is Your Example?                          6/7
Make God's Will Our Will                      6/8
Why Settle Down?                              6/9
False Pretenders                              6/10
Compromise Is Costly                          6/11
Christ Made the World                         6/12
Loving God Only                               6/13
No One Changes God's Law                      6/14
Ascription of Glory                           6/15
The Mystery in Worship                        6/16
"Yet Shall He Live"                           6/17
Truth Has a Soul                              6/18
The Conditions of Peace                       6/19
Our Wills Must Surrender                      6/20
God Understands Us                            6/21
Our Sovereign Lord                            6/22
Behind the Mask                               6/23
The Spirit's Gifts                            6/24
Christ Receives Sinners                       6/25
Lord of Our Living                            6/26
Christ Glorified in Us                        6/27

The Spiritual Essence                    6/28
Eternity in Our Hearts                   6/29
Prayer for Humility                      6/30

## July
Warning in the Gospel                    7/1
Critical Decisions                       7/2
Free to Be a Servant                     7/3
Only God Is Free                         7/4
God Touches Our Emotions                 7/5
God's Will: "Obey!"                      7/6
Discipline Is Dismissed                  7/7
Christians indeed                        7/8
Too Timid to Resist                      7/9
The Creator's Handiwork                  7/10
God's Saving Grace                       7/11
We Are too Comfortable                   7/12
Out of Balance                           7/13
Selfish Personal Interest                7/14
Repentance Is Rare                       7/15
God Needs No Pity                        7/16
Losing the Mystery                       7/17
Old Things Pass Away                     7/18
Obedience Is Better                      7/19
The Family of God                        7/20
Is Your Line Busy?                       7/21
Our Godly Conversation                   7/22
The Reality of Pride                     7/23
Two-way Traffic                          7/24
"Unfair! Unfair!"                        7/25
The Prophetic Voice                      7/26
God Needs No Adjectives                  7/27
A Worldwide Body                         7/28
Making Christ Wait                       7/29
Our Love for God                         7/30
Jesus Will Come                          7/31

## August
Just Plain Faithful                      8/1

God Would Stir Us                    8/2
Thank God for Conviction             8/3
Enjoying God Forever                 8/4
Giving Christ His Place              8/5
Christ Does Not Change               8/6
Christ, the Blessed One              8/7
God—Acting Like God                  8/8
A Heavenly Fragrance                 8/9
Chosen in Him                        8/10
Spiritual Suffocation                8/11
We Can Afford to Die                 8/12
How Do We Know Him?                  8/13
Our Inner Sight                      8/14
Blessedness to Come                  8/15
"Frozen" Unbelief                    8/16
Let Us Move Forward                  8/17
God's Eternal Work                   8/18
God Far Away                         8/19
Christian "Shrinkage"                8/20
Testing Our Faith                    8/21
God Gives Assurance                  8/22
Christ's Eternal Glory               8/23
Heir to All Creation                 8/24
Satan's Stratagem                    8/25
Prayer—and God's Spirit              8/26
Men Who Do Not Pray                  8/27
Trust—Not Adjust                     8/28
More Than Consolation                8/29
Human Psychology                     8/30
Prayer for God's Will                8/31

## September
Confidence in God                    9/1
Attributes of God                    9/2
Holiness Not an Option               9/3
"Be Thou Exalted"                    9/4
Meekness and Rest                    9/5
Weak In Discipleship                 9/6
A Lower Level                        9/7

What Do We Love?                        9/8
The World Is Scared                     9/9
God's Exhortation                       9/10
God's Validation                        9/11
Our Unworthy Attitudes                  9/12
God-hungry Souls                        9/13
Longing to See Jesus                    9/14
Humility—and Worship                    9/15
Heavenly Wisdom                         9/16
Guilty Silence                          9/17
Fun and Religion                        9/18
He Is Our Victory                       9/19
God Has the Answers                     9/20
Love Not This World                     9/21
God's Beneficiary                       9/22
Decision! Decision!                     9/23
Our Daily Problems                      9/24
We Trust God's Plan                     9/25
Root of Bitterness                      9/26
No Place for Fantasy                    9/27
Why Be Artificial?                      9/28
What We Shall Be                        9/29
Why Do Birds Sing?                      9/30

## October

"I Will Arise and Go"                   10/1
Unwilling to Yield                      10/2
A Christian Virtue                      10/3
"Toward the Mark"                       10/4
The Winsome Saints                      10/5
Failure of Religion                     10/6
Striving for Numbers                    10/7
"Someone" Is There                      10/8
Everyday Worship                        10/9
Misusing the Bible                      10/10
Game of Pious Words                     10/11
Light—and Shadows                       10/12
The Realities of Heaven                 10/13
God at the Center                       10/14

Resources That Endure                          10/15
Child of Two Worlds                            10/16
A Sacred Gift of Seeing                        10/17
Man's Empty Promises                           10/18
A Libel Against God                            10/19
Doting on the Past                             10/20
Faith and Prayer                               10/21
Problems and Pressures                         10/22
The Lonely Human                               10/23
Postponing Obedience                           10/24
Humans Judge the Lord?                         10/25
Cheap Religion                                 10/26
Brotherhood of the Redeemed                    10/27
God Is on Our Side                             10/28
"Top Side of the Soul"                         10/29
The Day of the Lord                            10/30
A Prayer at Communion                          10/31

## November
A Career—and Christ                            11/1
Rejoice—or Grumble                             11/2
Is the Church Weary?                           11/3
Claim Your Inheritance                         11/4
Worthy—or Unworthy?                            11/5
I Choose to Worship                            11/6
A Moral Pronouncement                          11/7
Mysticism Plus Theology                        11/8
Prayers: Too Late                              11/9
Moral Determination                            11/10
God's Place as Creator                         11/11
What Really Matters?                           11/12
Faith Must Be Restored                         11/13
Too Much "at Home"                             11/14
Answering God's Call                           11/15
Authority in Preaching                         11/16
The Unity of All Things                        11/17
Crossing over Jordan                           11/18
God and the Individual                         11/19
Saved from Idolatry                            11/20

Glamor Instead of Glory                          11/21
Getting God in Focus                             11/22
"A Cheerful Heart"                               11/23
Let Us Be Thankful                               11/24
God Gives—and Gives                              11/25
Faithful Stewardship                             11/26
Live for God's Glory                             11/27
"Why Am I Here?"                                 11/28
Nothing but Sweetness                            11/29
Thoughts on Communion                            11/30

## December
The Breath of God                                12/1
Life Flows from God                              12/2
Let Us Take It Personally                        12/3
Confused about Worship                           12/4
Let the Day Dawn                                 12/5
Everyone May Come                                12/6
Where Is the Radiance?                           12/7
More Than Pardon                                 12/8
Gifts and Graces                                 12/9
"Thus Saith the Lord"                            12/10
The Need for Reverence                           12/11
More Than a Name                                 12/12
Glory to God                                     12/13
Better Farther On                                12/14
Occupied with Praise                             12/15
The Secret Working of God                        12/16
Mercy: A Boundless Sea                           12/17
Give God the Control                             12/18
Revival—and Renewal                              12/19
Do You Love Beauty?                              12/20
If Jesus Came Today                              12/21
The Word Made Flesh                              12/22
Christmas Is Real                                12/23
Joy and Wonder                                   12/24
The Happy Morn                                   12/25
Christ's World of Nature                         12/26
Better Than Gold                                 12/27

Christ's Picture Everywhere                    12/28
The Lord of All Beauty                         12/29
God's Sovereign Plan                           12/30
The Perfections of God                         12/31

# Scripture Index

## Genesis

1:10 ..................... 2/1
1:21 ..................... 9/30
1:31 ..................... 12/2
3:12 ..................... 5/23
5:24 ..................... 4/26
6:8 ..................... 7/11
12:1, 4 ..................... 7/2
35:7 ..................... 10/14

## Exodus

3:2 ..................... 6/16
20:5 ..................... 11/20

## Deuteronomy

5:32 ..................... 4/21

## Joshua

1:5 ..................... 4/25
24:15 ..................... 5/26

## 1 Samuel

3:10 ..................... 11/15
12:18 ..................... 7/6

## 2 Samuel

24:24 ..................... 10/26

## Esther

4:14 ..................... 3/23

## Psalms

1:1, 2 ..................... 8/29
1:2 ..................... 2/24
19:1 ..................... 7/10
29:2 ..................... 12/31
34:8 ..................... 5/7
37:23 ..................... 2/11
39:4 ..................... 9/20
39:5, 6 ..................... 5/28
40:8 ..................... 6/14
46:10 ..................... 2/26
50:1, 21 ..................... 4/10
57:5 ..................... 9/4

66:16 ..................... 5/30
71:13 ..................... 10/28
71:17 ..................... 9/7
85:8 ..................... 5/12
89:7 ..................... 9/12
89:7 ..................... 12/11
95:6, 7 ..................... 3/13
104:29 ..................... 1/3
104:34 ..................... 4/17
105:4 ..................... 10/8
119:11 ..................... 1/17
119:35 ..................... 12/18
119:105, 106 ..................... 11/7
139:23 ..................... 2/12
140:13 ..................... 4/1
145:5 ..................... 1/23

## Proverbs

2:6 ..................... 9/16
2:6 ..................... 12/10
4:18 ..................... 12/5
8:13 ..................... 7/23
10:22 ..................... 3/19
15:23 ..................... 8/3

## Ecclesiastes

2:22 ..................... 11/12

## Song of Solomon

2:4 ..................... 4/24

## Isaiah

6:1, 5 ..................... 2/3
6:7 ..................... 7/27
6:8 ..................... 7/21
26:12 ..................... 12/3
35:2 ..................... 12/29
49:8 ..................... 10/20
53:7, 9 ..................... 7/25
57:15 ..................... 6/29

## Jeremiah

10:7 ..................... 7/16
23:24 ..................... 8/19
31:3 ..................... 1/13

## Lamentations

5:15, 16 ..................... 10/23

## Malachi

3:16 ..................... 7/22

## Matthew

3:17 ..................... 12/22
4:11 ..................... 12/26
4:19, 20 ..................... 7/7
5:5 ..................... 9/5
5:6 ..................... 8/2
6:33 ..................... 2/21
10:24 ..................... 6/2
10:38 ..................... 4/12
11:11 ..................... 4/28
11:27 ..................... 6/18
11:29, 30 ..................... 8/7
15:8, 9 ..................... 10/9
15:9 ..................... 10/25
16:18 ..................... 1/5
18:3 ..................... 9/28
19:22 ..................... 6/10
24:12 ..................... 6/13
25:41 ..................... 2/17
28:18 ..................... 4/6
28:18 ..................... 8/6
28:20 ..................... 4/9
28:20 ..................... 4/18

## Mark

6:31 ..................... 2/14
9:24 ..................... 7/24

## Luke

2:10 ..................... 12/24
2:11 ..................... 12/25
3:16 ..................... 3/15
8:14 ..................... 7/8
12:34 ..................... 3/10
15:10 ..................... 7/15
15:18 ..................... 10/1
19:14 ..................... 12/21
21:34 ..................... 1/20
21:28 ..................... 9/9
23:46 ..................... 3/2

24:5, 6................... 4/5
24:30, 31............... 11/30
24:45................... 12/14

## John

1:1......................... 1/2
1:12..................... 10/27
1:14..................... 1/9
1:14..................... 8/23
1:18..................... 8/8
3:7....................... 5/4
3:9....................... 3/25
3:17..................... 2/10
3:18..................... 7/1
3:27..................... 4/4
5:6....................... 3/11
6:63..................... 4/29
6:66..................... 3/18
6:68..................... 2/8
8:31..................... 7/13
8:31, 32.............. 2/6
10:27................... 8/4
11:25................... 6/17
12:2..................... 12/1
13:14................... 1/27
13:17................... 2/13
14:1, 2................ 10/13
14:23................... 2/7
15:9..................... 2/18
16:13................... 3/21
17:7..................... 7/17
17:15................... 6/11
18:36................... 10/16

## Acts

1:8....................... 5/6
1:8....................... 5/19
2:3....................... 9/2
2:17..................... 10/17
2:32, 33.............. 5/20
2:36..................... 2/5
4:10, 11.............. 5/29
4:19, 20.............. 9/17
5:31..................... 6/25
7:48, 49.............. 6/22
7:55..................... 11/22
9:6....................... 6/8
11:23................... 11/10
16:14................... 11/1
16:29, 30............ 6/19
16:31................... 1/26

16:31..................... 10/24
24:25..................... 3/6
26:18..................... 10/29

## Romans

1:25, 28.............. 11/28
4:8....................... 11/19
5:1....................... 2/20
5:12..................... 5/24
5:15..................... 6/1
5:20..................... 8/11
6:13..................... 10/2
6:16..................... 6/20
6:23..................... 1/12
8:15..................... 3/28
8:21..................... 8/18
8:26..................... 8/26
8:29..................... 9/29
8:35..................... 10/22
10:4..................... 2/22
10:13................... 1/18
11:5..................... 1/29
12:1..................... 5/9
14:13................... 5/14
14:18................... 9/3
15:6..................... 11/27

## 1 Corinthians

1:9....................... 3/4
1:23..................... 9/13
1:27..................... 8/30
1:30..................... 2/25
1:30..................... 3/5
2:5....................... 2/23
2:9....................... 6/27
2:12..................... 4/20
3:1....................... 4/15
3:8....................... 3/29
3:12..................... 12/27
3:13..................... 8/27
5:6....................... 5/16
6:20..................... 9/19
10:13................... 9/24
11:26................... 10/31
12:7..................... 6/24
12:13................... 6/3
12:14, 27............ 7/28
13:4..................... 10/12
15:24, 25............ 12/30
15:55, 57............ 11/18
16:2..................... 11/26

## 2 Corinthians

2:14..................... 1/15
3:18..................... 9/8
4:4....................... 9/21
4:10..................... 3/9
4:16..................... 12/19
4:18..................... 3/12
5:1....................... 8/15
5:17..................... 7/18
6:1....................... 9/23
6:16..................... 12/4
6:17..................... 3/26
7:10..................... 12/8
10:5..................... 1/22
13:5..................... 5/10

## Galatians

2:20..................... 4/22
4:9....................... 5/3
5:1....................... 7/4
5:13..................... 6/4
6:14..................... 3/31

## Ephesians

1:4....................... 8/10
1:10..................... 2/16
1:18..................... 8/14
2:8....................... 1/4
2:10..................... 5/8
2:12..................... 1/8
2:4, 5................ 12/17
3:14, 15.............. 7/20
3:19..................... 6/9
3:19..................... 8/17
3:19..................... 11/5
4:25..................... 7/9
4:25, 29.............. 7/26
4:30..................... 5/17
4:31..................... 3/27
5:1, 2................ 8/20
5:6....................... 1/16
5:17..................... 7/3
5:19..................... 6/6
5:19, 20.............. 11/23
5:20..................... 11/24
6:10..................... 5/1

## Philippians

1:10..................... 8/21
1:11..................... 10/5

2:11 ...................... 8/5
3:10 ...................... 4/8
3:13, 14 ................. 10/4
4:8 ........................ 10/7

## Colossians
1:20 ...................... 1/1
1:20 ...................... 3/30
1:23 ...................... 3/8
2:6 ........................ 5/11
2:9 ........................ 1/14
2:19, 20 ............... 11/17
3:2 ........................ 7/5
3:3 ........................ 8/28
3:16 ...................... 4/16

## 1 Thessalonians
1:5 ........................ 9/11
2:4 ........................ 3/1
2:12 ...................... 5/15
3:13 ...................... 8/9
4:12 ...................... 3/14
5:3 ........................ 10/18
5:10 ...................... 6/26
5:19, 20 ............... 5/18
5:23 ...................... 1/30

## 2 Thessalonians
2:15 ...................... 11/21

## 1 Timothy
3:6 ........................ 11/6
3:15 ...................... 1/28
3:16 ...................... 12/23
4:12 ...................... 6/7
6:3, 4 .................... 7/29
6:12 ...................... 11/25
6:17 ...................... 6/5

## 2 Timothy
1:12 ...................... 8/13
1:12 ...................... 9/27
2:2 ........................ 8/1
2:3, 12 .................. 9/18
2:19 ...................... 12/12
3:5 ........................ 10/6
4:2 ........................ 11/16

## Titus
1:2 ........................ 3/20
3:5, 6 .................... 6/28
3:7 ........................ 4/19
3:7 ........................ 12/16

## Hebrews
1:1, 2 .................... 8/24
1:2 ........................ 1/7
1:8 ........................ 2/4
1:12 ...................... 6/12
2:4 ........................ 12/9
2:10 ...................... 1/24
3:12 ...................... 8/16
3:12 ...................... 11/13
4:12 ...................... 3/17
6:1 ........................ 7/19
9:12 ...................... 3/24
9:14 ...................... 5/21
10:9 ...................... 2/19
10:22 .................... 5/5
11:5 ...................... 4/27
11:6 ...................... 1/19
11:13 .................... 11/14
11:35 .................... 7/12
12:1 ...................... 4/13
12:15 .................... 9/26
13:1 ...................... 10/3
13:8 ...................... 3/7
13:9, 25 ............... 1/10
13:13 .................... 9/6
13:14 .................... 8/12

## James
1:15 ...................... 4/11
2:20 ...................... 6/23
3:2 ........................ 10/11
4:8 ........................ 5/2
5:16 ...................... 10/21

## 1 Peter
1:4 ........................ 9/22
1:6 ........................ 11/2
1:15 ...................... 9/10
1:18 ...................... 6/15
3:8 ........................ 4/3
4:7 ........................ 1/25
4:11 ...................... 5/25
4:13 ...................... 4/23

4:14 ...................... 12/13
5:5 ........................ 5/27
5:6 ........................ 9/15

## 2 Peter
1:4 ........................ 2/2
1:12, 16 ............... 4/7
1:16 ...................... 8/25
1:21 ...................... 11/8
2:10 ...................... 7/14
3:11 ...................... 2/27
3:16 ...................... 10/10

## 1 John
1:9 ........................ 4/2
3:10 ...................... 11/3
3:18 ...................... 7/30
3:21 ...................... 9/1
4:16 ...................... 6/21
4:19 ...................... 1/6
5:4 ........................ 2/15
5:6 ........................ 5/16
5:7 ........................ 3/3
5:10 ...................... 10/19
5:10 ...................... 12/7
5:20 ...................... 1/11
5:20 ...................... 5/22

## 3 John
2 .......................... 10/15
2 .......................... 11/4

## Jude
20, 21 ................... 8/22

## Revelation
1:13, 16 ............... 1/21
1:17 ...................... 5/13
3:1 ........................ 4/14
3:11 ...................... 9/14
4:8 ........................ 12/15
4:11 ...................... 11/11
4:11 ...................... 12/28
6:17 ...................... 11/9
7:10 ...................... 9/25
7:14 ...................... 3/22
9:20 ...................... 3/16
10:6 ...................... 7/31

10:10......................11/29
14:13......................5/31
17:14......................10/30
21:27......................12/20
22:17......................2/9
22:17......................12/6

# Titles by A.W. Tozer
## published by
## Christian Publications

**Books (written/compiled by A.W. Tozer)**

*Born after Midnight* (compilation)
*The Christian Book of Mystical Verse*
*How to Be Filled With the Holy Spirit* (compilation)
*Keys to the Deeper Life*
*Let My People Go* (biography of R.A. Jaffray)
*Of God and Men* (compilation)
*The Pursuit of God* (cloth, paper, large print)
*The Pursuit of God—A 31 Day Experience*
*The Pursuit of Man* (formerly *The Divine Conquest*)
*The Root of the Righteous* (compilation)
*Wingspread* (biography of A.B. Simpson)

**Books of Sermons**

*Attributes of God*
*Attributes of God, Journal*
*Best of A.W. Tozer 1*
*Best of A.W. Tozer 2*
*Christ the Eternal Son*
*The Counselor*
*Echoes from Eden*
*Faith Beyond Reason*
*I Call It Heresy*
*I Talk Back to the Devil*
*Jesus, Author of Our Faith*
*Jesus Is Victor*
*Jesus, Our Man in Glory*

*Men Who Met God*
*Paths to Power*
*Rut, Rot or Revival*
*Success and the Christian*
*Tozer on Worship and Entertainment*
*The Tozer Pulpit I*
*The Tozer Pulpit II*
*Tozer Speaks to Students*
*Tragedy in the Church*
*Whatever Happened to Worship?*
*Who Put Jesus on the Cross?*

## Books of Editorials

*The Early Tozer: A Word in Season*
*God Tells the Man Who Cares*
*Man: The Dwelling Place of God*
*Next Chapter after the Last*
*The Price of Neglect*
*Set of the Sail*
*Size of the Soul*
*That Incredible Christian*
*This World, Playground or Battleground?*
*Warfare of the Spirit*
*We Travel an Appointed Way*

## Other

*Gems from Tozer*
*In Pursuit of God*/Snyder
*The Pursuit of God Study Guide*/Graf
*Quotable Tozer*
*Quotable Tozer II*
*Renewed Day by Day I*

*Renewed Day by Day II*
*The Pursuit of God Perpetual Calendar*

## Booklets

"A.W. Tozer and A.B. Simpson on Spiritual Warfare"
"The Bible: An Unchanging Book in an Ever-
    Changing World"
"Five Vows for Spiritual Power"
"God's Greatest Gift to Man"
"How to Try the Spirits"
"The Old Cross and the New"
"Those Amazing Methodists"
"Total Commitment to Christ: What Is It?"
"The Waning Authority of Christ in the Churches"
"What the Bible Says"
"Worship: the Missing Jewel"

## Audio Cassettes

*The Pursuit of God* (three-volume set)
*The Attributes of God Volume I* (six-volume set)
*The Attributes of God Volume II* (six-volume set)